❧ Whatever's Fair ❧

Whatever's Fair

The Political Autobiography of Ohio House Speaker Vern Riffe

VERNAL G. RIFFE JR.

with the assistance of Cliff Treyens

o o o

Foreword by Richard Celeste

The Kent State University Press

KENT, OHIO

Frontis: A pensive Speaker Riffe presiding over his very last session in 1994.

© 2007 by The Kent State University Press, Kent, Ohio 44242
ALL RIGHTS RESERVED
Library of Congress Catalog Card Number 2006028901
ISBN-10: 0-87338-726-0
ISBN-13: 978-0-87338-726-2
Manufactured in the United States of America

11 10 09 08 07   5 4 3 2

All photos are from the Riffe family collection.

LIBRARY OF CONGRESS CATALOGING-IN-PUBLICATION DATA
Riffe, Vern.
Whatever's fair : the political autobiography of Ohio House Speaker Vern Riffe /
Vernal G. Riffe, Jr. with the assistance of Cliff Treyens ; foreword by Richard Celeste.
p.   cm.
ISBN-13: 978-0-87338-726-2 (hardcover : alk. paper) ∞
ISBN-10: 0-87338-726-2 (hardcover : alk. paper) ∞
1. Riffe, Vern. 2. Legislators—Ohio—Biography. 3. Ohio. General Assembly. House
of Representatives—Speakers—Biography. 4. Ohio—Politics and government—
1951– I. Treyens, Cliff, 1955– II. Title.
f496.4.r54a3 2007
977.1'043092—dc22
[B]   2006028901

British Library Cataloging-in-in-Publication data are available.

Contents

To my wife, Thelma, whose love, support, and devotion to our family made all of this possible.

Foreword

"Whatever's fair, podnuh."

Over twenty years I must have heard that phrase hundreds of times, in party caucuses, on the floor of the legislature, in the Speaker's Office (and the governor's office)—negotiating bills, budgets, appointments, endorsements, even dates for events. It was hallmark Vern Riffe. I first met Vern in the flesh in November 1970 at the caucus of the Democratic members elected during Jack Gilligan's victory at the top of the ticket. Vern describes this caucus through his experienced eyes in this wonderfully revealing memoir. For me, as a neophyte legislator, it promised to be a stirring victory for the insurgents from northeast Ohio who backed Don Pease from Oberlin. We had agreed to a unit rule in voting from the twelve-member Cuyahoga County delegation, a move calculated to deliver a huge bloc for Pease.

As soon as the caucus began, I should have realized that something was up. A. G. Lancione turned over the gavel to Vern Riffe—his right-hand man ("because he is the next-most-senior member of the caucus," A. G. explained in an unchallenged ruling he made up on the spot). Then Vern enthusiastically accepted a request from one of our old-time Cuyahoga County members for a secret ballot. When the votes were counted, Don Pease only received eleven votes! We rookies from the big city had been snookered by our experienced colleagues led by Vern Riffe.

When I was introduced to Vern at the gathering after the caucus, I said, "I don't know whether they teach reading and writing in New Boston, but they sure as hell know how to teach math." Vern roared with laughter and said, "Welcome to the Democrat caucus, and let me know what committees you want to be on. We'll do our best to be fair."

Vern's description of his early life in New Boston and the remarkable role model his dad provided evokes vividly the 1940s and 1950s along the Ohio River. It was an environment of tight-knit family, nurturing community, and devotion to county that seems hard to find as we have raced into the twenty-first century. The politics that Vern describes—when candidates depended on shaking hands, speaking at every conceivable dinner, passing out literature at the county fair (or fairs, if you were running statewide), and when office-holders worked across the political aisle to get things done for their constituents—belong to a bygone era.

This book is an extraordinary window on more than thirty years of Ohio political history and a celebration of a man who loved his work and did it better than perhaps any other member of the Ohio House in our state's history. For the state legislature was the only political home Vern Riffe occupied. He resisted the calls to run for Congress and the urge to try his hand at statewide office.

It was the House whose unique rhythms and personalities he understood so deeply and led so fiercely. Vern's insight and candor help all of us, even those who shared the time and place with Vern, to understand our experience more clearly. He reminds us of those days when the best work was done by Democrats and Republicans joining together to tackle the big issues, whether it was initiating the income tax or resolving the savings and loan crisis. Vern knew how to put people together to get things done.

Let me share just one story that may help explain why Vern Riffe's name is on the state office tower on Capitol Square. The day before I was inaugurated in January 1983, I learned that Gov. Jim Rhodes had plans to break ground early the next morning for a not-yet-designed state office tower directly across from where my oath taking was to occur. No competitive bids, no publicity, just a last-minute deal with friends. I was outraged. Some of my advisers said there was nothing to be done. I called Mike DelBane, one of Vern's best friends, to my hotel room. I told him about what I had heard and said that it was unacceptable. I asked Mike, also a good friend of mine, to explain to Vern how unacceptable it was. And I added that, if the building went forward, I would have to cash in Mike's commitment to resign from the Public Utilities Commission.

I knew how much Vern wanted Mike to be reappointed to the Commission, and I knew how close Vern and Jim Rhodes were. I assumed that Vern would get my message to Rhodes. The message was one that Vern understood. The messenger was persuasive. No ground was broken on the state office tower on my inauguration day.

There will never be another Vern Riffe, able to influence and come to dominate our premier state legislative body for thirty-six years. Term limits have seen to that. So has the exploding cost of legislative campaigns. But most of all, it has to do with the sharply partisan and negative environment these two tectonic shifts in the political landscape have created.

Vern lived long enough to see these changes, even to wrestle with the money-guzzling element and emerge as the heavyweight fund-raising champion of his day. Yet he understood their devastating impact on the integrity and effectiveness of our democratic process. In an eloquent plea, Vern called for the repeal of term limits, recognizing the harmful, unintended consequence of a so-called reform that he had supported. Furthermore, Vern urged action to limit campaign spending, going so far as suggesting public financing. We would do well to consider Vern's valedictory advice as we watch a dramatic increase in partisanship and corruption in our state government.

Vern was raised by his daddy, the Mayor, to believe that government done properly could improve the lives of citizens, could ease burdens and open opportunities. Government was neither bad nor good; it was a tool to be used wisely. Few leaders in Ohio history understood how to use that tool better than Vern Riffe.

In his final days Vern knew that he was mortally ill. He feared our system of governance was mortally ill as well. In these pages, Riffe calls on us to respect our body politic and to devote ourselves to its healing.

After all, it's simply what's fair. Right, podnuh?

RICHARD CELESTE
Colorado Springs, Colorado

⚛ 1 ⚛

Homegrown Politics and
Other Early Lessons

You can be anything that you want to be in this country. I'm living proof of that. Even a hillbilly from southern Ohio can rise to the top and make a difference. When you get right down to it, success in politics and public service is about working with people, and you don't learn that from a textbook. It all begins in the family. That's where the die is cast.

My mother and dad came out of Kentucky. Both were raised on family farms just after the turn of the century in an era when farmers helped one another. They might work a week of plowing or pulling corn, and then they'd go to another farm the next week and work there. Everybody looked after each other. The times were different. They were hard times, but families were closer and people looked after one another.

Dad was born on September 21, 1900, right across the Ohio River from New Boston in Greenup County. His family later moved due west a little to Vanceburg. The first twenty years or so of his life were spent on the farm raising corn and tobacco for income. They also grew a garden for their personal use and had a butchery. The Riffes weren't rich, but they weren't poor either.

There were nine children in his family—five boys and four girls. Dad was the second oldest son, and he worked hard, a lot of it by hand or with horse-drawn plows and wagons.

Mother was born Jewell Emma Adkins on November 15, 1901, and raised on her family's farm in Sandy Hook, about seventy-five miles south of where Dad grew up. She was the oldest of six children— three boys and three girls. Her father died in the great flu epidemic of 1918 when she was only sixteen. It was the worst epidemic this country ever had. More than half a million people died.

Mother didn't have it easy growing up because as the oldest child, she was really the head of the family too. I've often thought that's where she got her independence. She was forced to grow up in a hurry and make the kind of decisions that a father would otherwise make.

When Mother moved to the Portsmouth area in 1922, she worked at Williams Manufacturing Company, a shoe factory. And after I was born, even after my sister and I were out of school, Mother continued to work. She was a dietitian at the hospital in Portsmouth and didn't retire from work until she was in her sixties. Today, it might not be unusual, but it wasn't nearly as common in Mother's day.

Dad and Mother left Kentucky in 1918 and moved to New Boston, which was surrounded on three sides by Portsmouth and by the Ohio River on the remaining side. The New Boston–Portsmouth area was where the jobs were in those parts. Unless you wanted to stay on the farm, you had to leave. I'd say 50 percent of the people in New Boston came out of Kentucky, maybe more.

At one time, Portsmouth was the shoe hub of the nation. It had more shoe factories and made more shoes than anywhere else. At the time the Depression hit, Selby Shoe Company was making nearly ten thousand pairs of shoes a day! The Norfolk & Western Railroad had its western terminal in Portsmouth, making it one of the largest yards in the country. That's where Dad had his first job in Ohio. Add to that the Detroit steel mill in New Boston, which had more than four thousand employees, and all the brickyards around, and ours was a booming area. There was a period after World War II when things slowed down some, but Portsmouth really didn't experience real hardship until the 1970s, when employment at the mill dropped to just a few hundred. The general state of the economy and foreign competition combined to hit our area very hard.

When Mother and Dad first met in 1923, he was a car inspector for the N&W Railroad and she was still at the shoe factory. They had gone separately to a big amusement park in New Boston called Millbrook. They made a striking couple. Dad was over six feet tall and, I've been told, was one heck of a handsome young man with personality plus. Even decades later, as mayor of New Boston, he would come into the office and some of those women would fall all over themselves.

Mother was a beautiful people person, inside and out, and something must have clicked because they were married the next year on June 28, 1924. On June 26, 1925, almost one year to the day later, I was born in our two-story shotgun house at 4236 Oak Street in New Boston. (They called them shotguns because you could look through the front door and see straight out the back of the house as if you were looking down the barrel of a gun.) And eleven months later my sister, Ilene, was born and that was it; Mother and Dad didn't have any more children. We moved to Spruce and Cedar streets nearby, and that's where I spent most of my childhood. I guess the acorn doesn't fall far from the tree because I lived within three or four blocks of the area most of my life.

There was always politics around our household. You could even say I got involved in politics from the day I was born. My middle name is "Goebel," just like Dad, my son, and one of my grandsons. It comes from William Goebel, a Democrat who was assassinated in January 1900 after running for governor of Kentucky the preceding November. It was an extremely close race, and the results were disputed. Finally the state elections board declared Goebel the winner; he was sworn in and died within the hour. Dad was born September 21, 1900, and it was my grandfather who wanted to name him after Goebel.

New Boston was a good place to grow up. It was small compared to Portsmouth. In fact, New Boston didn't even become a city until 1940, when its population reached five thousand. Just about all Mother's family was there; two or three on Dad's side lived in New Boston and the rest lived outside of Garrison, Kentucky, about an hour away. Sunday supper at our house was like a family reunion. We gathered to discuss family matters and politics.

Most of the people in New Boston worked at the factories, making it a blue-collar town. People worked hard, they played hard, they went to church, and they looked out for each other. That's the way I was raised. I believe much of a person's character is set early in life, so I'm glad I was raised in that atmosphere.

Some of my earliest childhood memories are of the Depression. We were luckier than most because during those years, Dad worked for New Boston and, as an employee of the city, he made a steady salary and a darn good one too, of $25 to $30 a month, sometimes in "scrip" instead of a check. (Scrip was a kind of credit stores would accept until they got their money.)

When the Depression hit, hardly anybody was working. Our area was particularly hard-hit because we were so dependent on industry for jobs. Everything was down, including the steel mill. There was no unemployment compensation. Nothing. If you earned ten dollars a month it was a big deal because you could buy a loaf of bread for three cents. People were so desperate; they went out and worked on farms for fifty cents a day.

Mother and Dad helped a lot of people who were less fortunate. They were a great pair. If a neighbor needed something, Mother made sure they got it, whether it was clothes, food, or anything else. If we didn't have what was needed, Mother somehow found it.

I remember Dad going around to the bakeries in New Boston. He would buy day-old or two-day-old bread and drop off loaves for people who didn't have any. Sometimes those people wouldn't even know where it came from. It didn't matter who they were, Dad would treat everyone fairly, honestly, and with respect. I was too young to realize it at the time, but those were the most important lessons I would learn in my lifetime—lessons that would be repeated over and over during my childhood.

Helping people was something Dad loved to do, and public service gave him a way to do it and make a living. He also loved politics. Dad's first public service job was on the New Boston Police Department. I couldn't have been but four or five years old at the time, but I can remember it like it was yesterday. Sometimes I'd take his handcuffs and handcuff my friends to the porch rail. Other times I'd disappear so my mother couldn't find me; then Dad would come looking and take me home on his police motorcycle. One of my proudest possessions is a painting of Dad in uniform on his motorcycle wearing his knee-high boots, pistol strapped to his side, and a wad of chewing tobacco in his cheek. Little boys always look up to policemen, so I was especially proud that Dad was an officer.

Dad's job ended when a Republican mayor was elected. Dad wasn't the kind to let things happen to him; he was a doer. He'd been on the force for three years, but rather than wait until the first of the year to get fired, he turned in his badge and his gun the day after the election.

About a month later he went to work as a watchman at the steel mill and stayed there until the mid-1930s, when Martin L. Davey was elected governor. Dad, being a strong Democrat, got a job as a "dry officer," which today is what we call a liquor agent. Even though Prohibition was over, a lot of people got used to making moonshine and other illegal booze. Dad would dress in old clothes and hunt out stills or buy illegal liquor in order to make arrests. It was dangerous business, and he always carried a pistol and kept a shotgun in his car.

By 1940 Dad was back in public service as New Boston's safety and service director. He had worked hard to elect Mayor Ted Stratton, and it was on that basis that he got the appointment. For nearly eight years, he was in charge of the police and fire departments as well as the service department. Then in 1947, Dad was elected mayor of New Boston after Mayor Stratton had resigned to become county commissioner. Dad served as mayor until 1971, making him the longest serving mayor in Ohio at that time.

I've learned a lot of lessons from my dad, but one of the most important was that you can be dedicated to your career and dedicated to your family at the same time. In other words, you don't have to sacrifice one for the other, not that there aren't some sacrifices involved. Too many people do that today, and I think it is one reason our society is in such bad shape. Even though Dad's responsibilities put heavy demands on his time, I always felt we had a tremendous relationship, the same kind I've tried to establish with my children.

When I was fifteen, the Detroit Tigers were playing the Cincinnati Reds in the 1940 World Series and Dad was going to the opening game. I wanted to go to the game more than anything, but he didn't have any more tickets.

"If that's the way it is, when I get to be twenty-one I'm going to vote a straight Republican ticket." I wasn't joking. Man, I was hot.

Dad felt bad about it, and I'm sure he didn't enjoy the game like he could have because he knew how much I wanted to be there. About 11 P.M. that night, I was in bed when Dad woke me up. He said, "Son, I want to send a note with you to school tomorrow to see if I can get you excused. I've arranged for John Counts to take you to tomorrow's game."

I couldn't believe it. I was tickled to death. John Counts owned a bakery in New Boston, and he was a strong Republican. Even so, Mr. Counts and Dad were good friends, because Dad was never one to let politics interfere with friendships. If he liked somebody, he was a friend; it didn't mean they couldn't disagree on political matters. I don't know if that's something I learned or whether it's just the difference in the times, but I always had a lot of Republican friends too.

Bucky Walters was pitching the second game of the series, and he won for the Reds, 5-3. Crosley Field was a small ballpark, so you could get close to the game, and we had good seats to boot. I was thrilled just to be there. The Reds ended up winning the series, 4-3. Dad was hurt because he couldn't take me to the game, but he busted his hump to get those two tickets. From that time on, I told Dad that if it hadn't been for that game, I might have become a Republican.

Dad was a great baseball fan and a pretty good pitcher himself. He was a lefty, and he could fire the ball. He even organized a semipro team. But one of his proudest accomplishments was starting the first little league program in Scioto County with the first lighted field in Ohio.

Now I was never a great baseball player, but it was in my blood too. I wasn't but thirteen years old when I helped form a team in what we called the "Knot Hole League." We sold doughnuts to buy jerseys and caps. Even in those days, once I took on a task, I was serious about it. Keith Gaspich, a doctor back home, still tells the story about how I came over to his house to repossess his jersey and cap because he had the measles.

"I got somebody else to play because you can't," I told him.

As long as I can remember, baseball and politics were a big part of the Riffe household. My first memories of politics were when I was five or six. Dad would come home with campaign cards or handbills, and we'd pass them out around the neighborhood. I'd go from door to door, up one side of the street and down the other. People knew they could get a rise out of me by calling me a Republican. I'd get as mad as a hornet and snap, "I'm a Democrat!" I went to political meetings with Dad too, and often I'd fall asleep on the bench right there in the meeting hall.

I always had an inkling that someday I'd be involved in politics. In high school, when we'd have political debates and choose Democrats on one side and Republicans on the other, I'd always head for the Democratic side. But nobody ever would have looked at me then and said, he's going to be a powerful politician someday. I was an okay student. I made As in math, which was my best subject, and Bs in government, history, and such. When it came to things like chemistry, I was just average, probably a C student.

I also played hooky from time to time. Once while in high school my friends and I were at the movie matinee downtown during school hours. It wasn't the first time I thought I was getting away with something when I wasn't. On the way home from classes on Friday of that week, I stopped by Dad's office to get my allowance, taking fifty cents or a dollar, I don't remember exactly, because I had planned on taking my girlfriend to the show Saturday night.

"You're not going to get an allowance this week," he said. "When you make up your mind to stay in school and quit playing hooky, then we'll go back to an allowance."

I always took a girl to the show on Saturday night, and he knew it. That's the last time I played hooky.

I wasn't totally dependent on an allowance; far from it. From the time I was able to work, I pretty much always had a job of some kind. My first job was as a paperboy for the *Portsmouth Times*. What I remember most was getting up at 4 A.M. on freezing cold mornings to deliver the Sunday paper, and afterward going back to bed only to get up again in time for Sunday school. We attended services and Sunday school every week at the Church of Christ in Christian Union. If there was a revival nearby, I was required to go with Mother to hear all the testifying. I can remember going to sleep in the back of the tent while there'd be all this shouting and witnessing.

When I was sixteen, I worked at the Kroger store for eighteen cents an hour; ten hours on Saturday got me $1.80, which was a pretty good day's work back then. I also used to chop kindling and sell it for ten cents a basket or three for a quarter. After Kroger, I really moved up to big money—eighty-five cents an hour doing construction work.

Those jobs put some spending money in my pocket. I wasn't thinking about a career though. Nobody was because we knew full well that after high school we'd be going into the service. I was eager to enlist, so much so that I went down to the Navy recruiting office and tried to enlist in the fall of 1942 when I was seventeen. The Navy would take you at that age only if your parents approved, and Dad wouldn't go along with it. That's the only time I can remember a big fight between us.

"You're going to have to go sooner or later, but you're the only son I've got. I want to see you graduate from high school," he said. I didn't like it, but that's what happened. I can see now that he was right, and I would have done exactly the same thing.

Dad never got to go to war. He just missed World War I because it ended before he turned eighteen. Once I was of age he supported me 100 percent, and I joined the Army Air Corps in 1943 right after graduating from high school, even then I was afraid they wouldn't take me because I was skinny as a rail, only 120 pounds. I would have been devastated if they hadn't accepted me. It was my generation's first chance to defend our country, and nobody was trying to get out of it; everybody was patriotic. Fortunately, the Army took me, and before long I was an aerial gunner in a B-17 serving in the European Theater.

There's no doubt about it: I went into the service a boy, but I came out a man. Like a lot of boys, I was babied at home, maybe even more than most, being the only son in the family. You never saw so much crying when I went into the service. Everybody was really upset—aunts, uncles, and everybody else in the family thought there was nobody like "June." That's what they called me, June or "Junior." Even today, the old-timers down home call me June or Junior. They'll say,

"Junior, I haven't seen you in a long time . . . but maybe I shouldn't call you Junior anymore." I always tell them, "No, no, no. I wouldn't think about being called anything but Junior by you."

The service was good for me because I was forced to take care of myself. At home, for instance, my mother would fry eggs and bacon for me in the morning and place a cloth over it to take the grease off. She'd fix me tea. Whatever Junior wanted, that is what she'd do.

The first time I asked for tea in a mess hall at Fort Thomas in Kentucky, a sergeant in the line blew his stack.

"What did you say you wanted, soldier?"

"Have you got any tea? I'd like some tea," I said.

"*Tea!* We don't serve no *damn* tea."

It was a new experience for me, not that I didn't get discipline at home. I got plenty of discipline, but it's different when it's coming from parents. To the sergeant, I was just a skinny, tea-drinking kid who needed to be toughened up before being sent to war. It was just what I needed.

Dad and I were closer than ever just before I was sent over; maybe because we both knew there was a chance I wouldn't come back. When I got my first furlough during basic training in Amarillo, Texas, Dad took time off as safety and service director to spend a week with me. I had to be on base during the day, but my sergeant, a good old boy from Louisville, Kentucky, gave me a pass and I stayed a couple of nights in Amarillo with Dad. Coincidentally, there was another fellow from New Boston stationed there whose Dad was on city council. He got a pass too and joined us. There wasn't much to do, but just being with each other meant a lot. Later when I went home on furlough, Dad traveled back to Cincinnati with me.

I served from 1943 to 1945 and during that time earned the African–Middle Eastern Campaign Medal with nine bronze stars. Those were very important years in my life. I've witnessed some terrible things. I've watched buddies die. I've seen bravery like you wouldn't believe, boys like me barely out of high school putting their lives on the line and not thinking twice about it. Beyond that, I've never talked much about my war experience. War is war. I served honorably, and

I'm proud of it. I'm glad I had the opportunity to defend my country. But if another American boy never had to go to war, I would be the happiest man alive.

It was a real honor to have served under two of the outstanding leaders of my generation—Franklin D. Roosevelt and Harry S. Truman. I'd have to say both of those men had a big impact on my life because they, along with my dad, really defined leadership for me.

Roosevelt was a great president, one of the greatest. People down home loved him for bringing us out of the Depression and putting people back to work. You could look around and see what he did. The post office in Portsmouth was built during the WPA, and the old American Legion Hall too. Roosevelt's New Deal built a lot of the streets, water lines, and sewers in New Boston when Dad was safety and service director.

My family never missed one of Roosevelt's fireside chats. If somebody on our street didn't have a radio or theirs wasn't working, our door was open to them so they could listen. Uncle Fred, who cried so much when I left for the Army, had a big picture of Franklin D. Roosevelt hanging in his living room. It said, "Daddy Roosevelt" beneath. Uncle Fred was cut off from the steel mill with a wife and children to feed during the Depression.

I was serving in Italy the day Roosevelt died. The whole squadron was called out for a memorial service. Some of the guys goofed off, and they caught hell for it. I don't know if they court-martialed them or not, but I felt then—and still do—that if a soldier doesn't pay homage to the commander in chief, something serious ought to happen.

Until Roosevelt died, you didn't hear much about Harry Truman. His name wasn't mentioned. But after he became president, I started to take notice of him. The Berlin Airlift was a fantastic move, and so was the Truman Doctrine. There's no telling how much of Europe the Soviets would have controlled if Truman had not done what he did.

What I liked most about Harry Truman was that he wasn't afraid to make decisions. He would listen to people, and when he got all the information he'd make the final decision. Simple as that. Sometimes he was right, and sometimes he was wrong, but he never flinched. Truman never second-guessed himself over the atomic bomb, even after the full extent of the damage was known. He said he would do it over again because it saved lives, American lives. In my view, he's one of the greatest presidents to ever serve this country.

I saw in Truman how a man from humble beginnings could lead the most powerful country on earth. In that way, you could say he was a role model for me. Truman worked his way up; nobody handed it to him. He wasn't the son of a rich person like Jack Kennedy. He wasn't a governor of a big state like Franklin Roosevelt. He started out as a precinct committeeman and earned everything he got every step of the way.

One of my greatest thrills was to meet Harry Truman during the Ohio Democratic Party dinner at the state fairgrounds in Columbus. It was 1958, and I was running for the Ohio House for the first time. What's more, U.S. Speaker of the House Sam Rayburn, a living legend himself, gave the keynote address. Talk about a good time. Just to be around them and listen to their stories was a real education. And I will never forget one of the statements Truman made. He said, "When it came time to make a decision, I never hesitated one minute because I always knew if I didn't make that decision I'd have two to make the next day."

But nobody influenced me the way Dad did. He was a great leader on a smaller scale, and anybody who remembers Dad as mayor will say so. No question about it: I got my leadership ability from Dad. Some people believe I got my feisty side from Mother, which may be true. She took the switch to me more than once as a child. The only way I'd avoid whipping was to hide behind Grandma's long skirt, and Mother would just wait and whip me later. I deserved it, of course.

Dad had a way about him, a presence, so that he never had to lay a hand on me. With one look he could put the fear of God in you or quiet a room. He didn't talk to hear himself speak like some people do; Dad could say more with silence than most people could with a whole lot of talking. But when he did speak, he had something to say, and people listened, including me. Call it body language, force of presence, whatever you want, but there is no doubt I inherited it, and it served me well as a legislator and leader.

I've always talked about the influence my dad had on me politically, but I don't underestimate the values my mother instilled in me as well. Dad was a "people's mayor"—he treated others with respect, decency, and, when necessary, discipline. Mother was a people person too, but in a different way. She was the one who organized an open house each election night. She was the one who made sure Dad kept in touch with constituents by telephone and that we mailed birthday, anniversary, and condolence cards.

When I got out of the service in 1945, I decided to open a small grocery store and become a businessman. I wasn't entirely new to the business. Dad ran a grocery store in the late 1920s, and I decided this was a way for me to earn some income since my "52-20" money was running out (when you got out of the service, they paid you twenty dollars a week for a year). My store was on Harrisonville Avenue and I called it V. G. Riffe and Son after my father and me. I ran the store for about a year and a half, but when the opportunity arose to sell it at a profit, I sold and cleared three thousand dollars. I've been fortunate never to have lost money in business, even when I was new at it.

I was still young and single, and my rambling days weren't over quite yet. The store tied me down a good bit, so after selling it I worked two years on the Norfolk & Western Railroad as an express messenger. The railroad had a hub in Portsmouth, and I ran routes through Ohio, Virginia, and West Virginia. My job was to put off U.S. mail, express mail, and baggage.

In those days we also delivered the remains of war casualties, usually to relatives waiting at the station. I remember times when we had as many as twenty boxes of remains on a car, each draped in an American flag. I've thanked the Lord many times for getting me through my military service unharmed, but never was I more thankful than when I looked into the eyes of those family members waiting to put their loved ones to rest. That part of the job wasn't easy, but I was honored to do it.

Railroading was hard work. I got my hands good and dirty doing it, and I have to say that there's no finer group of people than working-class people. I have fond memories of places like Williamson, West Virginia, where I'd often stay at Ma Diamond's Boarding House. She'd have eight or ten railroaders boarding there, and I was the pup in the group. They didn't have any showers, just a big tub to take a bath in, but it was all worth it just to eat the meals. In the mornings she'd have big breakfasts of biscuits and gravy, and at night supper was even better. We'd all sit at a large round table, and it was like one big family. I got along with everybody.

Just because I was on the go with the railroad didn't mean I lost touch with politics. I wanted to vote for Harry Truman so badly in the 1948 presidential election that I put in a request to be relieved that day. When I opened the door to my train car in Williamson on the Monday night before election day, there stood old man Bache, my supervisor.

"When you get through tonight, I want to talk to you," he said. I thought maybe I'd have my rear kicked because I wasn't wearing my gun; I had taken it off and put it in the safe.

After I got all the baggage out, I went to see him and was prepared for a tongue lashing.

"I don't understand why you would want to give up a sixty-dollar run to vote. You must have more money than you know what to do with," said old man Bache.

In my family, voting was not only a right but a privilege, so I didn't have any problem spitting it out.

"This is my first chance to vote for president of the United States, and I want to vote for Harry S. Truman. I feel real strongly about it," I said.

Well, I'll be darned if the old man didn't smile.

"I want you to know I'm the best Democrat in the State of Ohio. You go ahead and take your time off," he said.

My rambling days may not have been over when I started out on the railroad, but as time passed it got so that I couldn't wait to finish my run on Fridays so I could head straight home. There's no doubt about it: I was in love.

When I first got back from the service, I was a bit of a rounder and having a good time. I wasn't looking to get married, but while I ran the grocery store I began to notice Thelma Cooper walking by every day to her job at the hardware store down the block. I knew of her because I went to school with her brother and she lived within a block and a half from my family's house, but I didn't really pay much attention to her then. While I was gone, she really blossomed into a beautiful young woman with long, dark hair. It didn't take long before I knew I had to have a date with her.

Garnet Sturgill worked with Thelma at the hardware store, and they were good friends. You could talk to Garnet about anything; she was that kind of girl. So I called her up one day and asked if Thelma was going out with anybody, and she said no.

"Why don't you call her and ask her out on a date?" Garnet said. I could tell right then and there that Thelma was not going steady with anyone.

"I might just do that," I told her.

Not being one to jump into anything without thinking about it a bit, a month went by before I finally called Thelma. We went to the picture show in Portsmouth, and that got things rolling.

Thelma was a church-going gal, so one Sunday we'd go to my church, Christ and Christian Union Church on Cedar Street, and the next Sunday we'd go to hers, the First Church of the Nazarene. We went to Sunday school separately and sometimes we'd pass each other on the way.

It didn't take me long to pop the question; I was never bashful about it. I asked her directly one day, right in her living room, but she said I should talk to her dad about it. Her mother had already indicated to me it would be all right, so I knew that it was a formality, but I respected Thelma's father and went over one evening to get his approval. He was sitting in the living room, and as soon as I said I wanted to talk to him about Thelma, he grinned. I suppose he and everybody else saw it coming a mile away.

With his blessing, I bought the ring, and we were engaged. Then it began to sink in, not with me but with Thelma. Before long, the idea of marriage scared the daylights out of her, and Thelma took sick for about a week. Meanwhile, I just went about my business without any problem.

Then came the morning of March 6, 1948, our wedding day. I thought I wasn't going to make it out of bed. I'd been through a war and some other pretty tough situations, but I had never experienced anything like that before. Today you'd probably call it a panic attack. I considered backing out.

"Do I want to do this? Do I want to tie myself down? This is a serious thing," I thought to myself. We were to be married in her family's living room, but I almost wrecked my car on the way to the house. I was shook-up; there's just no other way to describe it.

Somehow, I don't know how, I managed to make it through the ceremony, and the next thing you know we were apartment hunting and setting up house, no honeymoon or anything. We paid cash for the furniture, using some of my money and a bunch of those new Roosevelt dimes she and I had saved together.

There's no question I enjoyed single life, but I always knew I wanted a family, because mine was always so important to me. There was never any question in my mind. Many years later, Jim Rhodes put it well when he told me, "The two most important things in our lives are our health and family, not necessarily in that order. You can have all the money in the world, but if you don't have good health and a good family, you don't have much." Fourteen months after our marriage, Cathy, our first daughter, was born.

Unfortunately the railroad was cutting back in 1949. I was let go and started drawing unemployment compensation from a system the railroad had set up. Twenty-five dollars a week was all I got, and things were tight with a baby and two adults to feed. When times were really tough, Dad would slip me a twenty-dollar bill. Naturally, he wanted to help me, so when we'd go to ballgames or out somewhere, he'd always pay the expenses. I went back to work for a brief time during the Christmas season of 1949, and on January 1, 1950, I began my six-and-one-half-year job on the New Boston Fire Department.

Being a fireman, I got to know everybody in town. And with Dad as mayor, I got the opportunity to work with him, the police department, and the service department. Looking back, it wasn't bad experience for someone who would run for public office someday.

I've been blessed to survive a war and six-and-one-half years on the fire department without a serious injury. I got shaken up once when a ladder went out from under me, and I almost fell off the roof of the steel mill during a fire. That's about it.

I sure saw my share of tragedy and joy though. I've dragged people out of fires who were dead, their feet burned just like a piece of bacon. I never will forget the time we pulled a young boy out of a pond at Shale Bank Hollow. I worked on him for quite a time while using mouth-to-mouth resuscitation, but it was no use.

Then there were people like old man Moore, who used to live down the street from us. He had a bad heart, and we made a lot of emergency runs on him. He'd always be upstairs. I'd start giving him oxygen and we'd wonder if he'd make it or not. Old man Moore would always come around. Dr. Dearth would arrive and the first thing he would do is give the old man a big shot of liquor.

"Have you given him whiskey yet?" Dr. Dearth would always ask Mrs. Moore. "If you haven't, get the bottle." Well I'll be darned if old man Moore didn't outlive the doctor, who died of a heart attack.

One thing about being a policeman or a fireman: Every time you go out, your life could be on the line. When the bell went off we'd jump in our boots, pull up our suspenders, get our coats and helmets, hit the pole, and we'd be gone without any idea what we were getting into. And no doubt every time we'd go out, my wife, the kids, Dad, and Mother would worry. Dad, more than the others, knew what a fireman's job was and how dangerous it could be. He saw some of his friends killed in fires.

If there was a major fire in the city, after the firemen and the policemen, Dad was one of the first to arrive on the scene. It wasn't just because of me. If there was a big snow during the night, he left orders at the police station to call home, and he was out there making sure the sand and everything was put on the streets. He'd go out there himself to see if the service department was doing a good job of garbage collecting, street cleaning, and the like. He would even get up at three or four o'clock in the morning to check whether policemen were spending too much time in the American Restaurant drinking coffee instead of being out in the cruiser.

I say this not because he was my dad but because I've known a lot of public officials and not one was on top of his job more than Dad. He could show up anytime. In fact, I remember one particular fire at the N&W Railroad tracks at about four o'clock in the morning. There was a big snow, and it was freezing. I turned around and there stood Dad.

"What are you doing here?" I asked.

"Son, I was doing this before you were born. It's a part of my job," he said. He was a people's mayor because he made sure the citizens were well served. Long after he retired, until the day he died, people called him "Mayor."

I've been accused of watching over my job in the same kind of way, and I always take that as a compliment because I learned it from the best.

When I started at the fire department, I was making two hundred dollars a week. Then one day a gentleman named G. M. Ross stopped by the fire station to ask if I would be interested in selling insurance. I thought a lot of G. M. He had an insurance and real-estate business in Wheelersburg and needed some agents to sell insurance part-time. Because I worked twenty-four hours on and twenty-four hours off, with an extra day off every fourth turn, it was a chance to make some extra money.

I moved right on it and got licensed to sell insurance. By 1954, I opened up my own office just a half block from the fire station. I was still working for the fire department, so I hired my sister-in-law, Shirley, to manage the office during the day. The extra money helped because our next two children were born during my fire department years—Verna Kay on June 28, 1952, and Mary Beth on June 12, 1956.

Also in 1956, I moved my insurance office to its present location and on September 1 that same year I formed a partnership with Don Sherman, a friend to Dad and me. Don and I both became independent agents.

About this same time I began to get interested in the Masons because some of my good friends belonged. You don't solicit Masons to join; they have to invite you. But I let my interest be known, and since I went to ballgames with these guys, bowled with them, and played cards with them, it was only a matter of time before I was allowed to petition to join and was accepted in 1957.

I really believe if everybody lived by Masonry, we'd have no problems. None. Masonry really boils down to a strong belief in God, country, and government. You'd be surprised by who is involved in the Masons. Harry Truman was one. So is Jim Rhodes. My longtime friend and former House minority leader Corwin Nixon is too.

The 33rd Degree is the highest you can go in Masonry. I was nominated for my 33rd Degree in 1979 and got it in 1980. At the ceremony they announced the nominees for the next year, and when they just about reached the end of the list, they read the name James Allen Rhodes. I went to the phone right away and got the governor at home about 9:30 P.M. I had never paid attention to his middle name, so when he picked up the phone, I said, "Who is James *Allen* Rhodes?"

"Where in the hell have you been?" he snapped. I told him about his nomination for the 33rd Degree to be awarded the following year in Philadelphia. He was pleased.

"Make me a promise you'll go with me," he said, and I did.

When it came time to go to Philadelphia the next year, we had yet to pass a state budget and were operating on an interim budget. I was prepared to stay in Columbus, but the governor, Chuck Shipley of the State Highway Patrol, and I were able to catch a three o'clock direct flight out of Columbus, get dressed in our tuxedos upon arriving, and make the 6:30 dinner ceremony. As soon as it was over, we hightailed it back to the airport and arrived back in Columbus by eleven o'clock. The first time I ever did see Jim Rhodes take a drink was on the trip home. It wasn't the hard stuff, but he did have a couple of beers, so I guess you could say he was celebrating.

You are presented with a ring upon receiving the 33rd Degree. When you die, two things can happen to the ring. It must either be returned to the lodge or you can be buried with it. Mine's going with me; that's how much Masonry means to me.

My involvement in Masonry began just before I ran for the Ohio House the first time. I hadn't planned it that way, but in 1958 the opportunity to run for public office finally presented itself—even if I didn't fully appreciate it at first.

Our House district was represented by Loretta Cooper Woods, a Republican who had been elected four times. She was a schoolteacher and a very popular person. In January 1958, she announced wasn't going to stand for reelection.

Don Sherman immediately wanted me to run; he said it would be good for business. Dad thought it would be a good opportunity too, since I wouldn't be running against an incumbent. The filing deadline was in February, so I had some time to think about it. But I told Dad I was inclined not to run, partly because I always thought I would replace him as mayor when he retired.

Meanwhile, some people approached Dad about running for the House seat. Also thinking about it was a young attorney named Charles Huddleston Jr. who was treasurer of the Scioto County Democratic Party and a Democratic committeeman. A lot of people thought he would make a strong candidate, but Charlie had a personality that was hard for some people to comprehend.

Dad kept putting off a decision but was getting pressure from his friend Burl Justice, the Scioto County sheriff, and others to let it be known whether he was going to run. One day Dad asked Don and me to meet with him.

"Son, if you're interested, you've got to make up your mind now. I'm going to make a call in the morning and tell them I'm not interested," he said.

Two years prior, Dad ran for state representative in the middle of his term as mayor but got beat in the Eisenhower landslide. He figured he had already had his shot at it. I've often thought how different things would have been if Dad had run for the House. (As it turned out, he was mayor for thirteen more years and I would have had quite a wait in order to replace him.)

My name had not even surfaced in the rumor mill, but I told Dad I'd think it through again overnight. I needed just a little more time to reach a decision because I had doubts about whether I really wanted to run. The more I thought about it, the more I began to look at it from the standpoint that if I didn't take advantage of an open seat, I might be sorry down the road. Nobody was better suited to go for that seat than me: I was active in politics, knew the county, and had been Dad's campaign chairman since I got back from the war.

If Mrs. Woods had been running, I wouldn't have been a candidate. Not only was she a good representative and a good candidate but I respected her personally. Years later, after I became Speaker, I always joked that I owed it all to her. We laughed about it, but the fact is she was always in my corner.

I sought Dad's advice my entire career, and right from the beginning he let me make my own decisions. At no time did Dad say, "Son, I think you should run." But when morning came around, I had talked myself into it. I went directly to his office at 9 A.M. sharp and said, "Dad, I'm ready to run."

We went straight to the Board of Elections to get my petitions. Charlie Huddleston had told people if Dad ran, he would stay out of the race. It came as a total shock to him when we walked into the courthouse and took out the petitions in the name "Vernal G. Riffe Jr." He was stunned. "I didn't make any commitment not to run if *he* ran," Charlie said. He stayed in the race, and it was the only time in eighteen elections that I had any opposition in the primary.

When I arrived at the courthouse to get my petitions, there were reporters there from the *Portsmouth Times*, a couple of radio stations, and the *Cincinnati Enquirer*. Dad had called them, so I went out in the hall and told them who I was and why I was running. I was green when it came to talking to reporters, but I managed not to stick my foot in my mouth.

Dad always had his bases covered, and now he was helping me cover mine. As mayor, when he wanted to get a levy or bond issue passed, for example, he did his homework before he'd even ask council to put it on the ballot. He'd meet with different groups and had his organization lined up. Dad showed me by example that a big key to success in politics is hard work, and people who try to take shortcuts usually don't get far. When I became Speaker, it was hard work that got me there and hard work that kept me there. I wasn't a big risk taker—most of the time taking a risk meant you either hadn't done your work on the front end or you were involved in something you shouldn't be doing.

Don Sherman was my campaign chairman even though he was a Republican committeeman. In fact, Don and my general election opponent, Charles Horr, were distant relatives. Sure, Don thought my election would be good for business, but he really believed I would be a good representative. And the beauty of it was that I could still be a full partner in the agency because being a legislator was a part-time job in those days. You spent about four to five months in Columbus, passed a budget, and you were done for the most part.

While I had come to terms with running, my decision didn't set well with everyone. Thelma was not happy about it one bit. I was a young fellow though, and sometimes the things she'd say went in one ear and out the other. After I made the announcement, she didn't speak to me for a week, and her sister Shirley wouldn't sign my petitions. Thelma wasn't too keen on politics at that time, no reflection on Dad. She knew he was a good officeholder—a nondrinking, honest, God-fearing man. But she wasn't crazy about seeing me trot off to a big city like Columbus while we were trying to raise a family and build a business. It took years after I was first elected for Thelma to see just how much I was able to help people. In 1962 after a term in the minority, I began to have doubts about running for reelection. You couldn't get any legislation of your own passed, which was frustrating, and I didn't see things changing anytime soon. I always had the insurance business to fall back on. Some people down home thought I might be interested in running for Congress, but Dad made it pretty plain what he thought about that.

"I do not think you even want to consider a run for Congress. You were just elected to the Ohio House," he said. Fact is, I never did consider it because I never had any desire to go to Washington.

At the same time, Thelma and the kids were pushing me to run for the Ohio House again. They could see how hard I had worked for the people in our area and how I had tried to build something. They knew I was discouraged at the time, and they didn't want to see me give it up only to regret it later. I might not have become Speaker if Loretta Cooper Woods had not retired her seat, but I sure as heck would not have become Speaker without the support of my family. That support helped me endure a total of twelve years in the minority before we finally won control of the House in the 1972 election.

Over the years, Thelma and I developed an understanding about a lot of things. For example, I'd never ask her to do something or go someplace for political reasons if she wasn't comfortable with it. In those days, women did not take part in politics with their husbands the way they do today. But make no mistake about it: Thelma contributed as much to my political career as anyone could. I simply could not have done it without her. I didn't have to worry about the kids when I was in Columbus because Thelma was home raising them. She got them to school, helped them with their homework, disciplined them when they needed it, and comforted them when they were hurt or upset. I called her every single day I was away from home, often two or three times a day. But the fact is she sacrificed a lot so that I could serve the public, and I am forever indebted to her for it.

Once I made a decision to run the first time, our strategy in the primary was pretty straightforward. There were really no issues in my first primary election. Without an incumbent, it ended up being more or less a popularity contest. Before primary election day, Huddleston and I met at the courthouse and agreed like gentlemen that whoever lost would back the other in the general election.

I would call Dad my secret weapon, but he wasn't such a secret; everybody knew he was the best politician around. Dad put my whole get-out-the-vote plan together, and let me tell you, he was way ahead of his time. The whole plan was built around targeting key Democratic precincts to make the most of our time and resources.

"Don't be wasting your time in strong Republican precincts because they won't vote for you," he said. It sounds basic today, but nobody then was targeting votes that way; Charlie Huddleston certainly wasn't. He was trying to roust up Democratic votes in heavy Republican precincts where there weren't but a handful. Targeting precincts was revolutionary in races of that size, but that's the way Dad was—no wasted time, no wasted effort, and always, always effective.

There was one other politician down home who was a mentor to me and he was Burl Justice. Elected to three consecutive four-year terms as sheriff, old Burl was a good human being as well as a good politician. He treated people alike, he didn't care who you were. If there was a fire somewhere in the county, he was the first one on the radio getting furniture to help the victims. Burl's bottom line was the same as Dad's—helping people. They were two of the best politicians ever to come out of Scioto County. The only difference between the two is Dad didn't drink and Burl would take a drink. Otherwise, they were the same. Nobody was more pleased when I decided to run for office.

Not too long before the primary of my first election in 1958, there was the annual Boy Scout Day at the Scioto County Courthouse. Every scout would serve in a county position for the day; one boy would be sheriff, another auditor, another county engineer, and so forth. That particular day Burl was showing his .38 caliber snubnose pistol to the scout who was sheriff for the day. When the scout was examining it, the gun accidentally fired, hit Burl in the back, and exited just below his heart. They rushed him to the hospital, and it was nip and tuck just to keep him alive.

Dad and I were sick over it. Burl was like family and the thought of losing him was almost more than we could stand. Shortly after the accident, Dad and I were getting ready to go to a Democratic meeting one evening. I had to make a couple of calls before we left, but Dad said, "Why don't you leave those two calls until tomorrow. Let's go by the hospital and see Burl."

When we got there the doctors wouldn't let just anybody in to see him, but they let Dad and me visit. Old Burl took my hand and said, "Junior, I want to wish you good luck and I want to tell you one thing: If you don't get more than one vote, you sure got one today. I voted absentee. I just wanted you to know that." He was so proud of me, and it just about broke my heart.

Burl Justice died on a Monday six days after the primary election, and the funeral was later that week. What a funeral it was. He had spent a lifetime helping people, touching so many lives, and people from all over the state traveled to Scioto County to pay their respects.

In the end I beat Charlie by a comfortable margin—3,790 to 2,472. On election night, some of the big Democratic precincts that we targeted came in more than 90 percent in my favor. We crushed him in New Boston, and when Charlie got only a scattering of votes in my home precinct, Dad didn't celebrate. He said, "I'll find out who those people are." And, somehow, he did. As for Charlie Huddleston, he never did keep his commitment to support me in the general election. He was even out there betting money against me, but I got the last laugh.

I'm sure he didn't expect me to win by so much because we had a lot in common: We were about the same age; we were both married and had families; and both our dads were committeemen. But I worked hard on the campaign, built up a lot of connections in the community, and had a huge advantage in my father.

We followed the same basic strategy during the general election that we did in the primary, and it worked like a charm. It didn't hurt that this was the year Gov. Billy O'Neill and big business put the "right-to-work" issue on the ballot, which would have prohibited labor contracts that require union membership as a condition of employment. The Republicans couldn't have picked a worse strategy for my area. It was like lighting a fire under labor and the Democratic Party, pulling out a heavy vote to defeat the issue and elect Democrats from the top of the ticket to the bottom.

The Democrats and labor argued that the right-to-work issue would break unions. This didn't set well around Portsmouth, where the steel mill alone employed four thousand people, not to mention the thousands of other unionized workers at the brickyards, the shoe factories, and the railroads. Even older people who had never voted in their lives got out and registered. They might have been seventy-five or eighty years old, but their sons and daughters worked in the plants, and they were going to help their children and their families at the voting booth.

Republicans all over the state took a beating. Mike DiSalle beat Billy O'Neill for the governor's office, John Bricker lost his U.S. Senate race, and Democrats took control of the Ohio House and Senate. It was a high point in the legislature during the early part of my career, since the House and Senate both went back to the Republicans two years later.

My general election opponent, Charles Horr, really misread the right-to-work issue. He wrapped himself in Governor O'Neill, telling voters, "If you're going to vote for Billy O'Neill, vote for me." Billy got the living heck kicked out of him in the district, and I won our race with just about 60 percent of the vote. Sometimes I wonder how I would have run without the right-to-work issue. I don't know for sure, but I might have gotten the same percentage because in eighteen elections I never had a tight race.

We spent maybe eighteen hundred dollars in that election, a lot of money in those days. We bought hand cards to pass out and big placards to put up along roads throughout the county, but even way back then the media was getting most of my campaign money. We did some radio and newspaper advertising and some direct mail to groups of people like railroaders, firemen, and teachers.

When the county fair was going on, I spent twelve hours a day shaking hands, and Dad was right with me, pushing me every minute, and I mean *every minute*. During the 1960s and '70s, I didn't have any opposition in a lot of the elections, but we were always doing radio advertising and giving out campaign materials at the county fair nonetheless. We did it to let people know I still was there. As long as I was Speaker, I always pushed our House candidates to do the same thing no matter how little opposition they might have. An old political saying goes: "There are two ways to run for office—unopposed and scared." I took it to heart. I always ran like I had opposition whether I did or not.

After our third daughter, Mary Beth, was born, I thought we had enough children. I had accepted the notion that we weren't going to have a son and joked with Dr. McAfee that we would have to switch doctors because of it. "That's your department, not mine," he said.

Thelma wanted another child though, and when she got pregnant again, I wasn't pleased at first. Of course, I grew excited as the weeks went by, and I'll never forget the day our fourth child was born. Shortly after five o'clock in the morning of April 15, 1960, Dr. McAfee came out of the delivery room with a big smile on his face and said, "Vern, you finally did it." We had a son, Vernal G. Riffe III, and we came to call him Skip for short.

As fate would have it, Skip would be the one to carry on the family tradition in politics. I always thought Verna Kay would be the one to run for office because she was interested in politics. One of her first jobs was to work in the Washington, D.C., offices of U.S. Representative Dennis E. Eckart and U.S. Representative Mary Rose Oakar. Later, as manager of the Cleveland Clinic's Columbus office, Verna continued to follow Statehouse politics closely. Both Cathy and Mary Beth became elementary-school teachers and showed little interest in politics. Cathy has always taught in Scioto County, while Mary Beth started out in the Cincinnati area but later moved back home to Scioto County. I am very proud of all my children and what they have done with their lives. Following in my footsteps was never that important to me. They made their own decisions and all have been successful in their own ways. I get no greater joy in life than being with my wife, children, and seven grandchildren.

Skip took out petitions to run for county commissioner in January

1990, the last year Dad was alive, and couldn't wait to tell him. It was Skip's decision. Fact is, I wasn't exactly encouraging him to run because I knew that as my son, he would be under tremendous scrutiny. Also, people were bound to compare Skip to me, and that wasn't fair because Skip was his own person.

Dad was in the hospital at the time Skip took out petitions. His health had been declining for a long while. We were able to keep him at home with Mother for years by getting a full-time nurse to watch after him, but later Skip assumed much of the responsibility by doing things like helping to bathe and feed him. Dad understood us at times, and there were many times when he did not. It was tough on all of us, but we did everything we could to keep things comfortable for him.

On that January day, Skip got right up to Dad's hospital bed and told him about taking out his petitions to run for office. We couldn't tell whether Dad understood what Skip was saying or not because he couldn't really talk at that point. Later though, one of the nurses told us she saw a grin, and somehow I figured Dad understood that his grandson and namesake would carry on the family tradition. And that put a smile on my face too.

2

The Rise to Leadership

"Be loyal."

"Be fair and honest."

"When you're a strong leader, everybody benefits; when you're a weak leader, everybody loses."

"What's good for the people is good for the party."

—*Riffe's Rules*

I'd say people underestimated me when I came to the Ohio House of Representatives in 1958. That's understandable, me being from a rural, southern Ohio county and holding elected office for the first time. What those people didn't realize is that I had had a world of education in politics. My dad taught me the importance of loyalty, teamwork, and serving the people before I ever took office. I understood the legislative system and how to work in it, and the House leadership took a shine to me early on because of it. They never had to worry about me: If our caucus leaders wanted something, I was for it.

Those in leadership also liked someone with backbone, and I had plenty of opportunities to show them that I had it. Dad always told me not to be afraid to take an unpopular stand if it was the right thing to do because you could explain a responsible position to the people. Or, if Republican legislation benefited my district, I didn't give one whit that it came from the opposite party, I'd support it. Some of my

Democratic friends didn't understand that, but that didn't bother me any. I'd tell them, "Listen, my district needs all the help it can get. We need every dollar we can get. If legislation is going to bring more money into my district, I'm for it. I didn't come here to be anti-anything or an obstructionist. I can't do that, and I won't do that." What's good for the people is good for the party, Dad would always say.

Politically, there were a lot of reasons not to support Gov. Mike DiSalle's tax increases in 1959. Voters didn't like tax increases then any more than they do now. But I supported every single one of them—increases in the corporate franchise tax, gasoline tax, cigarette tax, and tax on wine and mixed drinks, and a decrease in the sales tax exemption. I did it for two reasons: First, it was needed because many state services had been underfunded or neglected. Second, that's what the caucus leadership wanted. I felt duty bound as a member of the majority party in the House and of the Taxation Committee to support my caucus.

Back in those days, tax bills were separate; you just didn't fold them into the budget bill as we do today. The leadership tried to get freshmen to sponsor some of those bills, and they called a meeting with a bunch of us. Much later, when I became Speaker, I tried to protect freshmen from sponsoring controversial bills, but in 1959 and 1960 there were so many freshmen—we went from a minority of forty-two to a majority of seventy-eight—that leadership was hard-pressed for sponsors.

George Hook of Brown County, chairman of the Highways Committee, and A. G. Lancione of Belmont County, chairman of Taxation, tried to get freshmen like me, Myrl Shoemaker of Ross County, Charlie Jackson of Clermont County, Phil Collins of Hamilton County, and Harold Romer of Mercer County to sign on. The meeting was on a Thursday and they wanted an answer first thing the following week.

As we walked out of there, Myrl said, "Vern, you ought to talk to your dad about this. See what he thinks." When I told Dad what they wanted, he said, "Son, if you want my advice, don't put your name on those bills. I'm not saying that you won't have to vote for some legislation to raise more money. The state can't run without money, and you're the only people who can raise it. You have to assume your responsibility. But let the old-timers sponsor the bills." We followed Dad's advice, and am I ever glad we did.

The Republicans were working mightily to come up with a strong candidate to oppose me in 1960. Bob McAllister, who worked for the Ohio Republican Party, was always trying to get opposition for me. We were good friends even then and remain so today. His first attempt in 1960 was an attempt to get Loretta Cooper Woods to quit her job as a teacher for Clay High School and run for the House again.

"Well, Bob, let me think about it," she told him. Then she turned right around and called me to say what had happened.

"Well, just keep leading them on," I said. It was our little secret.

Eventually, Bob got around to talking to Bill Games, the state representative from Adams County.

"Bob, how dumb are you? She's just leading you on. Loretta's a good friend of Vern's. She is not going to run against him," Bill said.

Finally they got Cecil Burton to run against me. Cecil was older and in the real-estate business. Old Cecil was all right, but he had a low-key personality, not much of one to go out and make friends like you need to do in a campaign. Cecil took out big ads saying Vern Riffe supported "Tax Hike Mike," and he listed the tax bills that I voted for. There were even stickers on gas pumps that said, "Thank your state representative for voting this tax increase." But I explained myself to the voters just like Dad said and won reelection by almost the same margin as before, just shy of 60 percent. We might have survived it anyway, but Myrl always said until the day he died that Dad's advice about not sponsoring the tax bills was the best we ever got, and it's why we stayed in the House so long.

Not everyone survived it though, and we lost the majority in the House. A lot of the new people who signed on as sponsors were defeated in the election of 1960, and a lot of the ones who didn't were reelected, including Myrl and me. Two years later Gov. Mike DiSalle still couldn't shake the "Tax Hike Mike" nickname that the Republicans hung on him. Jim Rhodes beat him in a landslide and the Republicans ruled state government.

Also in 1962, the Republicans tricked a man named Ollie Webb, who owned a fried chicken business, into running against me. Roy Martin, Governor Rhodes's patronage chief, had offered me an appointment on the Ohio Personnel Review Board, which carried a salary. Since I had little seniority in the House, I thought I should at least consider it. I discussed it with my dad and family and decided to give legislative life more of a chance. Roy was from down home, so I went over to his house on a Sunday and told him thanks but I didn't want the appointment.

What Bob McAllister told Ollie sounded much different.

"We've got an appointment coming up we're going to offer Vern, and he'll take it because he's got an insurance business to operate. With the appointment, he won't have to run for office," they told him.

When I filed and stayed in the race, Ollie was none too happy about what his party had told him. He was a reluctant candidate, to say the least, and the month before the election, he more or less endorsed me in a joint appearance before the League of Women Voters.

"I don't know what I'm doing here because Vern Riffe has done a good job as our state representative. I was told I would not be running against him, and that's the only reason I filed," Ollie said publicly.

Later I came to find out from Jim Rhodes himself that it was not his idea.

"I told them you were too young to retire from the legislature," he said with a wink.

Years later I was at Buela Park, the thoroughbred racetrack in Columbus, having dinner with Bob McAllister. I left to place a bet, and on the way I decided to play a trick on Bob. When I returned, Bob was still looking at the program.

"Hey, guess who I saw up there?" I said.

"Who'd you see?"

"Ollie Webb. He was placing a bet, and we talked a bit," I replied.

"Oh no. Don't let him see us together. He's mad at me. I lied to him," said Bob, who literally ducked under the table. Boy, did I ever get even with Bob that night.

The next year, 1964, the Republicans were telling people I was going to be appointed postmaster and wouldn't be running for reelection. The fact is, I probably could have had the appointment if I'd wanted it because Jim Polk, a Democrat, was our congressman at the time. The Republicans made it sound like a sure thing. They got a gentleman named Don Covert, a local furniture store owner, to run, but when Don found out I had filed for reelection, he said, "I never would have run if I'd known Vern Jr. was in."

By the late 1960s they gave up trying to beat me, and my relationship with Jim Rhodes grew. When it came to getting money for state projects in my district, I did exceedingly well. The governor lived in Jackson County until he was eight years old, and he never forgot his southern Ohio roots. Since I didn't let partisanship get in the way of what was good for my district, Governor Rhodes often included me in his plans. My ace in the hole was that Roy Martin was from Portsmouth and he was always pushing for projects to be located in Scioto County. Even though we were of different parties, I got along fine with Roy; I even carried his insurance.

During Rhodes's first eight years as governor, my district got projects including Ohio University's Portsmouth branch building; Shawnee State Park lodge, golf course, and boat marina; and the Southern Ohio Correctional Facility. That's the better part of a thousand jobs in direct employment right there in the area, not including the boost those facilities gave to other businesses. We also got started on building four-lane highways in my district, and today—I don't care which direction you go—there's a four-lane highway to travel on.

No single project created more jobs for my district then the Southern Ohio Correctional Facility. In 1968 people down home didn't care that it was a maximum-security prison because five hundred to six hundred jobs were up for grabs; it's nearly double that now. Five or six other areas were competing for the prison, the closest being Athens about seventy miles away. Then one night about 11 o'clock the governor called me.

"Get your press release ready. I'm announcing it tomorrow," he said.

There was never a time, even from my very first day in office, that jobs weren't a bottom-line, pocketbook issue with me. It goes back to personal experience: Jobs are what brought Mother and Dad to Ohio from Kentucky; jobs are what made the Portsmouth-New Boston area boomtown during much of my youth; and the lack of jobs during hard times is what made me appreciate the importance of a job to a person's dignity and well-being. When early in my legislative career Jim Rhodes was preaching "jobs, jobs, jobs," I was already singing the gospel.

Whether it was a job on my staff or anywhere else in state government, I was always on the lookout to help constituents. Before leaving office, my staff added up all the state jobs and state spending in my district during my tenure. By the time I left office at the end of 1994, I had helped create more than two thousand state jobs in my district, and during my entire career, more than $2 billion had been spent there, much of it on payroll. More than two years after I left public office, the state still was building facilities in southern Ohio in which I had a hand. I worked hard at making sure my constituents got a fair return on their tax dollar.

While I had my share of success and fairly easy elections as a member of the minority, I was put to the test on some tough issues at the Statehouse. None was more difficult in the early years than the Fair Bus Bill. It wasn't a partisan issue. That would have been easy because if our caucus leader had asked me to take a position one way or the other, I would have done it, no questions asked. No, this was a case where each legislator had to decide what was right, and people all over the state including my constituents were worked up about it. As it turned out, all eyes would be on me.

It was 1965, and Sen. Tennyson Guyer from Hancock County introduced legislation requiring school districts to provide transportation to nonpublic school students who lived two miles or more away from school. The state would bear the cost of busing these additional children. The bill passed the Senate and turned into a big fight in the House. Back home, Protestants and Catholics had strong feelings about the bill—and believe me I heard from them. Jack Kennedy may have become the first Catholic to win the presidency, but Nixon won Scioto County.

I was on the Education Committee where the bill was being heard. I can remember nights when the State Highway Patrol would escort us to committee meetings, not because people were giving us a rough time or starting trouble, but because the halls and rotunda of the Statehouse were so packed that we couldn't get through.

When the bill first arrived in the House, I went to see the Speaker, Roger Cloud, one Thursday after session to ask what he thought of it. Roger knew the law backward and forward. And, like me, he was a Protestant and a Mason.

"I wouldn't worry too much about it," he said. "It has nothing to do with my religion. I just don't think it's constitutional," he said. Roger and others believed the state constitution wouldn't allow taxpayers' money to be used to bus Catholic students because of the separation of church and state.

I answered my constituent mail by saying I'd give their views very serious consideration. Never did I come out and say I was going to vote yes or no because I honestly didn't know at that point.

After holding some hearings on the Fair Bus Bill in early July, the committee moved on to other things without taking a vote. Some members were hoping it had stalled out, but before long the Education Committee chairman B. A. Broughton came to me.

"I just got some bad news a while ago. The Speaker wants to start hearings again on the Fair Bus Bill," he said. We were well into August at this point.

"I know you've got some problems with the bill where you come from, and you're trying to play fair with everybody. I'm disappointed the Speaker wants to start hearings again but that's the way it is. Something's happened," he said.

I went to the Speaker right away to see if he had changed his mind about the constitutionality of the bill.

"I've got to be honest with you. The governor said he wants the bill passed. He made a commitment to the Catholic people and he expects me to carry it out. I still think it could have constitutional problems," Roger said. Jim Rhodes pretty much ruled the roost in state government, so when he asked Roger to do something Roger generally responded.

Hearings resumed and then concluded on a Thursday, when the chairman announced that a committee vote would be taken, up or down, the following week. I had my work cut out for me over the weekend, and the first order of business was to get back to New Boston and talk to Dad.

We discussed the pros and cons, right and wrong, and how this would play politically in Scioto County.

"To tell you the truth, I don't know what I'd do if I was in your position," Dad said. "It's a decision you're going to have to make. But whatever you decide, I'm with you 100 percent."

Dad always wanted me to make my own decisions, but I usually could get some guidance from him. This time though I was completely on my own. I headed back to Columbus on Monday, still not knowing what I was going to do. That evening, A. G. Lancione, our minority leader, asked how I was going to vote. I told him the truth.

"I don't know. I'm debating it, but I'm just not sure," I told him.

"The reason I'd like to know is because Myrl Shoemaker is telling people he'll vote however you do," A. G. said. The way things were shaping up, it was going to be close.

About 8:30 the morning of the vote, I had just showered and was shaving in my room at the Sheraton when the Speaker called.

"When are you coming over to the office?" he asked.

"Anytime you tell me to, Mr. Speaker," I said.

"Well, why don't you come over now so I can see you for about five minutes. I need to talk to you about something. You know what it's about," he said.

I got dressed and went straight over. I didn't even stop for breakfast.

"I sure need your help. Myrl Shoemaker has indicated very strongly he's going to vote the way you do, and without your two votes, I don't think the bill will come out of committee," the Speaker said.

It just so happened that I had made up my mind only moments before.

"I'd appreciate it if you'd keep this to yourself, Mr. Speaker, because I'd prefer not to have people trying to change my mind for the next hour, but I'm going to support the bill," I said.

Roger could hardly contain himself.

"You know, I told the Catholic people, 'When the time comes, young Riffe, he'll do the right thing,'" he said.

Like Roger, it wasn't a religious issue with me.

"I'm not going to make any friends down in Scioto County by voting this way. I know that. I've lost some sleep over it. But I remember testimony about Catholic students, little kids, walking to school in the pouring rain, and the public school bus would go right by them and right by their school. That isn't right," I told him.

After I left the Speaker's office, I had to tell my boss. A. G., who was Catholic, never tried to influence me one way or the other. I respected him for that, since the caucus was not taking a position on the bill. But I knew he wanted that bill to pass, and when I told him I would be voting yes, he was one happy man.

When it was time for the committee meeting to start, I had to wade through a thick crowd to get into the room. Once there, Chairman Broughton indicated to us that the votes were not there to pass the bill outright. Instead, a motion would be offered to refer the bill to the more favorable Finance Committee without a recommendation. But first we had to dispose of a resolution to put the issue before the people for a vote, which would have meant sure death for the proposal. It was rejected by a vote of 11-13. That was the first indication to those watching that Myrl and I were for the bill.

Then the motion was offered to refer the bill to the Finance Committee. The committee secretary read off most of the names before getting to me.

"Riffe?" said the committee secretary.

"Yes."

"Shoemaker?"

"Yes."

When the final tally was taken, the motion passed 14-10. Our two votes had kept the bill alive. One week later, the Finance Committee passed the bill, 16-5, and eventually it was passed by the House and enacted.

Afterward, a fellow Mason from Pike County, Ray Evans, told me he was really surprised. "I didn't think you'd ever vote for a Catholic bill," he said.

"That had nothing to do with it, Ray. I'm a Mason. I believe in Masonry. But I also believe in the right thing for schoolchildren. That's the reason I voted for it," I said.

For some reason, there are those who believe the Masons are a Protestant organization. Maybe it's because Catholics have their own fraternal organization in the Knights of Columbus. But I've read about everything there is to read about the Masons, and there is nothing about excluding Catholics or drawing a distinction between Catholics and Protestants. I've never understood the dislike many Protestants and Catholics have for each other. (Years later, when I picked Father

Kenneth Grimes—now Monsignor Grimes—as the House chaplain, it probably bothered some people, but by that time I was Speaker and nobody ever said anything to me about it.)

Sure enough, there was a front-page story in the *Portsmouth Daily Times* with the headline: "Riffe for (Fair Bus) bill." The following morning Roscoe Bussa, a police officer in Portsmouth, stopped by to see me. Roscoe was a Baptist and a Democrat.

"Junior, I'm really surprised at you. If you think for one minute you made some votes supporting that bill, I'm here to say you lost at least a thousand Baptist votes. This is going to hurt you; it might even defeat you next election," he said.

While his prediction didn't scare me, I nevertheless worked hard and made sure the voters understood why I voted the way I did. I won reelection easily in 1966, taking 63 percent of the vote. I also won the respect of Republican and Democratic leaders in the House.

By now I had developed a reputation as someone people on both sides of an issue could deal with and trust. Jim Rhodes must have thought so in 1963 when he asked me to cosponsor the bill that allowed multicounty joint vocational education districts. That bill was very important to the development of vocational education in Ohio, and I considered it an honor to be asked to participate on the front end by a governor of the opposing party. That was not an opportunity that came along every day for a member of the minority in only his third term.

Two very important issues that Jim Rhodes and I always had an intense interest in were education and jobs. Those should always be above politics, at least that's the way I always tried to look at it. And it was Jim Rhodes who really played up the connection between those two issues.

When I went to Columbus to take my place in the Ohio House, education was my number one priority. When Speaker Jim Lantz of Lancaster asked for our committee preferences, I put the Education Committee at the top of my list and got it. That very first term, four of us from southern Ohio—Charlie Jackson of Batavia in Clermont County, Paul Siple of Ironton in Lawrence County, Myrl Shoemaker of Bourneville in Ross County, and me—introduced a bill to increase the minimum salary for schoolteachers. We were all Democrats, we were in the majority, and our bill was enacted.

It was also that first term that the four of us got behind the idea of true equalization of school funding throughout the state so that children in tax-poor school districts would not get an inferior education to those in tax-rich districts. The bill worked so that taxes collected locally on industrial property and utilities would be forwarded to a state school equalization fund. The state would make payments from that fund to school districts to equalize funding.

We thought it was a great idea and something that was badly needed in our districts. It was wrong then—and it still is wrong—that children in a poor, rural area of southern Ohio are at an educational disadvantage because of the place of their birth. This bill was a way to do something about it, and we were ready to go forward with it.

Then one day we got a call from Mark McElroy, the state attorney general, who wanted to meet with us.

"Fellas, some people question whether your bill is constitutional or not because you can't take taxes approved by voters in one school district and spend it in another district. You might have a tough time if someone requests my opinion as attorney general," he said.

McElroy was a Democrat, and we appreciated him being honest with us, even if we were terribly disappointed. We just dropped it. That was my first experience with the school funding formula. As I would find out later, constitutional and political problems would stand in the way of the kinds of changes that some of us legislators thought were needed for the next thirty-five years of my career and beyond.

I always regretted not doing more to further my own education. Some of it was my fault, some of it was the times, and some of it was a system of education in Ohio that was not responding to the needs of people in Scioto County who were going to college. I could have easily gone to college under the GI Bill, but there were a number of reasons why I didn't. One of them was that we did not have a university down home. The closest was Ohio University in Athens, and that was sixty to seventy miles away. There was just no opportunity for many young people in our part of the state. If I had to do it all over again, there's no question that I would get a college degree. When my children graduated from high school, I made sure they all went to college. They could have gotten scholarships because they had the grades—Cathy graduated valedictorian, so did Verna Kay—but I paid for every dime of their educations. I didn't want to deprive some other young person who didn't have the money from going to school.

My experience was not a whole lot different from most people in my hometown. Getting a good education meant getting a high school diploma. You learned the basics—reading, writing, arithmetic, history—and that was it. Most of the time there were plenty of jobs in my area, particularly in manufacturing, so a high school education was enough for most people.

School districts in my part of the state didn't have the resources that the metropolitan areas did. There was only one well-off school down home, and that was New Boston. The steel plant paid 80 to 85 percent of all the tax revenue. Our schools didn't qualify for state aid because we were getting all kinds of money. Whenever Dad ran for reelection as mayor, his letters would always say, "Lowest tax rate in the State of Ohio." Eventually things changed in New Boston when the steel mill pretty much shut down starting in the 1970s.

In spite of my own experience, I knew education would be increasingly important to the future of the people in my district and the state. Businesses wanted the best workers they could get, and jobs, including those in manufacturing, were getting more technical. By the late 1950s, the space race and the atomic age were in full swing. We might not have been able to see exactly what the future would hold, but it was pretty clear that our children would need more education than my generation.

Even so, there was much more to be done in education, and one area that I was very interested in was vocational education. Since so many of the young people in my area were not going to college, I felt the state needed to do more to prepare them for jobs. Too often, high school wasn't giving them the skills they needed to get and hold a good job.

My strong belief in education didn't mean that I was for every proposal that came down the pike. What I wasn't sold on was the call for a centralized board in Columbus to oversee the whole system of higher education. In his first month as governor, Jim Rhodes proposed the creation of the Ohio Board of Regents as a way to help put together his vision of a higher education system in Ohio. The university presidents would try to work things out among themselves, sometimes successfully and sometimes not. They all had their individual agendas and boards to deal with, so the fact that there was no statewide planning to speak of was no surprise. Of Ohio's six universities at the time, only Ohio State was located in a metropolitan area, and there were only two community colleges in the entire state. Not only was access a problem but also there was virtually no technical education at the postsecondary level.

I was on the Education Committee that was hearing the Board of Regents bill at the time, and a lot of people, including me, didn't understand why it was necessary and what it would accomplish. It was brand-new as far as Ohio was concerned. It sounded like so much bureaucracy to me. Besides, the university presidents were dead set against it. Even though the Board of Regents would only be an advisory body to the legislature, the presidents were threatened by anything that would interfere with the way they did business.

After some hearings, the governor seemed to ease up for a while. Then sometime later John Millett, the president of Miami University, came before the committee and supported the bill. I forget who was sitting next to me, but I punched him in the side and said, "There's your first chancellor." Sure enough, the bill was enacted and John Millett became the first chancellor of the Ohio Board of Regents. Jim Rhodes was a master politician. He knew which buttons to push and had promised the university presidents $175 million of a $250 million bond issue if they'd get behind the Board of Regents legislation. Eight months after he took office, the Board of Regents was law. The two bond issues he proposed in 1963 and 1965 provided a total of $330 million for state capital improvements, most of which went to finance some 120 higher education projects.

During my first two terms, Ohio created three new urban universities: Cleveland State, Wright State, and Youngstown State. It added the universities of Akron, Cincinnati, and Toledo to the state system, and it established eight branch campuses, seven community colleges, and eight technical schools. It was an unprecedented time of growth in the state's higher education system.

The Board of Regents proved helpful in making the governor's vision a reality. One of the board's early recommendations was that there would be an institution of higher learning within easy commuting distance of every Ohioan. But in the master plan completed in 1966, the Regents also called for a whole new system of two-year technical schools to be a part of higher education. For the first time, the state government was looking at the state as a whole, both in terms of access to higher education and the needs of local citizens.

Ironically, one of the first things Jim Rhodes asked me to do when he was elected governor for the third time in 1974 was to consider abolishing the Board of Regents. He also wanted to abolish the State Board of Education. The governor asked me to meet him at the Athletic Club in downtown Columbus on a Sunday night, just the two of us. It wasn't even open, so when I arrived a state patrolman directed me in. We sat at a table with hardly any lights on and discussed a lot of things.

"Vern, we just don't need the Regents any longer. Back when it started, we needed it," he said.

"Governor, to tell you the truth, I didn't vote for the Board of Regents to start with," I said.

A lot of people were down on the Regents in those days, saying it wasn't working and the universities weren't listening to them anyway. The State Board of Education had been criticized for the same reasons, and still is today.

I'll tell you this: it could have very easily been abolished in 1975. As I look back on it, I think the Board of Regents has turned out all right in terms of planning for our system of higher education. Whenever I had a problem with the Regents, I was able to get it resolved because eventually they would have to answer to the House anyway. After the governor was sworn in, in 1975, the subject never came up again.

While I was in the minority, my interest in economic development legislation, perhaps more than education, helped me build connections with constituencies not normally aligned with Democrats. Democrats, for instance, were supposed to be prolabor and antibusiness, but I didn't fit that mold, not by a long shot. I never considered myself antibusiness or antilabor. If anything, I was probusiness and prolabor. The way I saw it, business needed a good workforce and all labor was doing was looking out for the needs of working people. I developed very good working relationships with both sides, and why not?! I've belonged to unions as a railroader and fireman, and I've run businesses.

When the Portsmouth Chamber of Commerce asked if I would be on its board of trustees my first term in office, I jumped at the opportunity and became one of the first Democrats in the history of the board. At the state level, the Ohio Chamber of Commerce thought there was nobody like me because I was a conservative Democrat who had the gumption to support them if I felt they were right. My involvement with the chamber was just a part of the long process of building mutual confidence and trust with the business community in Ohio. There's no doubt Jim Rhodes helped with that because even in 1959, Jim Rhodes knew me through my dad. Anyone who knew southern Ohio politics knew Dad.

As for labor, it was a union that gave me my first contribution and my first endorsement. Over the years, particularly when I became a leader, labor was critical to keeping a Democratic majority in the House. They may not have liked it when I took the side of business on an issue, but they almost always came through when it counted.

If something was good public policy, I didn't care who was pushing legislation—I'd support it. Most of the time that wasn't a problem because very few bills were policy bills that required a party-line vote in the first place.

I must have been doing something right because I landed a spot on the Rules Committee in 1963. That position was a real plum; the Rules Committee set the House calendar and it also was a closed committee. That meant members of Rules knew more about what was going on in the House than almost anybody else.

That was my real introduction to leadership, and I served continuously on the Rules Committee for thirty-two years, which is a record.

Even before I got on the Rules Committee, I was getting to know some of the top House leaders on a personal level at the poker table. I love poker, always have. I just didn't know how useful it would be to me in building friendships that would help my political career.

I had scarcely arrived in Columbus in 1959 before I started up a regular poker game in my corner room at the old Deshler Hilton Hotel at Broad and High streets across from the Statehouse. Two of the regulars were Jim Lantz and A. G. Lancione.

When I'd arrive in Columbus on Monday, the first thing I'd do is get a bellhop to bring a big, round table up to my room so we could play after session that day. We'd put a white tablecloth down, get a tub of beer and ice, and start around nine o'clock in the evening. Sometimes we wouldn't finish until six in the morning, when it was time to shower, shave, and go to work.

The Deshler and Neil House hotels, and later the Sheraton Hotel and the Galleria Tavern, were all places where legislators, lobbyists, executive branch people, and reporters would go. A lot of problems got worked out in those places, and people really got to know you on a personal level. I thrived on it, but A. G. didn't take to socializing much. I believe that's one reason why, as the years went by and I took on greater responsibility, members of our caucus were more comfortable coming to me with their problems than they were going to A. G.

A. G. was an attorney, and a darn good one, but when the session was over at noon on Thursday or whatever it was, he was already checked out of the hotel and ready to go home to practice law. I stayed in Columbus much more of the time, taking care of caucus business and working with members on their problems. That, as much as anything else, is responsible for me becoming a leader. Plain, old hard work is what helped me to get to the top and stay on top. Win, lose, or draw, nobody can say they outworked me during my legislative career.

I might not have survived the 1960 election after casting all those votes for tax increases if I hadn't worked like the dickens to support my district. I answered every bit of mail, attended public meetings, sent a baby card to the family of every newborn in the district, worked the fair—you name it. If a constituent had a problem, I'd often go to their house or call them on the phone, sometimes as late as nine or ten at night. People were impressed with that. They'd think, "Here's a state representative still working, interested in my problems." I'd also send out surveys to teachers, attorneys, clergy, and other groups of people to find out how they felt about certain legislation.

Dad was always pushing me to stay on top of things. The day after the general election in 1958, he and I went to Johnson's Restaurant in Portsmouth to have breakfast. A family friend, Paul Soltis, came in, and Dad immediately said, "Put it on my check."

"Wait a minute," Paul said. "Vern Junior bought my breakfast last week. The election's over."

Dad said, "The election was over yesterday. Now we're thinking about the next one." That's the way Dad was.

Jim Rhodes and my dad both believed when you're in politics, it's just like a business: You work at it every day of the year, every minute of the day, all the time you're awake. Dad hammered that into me.

While in Columbus, I would work until eleven o'clock or midnight sometimes. If members had a problem, they'd come in. If lobbyists had a problem, they'd come in. That's when Dick Celeste and I became real close. He was in his office across the hall at the Statehouse, and he also worked late into the night. Members took notice, and when we won the majority, they knew they needed that kind of hard work if we were going to keep it. Maybe I didn't know any better, but I was eager to do caucus work; I had patience, good political instincts, and I saw opportunity where others didn't.

Bit by bit, I began to take on more and more responsibility. When A. G. ran for minority leader in 1963, I was his campaign manager. After he was elected, I became his assistant and confidant and probably should have had a title of administrative assistant because that's basically what I was.

A. G. put a lot of matters into my hands whether it was legislation or private business. He wanted me involved to the point of putting a desk for me in his office. Anytime a member or anyone else had a problem, I was right there to handle it.

He turned over most of the personnel matters to me by making me chairman of our caucus's Personnel Committee. We had our own secretarial pool, and everything relating to it had to go through the committee.

I even put together committee assignment recommendations for the Democratic Caucus members in 1963 and 1965, when Speaker Cloud asked A. G. for his preferences. A. G. asked me to work it out, and he checked it over before we turned it in.

There are few leadership responsibilities more critical than committee assignments, and when problems arose I would be the one to smooth things over. Much later in 1973, when I was Speaker Pro Tem and A. G. was Speaker, C. J. McLin had told Ed Orlett he would get him on the Judiciary Committee. They were both from Dayton, and C. J. was looking out for Ed since it was his first term. I made up the list, but there must have been a miscommunication because Ed wasn't on Judiciary. They were both upset, and we didn't need problems like that since we were trying to establish ourselves as the majority caucus after twelve years on the sidelines.

I got the list again and quickly saw a way out. We had put Claude Fiocca back on the Judiciary even though he was a new member of the Reference Committee, which was considered a prestigious assignment. I went straight to A. G.

"You've already rewarded Claude, but you've got to look after your new people. If we're going to build this caucus, we need to put Ed on Judiciary instead," I told him.

A. G. didn't like it one bit. Claude was very loyal to him, and they were good friends. Claude raised all kinds of hell about it too. He said it was a dirty deal and he wouldn't drop Judiciary. They simply didn't understand that this problem had to be solved or it could create even bigger problems down the road. Our credibility as leaders was at stake. That's when I put it to Claude.

"Are you thinking about yourself, or are you thinking of the caucus?" I asked. "This is a way to work things out, solve some problems, and keep harmony in the caucus."

That stopped them in their tracks. They knew I was right, and just that quickly, it was done.

Now, I've made my share of mistakes just like anybody else. But when it came to something really important I had usually considered all the angles and I felt like I knew what the outcome would be. That's why A. G. liked having me around, and on the rare occasions when A. G. didn't follow my advice, he paid the price. When I was directing his reelection effort as House minority leader in 1966, for instance, I was concerned about his chances against Frank Pokorny of Cuyahoga County. I had been talking to a lot of members and knew A. G. could lose it. One day, after I had just finished traveling the state on A. G.'s behalf, I ran into Tony Russo of Cleveland at the Red Lion in the Neil House. Tony said he would vote for A. G., but he wanted a commitment to put him on the Rules Committee before he would agree to support him. I told Tony to wait right there while I checked with A. G., who was upstairs.

When I walked into A. G.'s room, Rep. Dick Christiansen from Richland County was there. I strongly advised A. G. to take the deal, but Dick said A. G. had it wrapped up. Now, I liked Dick as a friend, but he didn't know what he was talking about when it came to putting together votes, and I told them so.

"I just got back into town from traveling the state, and it's tight out there. A. G.'s in trouble. We have to make any deal we can make," I said.

A. G. didn't listen; why, I don't know. I had to tell Tony there was no deal, which was too bad because Tony's word was good. When it came time to caucus and the votes for minority leader were counted, A. G. lost by one vote. One. Tony would have been the difference.

In 1970, when A. G. wanted me to direct his campaign for minority leader again, I made him promise to follow my advice before I'd sign on. He did and went on to become minority leader again and, two years later, Speaker.

One mistake that has always bothered me was in 1969 when I joined the caucus in walking off the floor of the House in protest of how we were treated on the budget bill. John McDonald of Licking County, our minority leader, wanted us to boycott the vote, and we were unified in carrying it out. But no sooner did we walk than it started to really gnaw at me. I knew deep down inside that you're not doing your job when you fail to vote. That's why citizens send you to Columbus, to consider and vote on legislation that affects their everyday lives. We simply weren't doing our jobs that day, and I vowed right then and there never to do it again. I believe if A. G. had been minority leader at the time, I could have stopped it and probably would have.

With few exceptions, I got along famously with A. G., but he had a way about him that some people simply misunderstood. Art Wilkowski of Toledo used to get so mad at A. G. Lancione because he would go in to talk to him about something, particularly when A. G. was Speaker, and A. G. would sit there and read a newspaper. To make matters worse, Art was liberal as hell and A. G. was downright conservative (depending on the issue).

Even though I had been working my tail off for the caucus for years, I didn't begin to think seriously about a leadership position until the late 1960s. There had always been people ahead of me with leadership experience. Besides, coming from a rural county, I had been at a disadvantage in running against people from large metropolitan counties with big legislative delegations. I knew you couldn't come to Columbus and have everything overnight; you had to be patient and be part of a team.

I developed my own niche and worked over many years to strengthen the caucus. Dad was absolutely right when he told me that you have to have an organization to be successful in politics. Too many good people won't run if there's a weak organization or no organization behind them.

For years I kept a low profile on the floor of the House. Mostly I sat back, listened, and watched. In my view, it was up to the leaders and chairmen to take the lead on legislation on the floor. I may have gotten up once or twice to speak to a land transfer bill involving Scioto County, but that was about it. I always believed you didn't have to make a lot of floor speeches to be a successful legislator. The one big thing you had to do was take care of your people back home. Ninety-five percent of the people didn't know anything about voting records because they weren't publicized then like they are today. But if a constituent had a problem, I was always available.

I was more active in committees, and I had some good ones—Insurance Committee, Highways Committee, Education Committee, and Rules and Taxation Committee, as it was called then.

Our fortunes as a caucus began to change in 1970. When Jack Gilligan became governor, Democrats swept the statewide offices and we picked up ten seats in the House. We were within striking distance with forty-five Democrats to fifty-four Republicans. Most important of all, Democrats now controlled the state Apportionment Board, which drew the lines for legislative districts. We knew our long dry spell in the House could soon be over.

After four years out of the minority leadership, A. G. was running for minority leader again and he wanted me to handle his campaign.

John McDonald had run unsuccessfully for attorney general in 1970, losing to Bill Brown in the Democratic primary. After the election he took position as Governor Gilligan's legislative liaison, so there was no incumbent House minority leader. Don Pease of Oberlin was going for it, and so was Myrl Shoemaker. I tried to talk Myrl out of it because I knew he didn't have a chance, but he had convinced himself that if A. G. and Don could not get a majority of the caucus, he could be the compromise candidate.

The first thing I did was talk to Jack Gilligan about getting his support, and he said he preferred to stay out of it.

"Vern, I promise you I won't get involved because that should be up to you guys. You elect your own leader," he said.

"If you do that, I'll be satisfied," I said, and he agreed to stay neutral.

Three days before our caucus meeting, tragedy struck. A. G.'s wife, June, died of a stroke. I was with A. G. the day she passed away and told him not to worry about the caucus election, that I would take care of everything. I wanted him to be able to make arrangements, be with his family, and grieve.

But as the day of our caucus meeting approached, it was no secret that John McDonald was working to elect Don Pease. On the morning of the vote, I realized something had to be done, so I got on the telephone and called the governor's office.

"Governor, I thought you told me you were going to stay out of our leadership race," I said.

"I am."

"Have you read the papers?" I asked, pointing out that his legislative liaison was clearly identified as working to elect Don. "If you're supporting Don Pease, it's going to break the caucus in two."

"That's not true that I'm supporting Don Pease," he said.

"Then you need to come to our caucus this afternoon and tell them that," I said.

"I've got another event to attend this afternoon, but as soon as it is over, I'll be there," the governor said.

Since A. G. was a candidate, I had seniority in our caucus. By tradition that meant I would preside over the caucus meeting. This was important because the governor had to give a speech first and might not be able to come to our caucus right at 2 P.M. I sure as hell didn't want a vote to take place before he arrived.

Just before two o'clock, Jim Flannery of Cuyahoga County said some people in the caucus didn't think I ought to preside since I was A. G.'s campaign manager. I could see what they were trying to pull.

"Let me tell you something, Jimmy. We've had this unwritten rule for years and years. If you want to object to it, you can do that on the floor of the House before the caucus, but I'm going to preside today."

About 2:15, Jack Gilligan walked in, and I thought John McDonald was going to drop. He was standing behind the rail at the back of the House. Since it was the first time he had appeared before our caucus, the governor gave a short talk, saying how he was happy we had picked up ten seats and so forth.

"I want you to know that whomever you choose as your leader, I will be happy to work with him. That's a decision for you to make. You have all good people here," the governor said.

With that done, I appointed two people to count ballots, we took the vote and it was all over. A. G. got 23 votes, Don got 16, and Myrl got 6. It takes a majority of the caucus—not a plurality—to win, and A. G. took it by one vote. Had he lost, there's no telling what would have happened to my career.

It wasn't the last time I would outflank Don. After we won the majority in 1972 and I was Speaker Pro Tem, he had authored legislation to create so-called "Education Service Districts" to provide special education and administrative services to a county or multicounty area. There were a lot of us from the more rural parts of the state who saw this as an attempt to take some local control away from our schools.

"This bill threatens the very foundation of our locally controlled school districts and substitutes, instead, a state-controlled level of bureaucracy that is simply not necessary and, more important, not wanted by a large segment of our population," I told the full House as it prepared to vote. "I don't think we should rush to centralize everything because centralization is not, by definition, better or more efficient. We sometimes lose important qualities [local] when we consolidate."

This was not an issue that divided along Democratic and Republican lines. It really depended on how each member's school districts might be affected. Because of the number of legislators from urban areas, I was concerned about whether the bill could be defeated on an up-or-down vote. So instead, I moved to refer it to the Finance Committee, where I knew my friend, Myrl Shoemaker, would make sure it never saw the light of day.

Don Pease opposed my motion, saying, "The Speaker Pro Tem is calling in his IOUs." He knew members had reason to support me because I helped make the committee assignments, hired the personnel, and spent a considerable amount of time attending to the individual needs of our caucus members. You bet I called in those IOUs, and the bill was never heard of again.

This was a pivotal time for us in terms of capturing the majority, so I wasted no time in doing anything I could to set us up for the 1972 election. First, I was A. G.'s point man in drawing up new House district lines. I was the one who tended to the details, worked with other legislative leaders, and made sure decisions were made on our end.

Next, I turned my attention to fund-raising. There was no such thing as caucus fund-raisers in those days; the party was strapped for money, so our candidates were more or less on their own. Of course Jack Gilligan was helping with money and organization, which was a boost since we hadn't had a Democratic governor for eight years. As for my part, I decided to travel the state and use every connection I had to raise money for our candidates. It wasn't much by today's standards but, as I found out later, it meant a lot to our candidates that I was out there trying to help them.

I also helped recruit candidates wherever I thought it could help, and for the first time the governor's office was involved in a significant way in recruitment under the direction of John McDonald and Bill Chavanne. Traditionally the caucus had done little in the way of candidate recruitment and the party hadn't done much more. Bill called legislative candidates "the orphans of candidates," which was pretty much the truth. If ever there was a time to field strong candidates, it was the election of 1972 with the majority in the balance.

When the votes were tallied on election day, we had won the majority in the Ohio House for only the third time since 1949. We picked up thirteen more seats for a 58-41 margin. The majority may have been ours based on the new lines alone; I was never one to underestimate the power of the pencil. The real work was just beginning in my view, however, and some things would have to be done differently if we were to hold on to the majority. Like Dad had taught me, I was already thinking about the next election.

Right after the election, the caucus convened to elect our leaders for the 110th General Assembly to begin two months later. A. G. was due the Speakership, since he was minority leader before the election. I was elected Speaker Pro Tem so that I could continue the working relationship I had with A. G. Also elected were Barney Quilter of Toledo as majority floor leader and Bill Mallory of Cincinnati as assistant majority floor leader.

If we wanted to protect our incumbents and increase the majority, we couldn't count on anyone else to do it; we'd have to do it ourselves. I took it upon myself to put the program together. Ohio House races still were not expensive compared to today. Big TV buys hadn't started in legislation races, there was less polling, and direct mail was used more sparingly. But I was looking further down the road, and what I saw in newspapers and on television was that money would be the key to holding power.

Thirteen months after the 1972 election, I put on the first-ever House Democratic Caucus fund-raising dinner at the Neil House Hotel. In fact, no legislative caucus had held a caucus fund-raiser before. We took in $85,000, maybe the biggest political fund-raiser ever in Columbus outside the state political party organizations. Things really started to gel after that.

I put together a candidate recruitment program with the goal of fielding someone in every district, something that had never been done in my experience. We looked for electable candidates where we had a shot at winning and strong candidates in uphill districts to at least make the Republicans work and use some of their money. Never again would we give seats away if I had anything to do with it.

For the first fifteen years, I had learned a lot watching the old pros such as A. G., Jim Lantz, Roger Cloud, and Chuck Kurfess. Then, when the opportunity presented itself, I made a move. A. G. had let it be known that he wanted to retire at the end of one term as Speaker and he and many of the caucus members wanted me to be his successor.

Then in 1974, A. G. attended a national legislative conference in Arizona, along with a lot of our members, while I stayed behind and took care of House business. When Art Wilkowski returned from the conference, he called me.

"I heard A. G. make a statement out there I don't like. He indicated he was running for the House again and he wants to be Speaker," Art said.

A. G. had told me the same thing that morning. He said his plan was to hold the seat for his son until after the election. "I'm going to retire. I've had enough. I just want to make sure my son succeeds me in my district, and I want you to make sure it's done," he told me.

It was the prerogative of the caucus to fill vacancies, and I had no problem with it. "If that's who you want to succeed you, absolutely. I'll make sure it's done," I said.

A. G. remarried the same year and, following the legislative conference, he and his new wife, Madeline, went on a trip. After that trip A. G. seemed to change his mind about retirement. The speculation was that his new wife had talked him out of it. I also assumed that his brother, Nelson Lancione, had something to do with it. Around the same time, Nelson was running to become the next state chair of the Ohio Democratic Party and his chief competitor was Paul Tipps, the Montgomery County chairman.

When Art first came to me about this, I told everybody, no, I wasn't going to seek the Speakership based on what A. G. had told me about his plan. Now Art Wilkowski, Barney Quilter, Mike DelBane, and Tom Carney, among others, were saying: "Vern, you either go after the Speakership or we're going to get somebody else to do it. We're not going to support A. G. again." They felt that A. G. wasn't keeping his word about retiring. They also felt I had worked hard for the caucus, and I deserved it. They weren't the only ones.

Such people as Pete O'Grady just couldn't understand what was holding me back. Pete was the executive director of the Ohio Democratic Party until accepting a cabinet position in the Gilligan Administration.

"When are you going to wake up and start running for leadership yourself instead of carrying his [A. G.'s] water?" he said. "Don't you think it's about time, with your talent and the way you've gone out and campaigned for him, that you start doing that for yourself?"

Still, I was reluctant to run against my friend.

Art was leaking things to the press, and one day a story hit the papers about a letter Art had written talking me up as a candidate for Speaker. A. G. was furious. Since Art was not in town that day, A. G. called Barney to his office to lay into him. But, as Barney told me later, he was the one who laid it on the line.

"Say what you want to. You're entitled. But you told members of this caucus two years ago that you wanted to serve as Speaker for one term and then retire. We voted for you on that basis, and now we're going to hold you to that commitment," Barney said.

One day in December of 1974, I met Barney in the lounge at the Fort Hayes Hotel on Spring Street. Barney was pressuring me to run for Speaker, and we must have spent the better part of two hours hashing it out over popcorn and drinks. When we left to walk down High Street toward the Capitol I still couldn't make up my mind. Barney told me that Art Wilkowski had drafted a letter to A. G. saying the votes were there to elect me Speaker, but he wouldn't deliver it without my okay.

"He's waiting for a call from you. What do I tell him?" Barney asked.

"If that's the way it's going to be," I said, "tell him I'll run." I knew I could do the job and wanted to do it. The only part I didn't like was running against A. G. The caucus wanted a change, however, and I didn't see any alternative at that point.

I worked hard at my campaign for Speaker just like I did everything else. A majority of the members were lined up behind me, but I wasn't taking anything for granted. I really wanted to have the Cuyahoga County delegation locked in, so I met with the top people who controlled Democratic politics there, including George Forbes and Tony Garofoli, cochairs of the Cuyahoga County Democratic Party. I'm not sure how much convincing I had to do. They knew me and had done their homework. When the meeting was over, it was a done deal.

When word got out that the Cuyahoga County delegation was behind me, I got a call from A. G. "I know I don't have the votes," he said. "What happens to me now?"

I had already thought about it, and I figured that I needed to smooth over any hard feelings if I wanted a unified caucus (plus, A. G. was a friend). Things were going to be different under my leadership, and I wanted everybody pulling in the same direction as quickly as possible.

First, I asked A. G. to be chairman of the Rules Committee, the first time anybody other than the Speaker would serve in that position. Then I asked him to chair the Legislative Service Commission, which was the research arm of the legislature. He'd have his own office, secretary, whatever he needed.

"You'd do that?" he asked.

"Absolutely," I said.

Art and the others tried to talk me out of it, but I wouldn't hear of it. "He's the dean of our caucus. If he wants those appointments, they're his," I said.

The caucus accepted that, and when it came time to elect the leadership, A. G. wouldn't let his name be put in nomination for Speaker. There's no question he was hurt by the experience, but he remained a loyal member of our caucus. From then on, there was no stronger supporter for me than A. G. Lancione. He was always the first to say "I support the Speaker" on an issue. We remained friends, but those were tough days for us both, no question about it.

As for the chairmanship of the state party, I supported Paul Tipps over Nelson Lancione. Whatever involvement Nelson had in the Speakership race made no difference to me because all he was doing was supporting his brother. I'd expect him to do that. Paul and I got along well together, and I sincerely believed that he would make a great chairman, which he did.

Once I became Speaker, I was in the strongest possible position to make changes, and I did. For the first time, I had complete authority to make committee assignments: I could make them and take them away. Naturally, I took care of people who were good soldiers, those who were there when you needed them. I knew each individual better than anybody else in terms of their interests and the role they could play in a committee. I also took the geographic location of each member into consideration when I made committee assignments.

One thing I always did was send out a form and ask members to give me their first four committee choices. I always kept their requests in case a member came in to complain, and it's a good thing I did.

One time Pat Sweeney charged into my office upset. "Boss, you didn't treat me right on committee assignments," he said.

So, I took the request sheet out of my desk to check because half the time I couldn't remember their requests.

"There it is. You got three out of the four committees you requested. What are you complaining about?" I said.

"Is that mine?" he asked.

"You're darn right it's yours. Is that your handwriting up there with your name?"

"Yeah."

"Then it's yours," I said.

If I hadn't kept those requests, neither one of us would have known who was right or wrong. But the point is this: I worked hard at honoring those requests and putting members on the committees they were interested in. Members are more loyal if you're fair and honest with them, and that's important because committees are where members spend most of their time.

As the work of the legislature increased, there were opportunities to create new committees. From the time I first took office until the time I retired, the number of committees almost doubled (from seventeen to thirty-two) and I'd say the workload doubled too. In 1959 the state budget was $1 billion; when I left it was $34 billion. Thirty years ago, there was no Environmental Protection Agency, the prison system was a lot smaller, and utility rates weren't shooting through the roof. Our university system was smaller. We had fewer roads. Over the years, the problems became bigger and more complicated. Some of my committee chairmen complained they were overloaded and there was no way they could give bills proper consideration.

I also thought some areas, such as veterans affairs and children, deserved more attention than they had received in the past, and so I created committees to deal specifically with those issues. I'm proud to say that the Ohio House created one of the first legislative committees in the country devoted solely to children.

I'd be less than honest if I didn't acknowledge that by increasing the number of committees, it also increased the size of my leadership team. I expected committee chairmen to be loyal to me, since I appointed them and they were receiving additional pay along with the additional responsibility. And with roughly half of the House Democrats being a part of leadership, loyalty and teamwork were never a major problem as long as I was Speaker. But I never would have increased the number of committees if there wasn't a positive public purpose to it.

I saw other needs among members over the years, and when I got into a position to do something about them, I did. When I first started, for instance, members didn't have offices and worked right from their desks in the House chamber. We didn't have personal secretaries or staff either, just a stenopool.

Today every House member has staff support and an office. As recently as 1989, Ohio had the lowest per capita expenditures on the legislature—$2.28 per person—of any state in the country, according to the National Conference of State Legislatures.

More importantly, in the old days, legislators didn't have the responsibility or authority they do today. I can remember when the legislature was what you might call a "weak sister" to the executive branch. A lot of governors had their way with the legislature, and none was better at it than James A. Rhodes.

During his first eight years, Jim Rhodes called the shots. Every state office was Republican, and anytime you wanted to get a bill passed you went to the governor's office; you didn't go to the Speaker of the House or the President of the Senate. I put a stop to that.

If there's one thing people have to give me credit for, it's that I regained the rightful authority of the legislature. Pat Sweeney recognized it, and he was one of the first to support me for Speaker. I think he saw, by gosh, a guy doing what a leader should be doing. I can't tell you how important that was to creating loyalty and a strong caucus.

As early as 1973 as Speaker Pro Tem, I let it be known that the budget was going to be written by the legislature, and it was going to start in the House of Representatives. This was the first big step toward restoring the power of the legislative branch.

About this time, Bill Chavanne with Governor Gilligan's office was lobbying my members on the budget after hours one day at the Statehouse. I said, "Bill, do you know what time it is? It's five minutes after five. Get your butt out of here. Those kinds of decisions will be made by the Finance Committee and then on the floor of the House. Now, get out of here."

I'm sure it startled Bill. It wasn't that I didn't check with the governor's office. I had a good working relationship with Jack Gilligan. Besides, you never ignore a governor when he has the veto. But I was trying to make a point, and I think the point was made.

Later, in my first speech as Speaker, I served notice that there were going to be more changes. "The governor-elect, while receiving a plurality of the votes cast in his race, did not receive a majority of the votes. In contrast, the Democrats in this House received a clear majority of the votes cast in House elections, while the Democrats who ran for election to the Senate did likewise. Additionally, the total vote for Democrats running for this House exceeded the total vote for the governor-elect.

"Given these facts, I believe the people of this state expect the Ohio General Assembly to be at least an equal with the governor in leading the government of this state. I believe they expect this General Assembly to have its own ideas about how Ohio should be governed. Accordingly, this House, together with our friends in the Senate, will move vigorously forward with an agenda for Ohio."

We made other changes that put a tremendous amount of power back into the hands of the legislature. One involved the Joint Committee on Agency Rule Review (JCARR), which has to sign off on executive agency rules to make sure they meet the intent of laws passed by the legislature. The other involved the state Controlling Board, which authorizes the release of state funds for budget expenditures.

Prior to JCARR, the legislature had no direct control over the rule-making process. The problem was that only the legislature could enact laws, but agency rules had the force of law. As far as I was concerned, no body should be making laws in the State of Ohio except the General Assembly.

During my second term as Speaker, Rep. Tommy Gilmartin of Youngstown put together a bill to create JCARR. He got the idea based on some model legislation he had heard about at a legislative conference. Under Tommy's bill, if rules didn't follow legislative intent, JCARR could invalidate them. Even though the bill had bipartisan support, Governor Rhodes vetoed it. The governor heretofore had been successful in making his vetos stick, but this time both the Senate and House voted to override, and the bill became law. Next session, the legislature passed the bill again and this time the governor allowed it to become law without his signature. The fact is, the legislature would always have the last say by enacting new laws, and I guess the governor realized that.

Today an agency can hardly do a thing in the way of new rules or rule changes without JCARR approval. In later years, I often thought we could make the process work even better by authorizing JCARR not only to invalidate rules but also to rewrite or amend them. I never got around to trying it though.

The Controlling Board was established to authorize the expenditure of money for emergencies when the legislature was not in session. In the old days, the legislature would adjourn *sine die* and could only reconvene if the governor called it back in a special session.

The Controlling Board had very limited authority, but legislators were in a minority on the board. I never thought that was right, since the legislature enacts the budget. When I became Speaker, I promoted legislation creating a legislative majority on the Controlling Board. We also began putting language in the budget that made certain expenditures subject to Controlling Board approval. Over the years, the Controlling Board became more and more involved in the release of

more and more money. It's to the point now where individual contracts between executive agencies and consultants or vendors have to
clear the Controlling Board.

Even with the legislative majority on the Controlling Board today,
I'm not so sure it is constitutional because under our state constitution, the legislature cannot delegate its authority. Having just one
person from the executive branch of government with a vote on the
Controlling Board could mean we were doing just that—delegating
legislative authority.

Like I said, governors were used to having their way with the legislature, so I thought it was high time the executive branch was a
little more responsive to us. Even before we won the majority again,
I was going to bat for members when it came to dealing with the
governor's office or agencies. When you're in the majority, it's easier
to get things accomplished. I'd think nothing of calling the director
of a department or agency and getting him to sit down with us to
discuss a problem. It wasn't a matter of strong-arming anybody: If
a member was wrong about something, I'd be the first to say so. But
if I thought he was right, I supported him right down the line with
whatever executive agency it was.

I wasn't beyond using my position to benefit my district when I
thought it was fair. In 1976, for instance, the state Department of Education ruled that Pike County could not have its own joint vocational
school because it did not have a large enough student population. Students would have been sent to Scioto or Pickaway County instead.
True, its enrollment was smaller than many of the other joint vocational schools, but I felt strongly that the people of Pike County had
a right to try and make it work if the commitment was there. I asked
State Superintendent of Education Martin Essex to come to my office.

"Now, Martin, you're not going to do that. At your next state board
meeting, I want a resolution grandfathering in Pike County's district.
If you don't, I'm going to do it by legislation in the budget bill," I said.

He took it to the board the following week. After the meeting,
Martin called. "It's done," he said.

Shortly thereafter, the Pike County Joint Vocational School District got funds from the state and the Appalachian Regional Com-

mission to build a new facility. It opened in the fall of 1980, and I am extremely proud that they chose to name it the Vernal G. Riffe Joint Vocational School. Most importantly, the school is thriving, and today it serves between 50 and 60 percent of the eleventh and twelfth graders in Scioto County as well.

The shift of more authority to the legislature was no big deal for Jack Gilligan. He came out of the legislative branch of government as a city councilman in Cincinnati. He did a yeoman's job down there and made sure the council was the dominant factor in government in the city. When we started to give the legislature a stronger role in decisions, I think the governor accepted it.

It was a lot harder for Governor Rhodes to handle when he returned for his third term. Things had changed completely from his first two terms, when he had a Republican House and Senate. By 1975 it was just the opposite, and it took him a couple of years to accept the fact that he couldn't get much done without us. But I'll say this: Once he did, no governor got along better with the House.

After I had been Speaker going on five years, I received a call from the Speaker of the U.S. House of Representatives, Tip O'Neill. He was trying to entice me to run for the seat being vacated by Bill Harsha, who was not running for reelection in 1980.

"I've been told you can win that," he said.

In fact, I had one heck of a shot at it. There were Republican chairmen down there telling Bob McEwen, who eventually won the seat, that if I ran that's who they'd have to back. Then Bob himself came to see me and said he wouldn't run if I decided to.

"Mr. Speaker, why would I want to run for the U.S. House of Representatives over there to be just one of 435 with that seniority system you've got?" I asked him.

"Well, from what they tell me you wouldn't be just one of 435 here. You'd move up quickly the way you operate," he said.

"If you changed the rules a little bit I might just do it but, no, I'm not interested," I said.

"You're just not interested in coming to Congress?"

"Maybe at one time, but not now. I like state government," I said, and that was it.

At that stage of my career, Washington had no appeal for me, nor did any other office for that matter. I flirted with running for governor a couple of times, somewhat seriously in 1990, but there was one fact I simply could never escape: I loved being Speaker.

⊚ 3 ⊚

Loyalty and Discipline

I guess you could say 75 to 80 percent of what I learned about politics came from Dad. Maybe all of it. He always told me to be honest and fair and tell the truth, even if it hurt. He'd say, "People might disagree with you, but they have to respect that."

Dad was tough when he had to be, but that's not what people remember. Folks would do just about anything for Dad because he would do anything for them. I can't count the number of people he helped in his lifetime, but I know this much: They never forgot it.

That's really where I learned about loyalty and discipline. My old friend Barney Quilter always said that you accomplish more with honey than with vinegar, and that's really true. There's a time when every leader has to use discipline, but nine times out of ten you get people's loyalty by helping them, not punishing them. That's what Dad did, and that's what I tried to do.

Dad created a loyal following, not just by the way he did his job but by the way he lived his life. During the Depression, for instance, when I was only four or five years old, I can remember Mother and Dad going to the store. They'd come back to the kitchen where we had this big, round table and put the groceries—flour, potatoes, sugar, whatever it was—in three different piles. I remember asking why they did that.

"Son, you see this one here? That's for Mr. Sims next door," Dad said. Mr. Sims was laid off from the steel mill and had three or four children to feed. "This other one here is for your Uncle Fred." Uncle Fred also was laid off from the steel mill and had a family. "The third one is for us."

But it wasn't just during the Depression. Dad did things like that for people all his life. He wasn't seeking anything in return. He was just a good person who believed that you do good things for other people. I learned from that. I also learned that sometimes loyalty is betrayed. Dad would not tolerate lying or disrespect for authority. It didn't matter if you were friend or enemy; he held everyone to the same standard.

One time when I was a kid, Uncle Elmer (my mother's brother) having had one too many drinks, got in a fight at a pool hall on Park Avenue in New Boston. Dad was a police officer, and he arrested Elmer and another man.

Elmer looked at him and said, "Vernal, I'm not going to jail."

"Elmer, you're either walking out of here or I'm going to drag you out," Dad told him.

After several attempts, Elmer still refused to go and that was it; Dad coldcocked him. Elmer bit his lip and went right to his knees, blood was running all over. He got Elmer out of there and locked him up with the other fellow. Dr. Mills had to come over and put stitches in Elmer's head.

Mother heard about how Dad hit Elmer on the head, locked him up, and so forth, and she jumped on him about it. Dad looked her right in the eyes and said, "Jewell, don't interfere." He had no double standards.

Unfortunately, Elmer wasn't the only one in our family to have a drinking problem. Mother's youngest brother kept getting jailed for drunkenness. One time Dad sent him to the county jail for thirty days. He got out on a Friday and was back in jail the next night. On the following Monday he had to appear in court before Dad, who was mayor then, and Dad lit into him.

"Mister, if you think you're going to get drunk and lay around in jail so the taxpayers can pay your room and board, it's not going to work. You've got twenty-four hours to either get out of town or you're going to the workhouse in Cincinnati for six months. I'm not putting up with it anymore," he said.

He knew Dad meant what he said, so he left for Anderson, Indiana, the next day. My Aunt Grace and I took him down to the train station and paid his way. He didn't show his face in New Boston for twelve years. He finally called one day while Dad was still mayor and said, "Vernal, I'd sure like to come over to pay a visit. I haven't seen some of the family for years."

"Are you still drinking?" Dad asked him right away.

"No. I'm going to church, and I haven't had a drink in six months," he said.

"Well, I've got no problem with you coming over here, but I'll tell you one thing: If you take one drink out on the street, I'll do what I said," Dad told him.

He never touched another drop in his life as far as we know.

Dad had two brothers with drinking problems, and all those incidents were tough on both Mother and Dad. I asked Dad if he'd ever taken a drink, and he said, yes, when he was eighteen years old and out with a bunch of guys. He took a swig of booze, didn't like it, spit it out, and never tried liquor again.

"Son, why would I drink something I didn't like?" he said.

Dad could have used his position to get me out of a jam many a time, but he never did. He knew if you started making exceptions, people wouldn't respect you.

Once when I was a young man, I got caught speeding in Waverly on the way to an insurance convention in Columbus. I had a nice blue, Chevy BelAir and I was probably going 60 or 65 in a 45 mph zone when the State Patrol got me. They set my hearing for a few days later before the mayor of Waverly.

I was explaining what happened to Fred Brown, the police chief in New Boston, when in walks Dad. It was about six o'clock in the evening, and he had just finished trying a State Patrol case in mayor's court.

"They got Junior for speeding in Waverly the other day and he's set to go before the mayor. You know the mayor there. He's a good guy. Why don't you see if you can get Junior off," Fred said.

"Son, were you speeding?" Dad asked.

"Yes, I was going too fast. No doubt about that."

"Let me put it this way: You're no better than anybody else, and you need to go up there and appear before the mayor. If you don't have the money to pay the fine, I'll lend you the money. Remember who you're talking to. I've got to hear cases the patrol brings before me and act on them."

I knew better, but Fred didn't think there was any harm in asking. I entered a plea of guilty and paid a fine of ten dollars and court costs. As I recall, the mayor suspended the fine.

The reason I wouldn't ask Dad myself is because a friend of mine was arrested once for driving while intoxicated. He had been in the military, and he asked me if I could talk to Dad about his service record in the hopes that he would get a break. I did, and Dad let me know right away what he thought about that.

"Son, if he had been walking around drunk and the police picked him up, that's one thing. But he was driving a vehicle drunk. I don't go for that, and don't you ever come to me again and ask me to ever give a break to someone who is charged with a violation."

My dad never whipped me in his life; never laid a hand on me. But when he told me, "Junior, do this," I did it. No questions asked.

Dad also taught me that when people work for you, they have to be loyal. If they're not, it'll only get worse and soon enough you won't be able to get the job done. When my time came, I understood that to be a strong leader and a successful leader, people had to be loyal to me.

My upbringing helped me out a lot when I first got elected to office. The leaders in the House really took to someone who was honest and loyal to them, and my loyalty to leadership helped get me my first big break in the House.

Just before I took office, Governor-elect Mike DiSalle came out for Jim Lantz as Speaker. Lantz was running against Jim McGettrick of Cleveland. The governor called Dad about getting my support. Dad was good friends with the governor, as he was with most of the top state politicians of his time. Nobody knew Scioto County like Dad, and he was always helping the top Democrats in campaigns there.

"Governor, I'll be happy to tell him you called, but I'd call back and talk to him because he's the state representative, and I want him to start out that way," Dad told him. Sure enough, I got the call, and I committed to him that I'd support Jim.

Jim won the Speakership and was appreciative of my support. Increasingly, I became known as the fair-haired boy because I'd do anything Jim asked me to do. My dad said, "If you want anything for your district, you can't just be an individual. You have to go up there and be a part of a team." That's exactly what I did.

Unfortunately, our caucus's support of the DiSalle tax bills put us back into the minority in the 1962 election at forty-nine Democrats and eighty-eight Republicans. To make matters worse, our caucus was without a leader because Jim Lantz ran for lieutenant governor, and he lost. I was part of a team, but our team had suffered a major setback.

We were not without leadership material, however. When I first came to the House, Dad said, "Son, there are three people I'd like you to pay attention to because you can learn from them. Duke Tablack is one, George Hook is another, and A. G. Lancione is the third." Dad knew all three personally. G. D. "Duke" Tablack was a longtime representative from Mahoning County and a real expert on tax law. His son George Jr. was later elected to the House after his father retired. George Hook was from Brown County and chaired the Transportation Committee. As for A. G., well, Dad just liked the way he conducted himself. A. G. was smart and when it came to speech making, nobody could hold a candle to him. All the Republicans had the highest respect for him because he was always fair and honest with them. He was good!

A. G. had grown to like me in those first two terms. When he decided to run for minority leader following the 1962 election, he asked me to help manage his campaign. A. G. was elected and, by gosh, he showed loyalty if you were loyal to him. He asked to have me put on the Rules Committee.

In those days, the Rules Committee met behind closed doors. We made up the agenda, and we didn't keep any committee records. It was the most powerful committee in the House, and everybody was running after you to support their bill. You didn't go outside the committee room to discuss how a certain person felt or what was said. Being on Rules gave you a chance to know exactly what was going on because nothing passed in that House until it went through Rules. I learned a tremendous amount about politics, individual members, strategy, and so forth.

As Speaker, Roger Cloud was chairman of the Rules Committee. He taught me a lot, and we became very good friends. He called me to his office many times and we'd sit for hours on Thursday afternoons after session to talk about things. It didn't matter that he was a Republican and I was a Democrat.

Roger Cloud reminded me a lot of my dad. They both knew what they were doing. I remember back many years when Dad was mayor; he used to try a lot of State Patrol cases. I've had many a state patrolman tell me that my father was one of the fairest people they ever went before. He explained their rights to them, and he conducted a court better than some judges. Roger Cloud wasn't a lawyer, but he knew the Ohio code like some people know the Bible. When I first came to Columbus, Roger Cloud knew more about state government than anybody around.

When we were in session, I'd study every move the Speaker made. When it came to discipline and loyalty, he demanded it. I never will forget one Rules Committee meeting when Terry Drake of Crawford County, a Republican member, voted against the Speaker on a matter. Roger looked over at him and he said, "Let's take one more vote and, Terry, I want to see that hand in the air." He took the vote, Terry voted with the Speaker, and the bill came out.

When I became Speaker, I'd say I had about the same style as Roger. There was simply no hanky-panky taking place on the floor of the House of Representatives. There was no cutting up. Roger wouldn't put up with it. When I became Speaker, I said there would be no more newspaper reading on the floor, no more coffee at your desk, and I was very strict on noise. I always thought it was in very bad taste for that sort of thing to be going on in front of high school students or anybody else in the gallery.

Those rules applied to everyone, no exceptions. Once some members brought to my attention that a reporter, a member of the Capitol Press Corps, was not standing for the Pledge of Allegiance. They said, "I thought you had a pretty strong rule that whatever applied to members on the floor also applied to the press corps and staff people." So the next time we said the pledge, I watched and, sure enough, the reporter didn't stand. I presided over the session and afterward I came down to the floor and called him over.

"I don't know what kind of a problem you might have, but I noticed that you're not standing for the Pledge of Allegiance to the flag. One of the rules of this House is that you do that. I don't want you to be embarrassed, but I don't want to be embarrassed either. If you're going to be on this floor for the pledge, I expect you to stand." He said he understood, and he always stood for the pledge after that.

I served one term under Jim Lantz, four terms under Roger Cloud, three terms under Chuck Kurfess, and one term under A. G. Lancione. They were all good Speakers in their own right. I learned something from each of them about using discipline and maintaining loyalty.

One of the most important lessons I learned was from Chuck Kurfess in 1971. He took a strong stand in support of the state income tax proposed by Jack Gilligan, even though the governor was a Democrat. This was important because the Republicans also were in control of the Senate, and the two chambers could have blocked the legislation. Chuck felt very strongly about increasing money for education and other services that were needed. The only difference between him and the governor was over whether it should be a flat or adjustable tax, but that was ironed out.

It was a major decision for Chuck, and he stuck with it. But he caught a whole lot of flack from his caucus. I mean a lot of flack. Even Charlie Fry of Clark County, Chuck's Speaker Pro Tem, fought him on it. There were stories in the newspapers about members of his caucus calling on him to back off the income tax or step down as Speaker.

He had some strong people in his caucus who were behind him— such as Corwin Nixon and Ed Lampson, among others—but a lot of his chairmen as well as rank-and-file members ran from him on that issue. He couldn't have passed the income tax with just the Republican caucus. When the final compromise was voted on, all but two Democrats—Pat Sweeney of Cleveland and Art Bowers of Steubenville—supported it. In the end, that was enough.

After the Republicans lost the House majority in 1972, Charlie Fry challenged Chuck for the minority leader position, but Chuck won easily. Even so, he continued to have problems with his caucus. Some of his members just wouldn't let go. It was terrible the way they treated him, people he'd been so loyal to over the years, people he had made chairman. I always admired Chuck for his stand. It took real political courage. He thought the income tax was right for Ohio, and it was.

We discussed many times how his caucus treated him. I think Chuck was hurt personally by it, but if he had to do it all over again, I don't think he would have changed his position one bit. Whether he would have handled his caucus differently, I don't know.

You have to keep in mind that all this was new to Chuck, and Roger Cloud before him never had that kind of experience. I learned from that. If I had been confronted with the same problem, I would have demanded loyalty from my caucus so long as I had the votes to back it up. I once advised Corwin Nixon that you can do anything if you have the votes. He called it "the Riffe Rule."

Rarely did I bluff. I much preferred to do my homework so that I could operate from a position of strength, whether it was behind the scenes or on the floor of the House. But I wasn't beyond bluffing if necessary, such as the time I was asked to chair the state Democratic Party convention in 1974.

The party had given me an agenda to follow that it had put together in conjunction with Governor Gilligan. I was trying to stick to it, but the delegates were trying to head off in other directions. One group in particular was trying to get a gay rights plank in the platform, and there was no way I was going to let that happen under my watch. Time after time I had to gavel them down; one reporter said he saw splinters flying. Before long, delegates were yelling, booing, and accusing me of not being able to hear—the way you accuse an umpire of not being able to see. Paul Tipps, the Montgomery County chairman at the time, came up to me and said, "You have the fastest gavel in the West. Watch out. Things are getting out of hand."

That's when I knew I had to do something, so I reached in my back pocket and grabbed my wallet.

"Delegates, somebody has found a wallet," I announced, holding it high. "Let's take a five-minute recess so that it can be claimed."

Instead of five, I took fifteen minutes until I was sure they were sufficiently settled down. During the recess, Frank Lavelli, the Belmont County chairman, came up and removed his hearing aids, handing them to me.

"You're the one who needs these things, not me," he snapped.

Quick thinking and several shots of Canadian Club Whiskey were all that got me through that convention.

The same type of thing can happen in a caucus meeting. Too often it was just an opportunity for people to make a show and incite other members. That's one reason I said to myself early on that I wasn't going to be caucusing much in the future. It got so that the last few years of my Speakership, I didn't caucus except to explain the budget.

There were people who didn't like it, but they didn't let it be known to me. It wouldn't make any difference because I had made up my mind. I just didn't see that there was any advantage to calling a caucus and letting people, mostly from the liberal wing, get up and spout off about their own interests.

The fact of the matter is that a lot of caucus members didn't like the grandstanding either. I had members coming up to me and saying, "Why do we have to put up with this?" I probably made a lot of friends doing what I did.

It wasn't always that way. Back in the old days, caucusing was a way for leadership to give its views as to what was going on and to explain the strategy that we'd use on the floor. There was more trustworthiness back then. When you discussed something in the caucus, it stayed in the caucus. You didn't go outside and tell everybody what was said about this or that.

Today everything's changed. Society's changed. Trust has changed. Some people today tell you that they're for something and then, when they don't vote that way, they don't think they've lied about it. They just think it's part of the process: "I'm the state representative. I can change my mind whenever I want to and get by with it." Teamwork is on the way out.

Like Chuck Kurfess, I had some on-the-job training when I became Speaker. I faced a different situation than the Speakers before me. I had to manage an inexperienced caucus. Many, many times I've thought, how did I get it done? I honestly believe that if I had not exercised strong leadership, I would not have survived.

Instead of having caucus meetings, I relied on my leadership team. If there was a bill I needed to check on, I would get the leadership in and ask them to count votes. And when the time came for a vote and certain votes weren't there among people who had gotten chairmanships, I decided to exercise some discipline.

To say I forced my caucus members to vote a certain way is wrong. I couldn't force a member to do anything. In fact, there were plenty of times when a member would come to me and say he or she had a very serious problem back in the district on a vote. If I thought I had the votes on an important issue, I didn't try to twist arms. Often I did it by reaching over to the Republican side, whether the minority leader was Chuck Kurfess, Corwin Nixon, or Jo Ann Davidson. There had to be something in it for the Republicans, of course, as in the case of tort reform in the 1980s and workers' compensation reform in the 1990s.

The fact is 90 to 95 percent of all bills that come to the floor of the legislature are nonpartisan and don't amount to a policy vote in the first place. In twenty years as Speaker, I doubt very much there were more than thirty or forty policy votes where I had to have the support of my caucus. Now that's a pretty darn good record.

I didn't interfere with the way chairmen conducted their meetings on legislation, but when I needed something done I expected them to be with me. I was the one out there raising the money, seeing that people were getting their legislation through, and helping them back in their districts. I was the one who had to do that. Nobody else. If this was my responsibility—which it was, and I was ready to accept it—then it was their responsibility to back me when I needed their help. It very seldom came to that.

A lot has been made in the press over my taking chairmanships away from people. That never bothered me. During my twenty years as Speaker, I probably only stripped members of chairmanships six or eight times. I did what I had to do.

In my judgment if you were made a chairman, that was a part of leadership and you were to be loyal. When I needed loyalty and it wasn't there, then I usually did something about it. Otherwise, it would get out of hand and people would say, "Well, John Jones got by with it. Why can't I, if I'm a chairman?" The first thing you know, I wouldn't have the votes when I needed them.

Ron Suster of Cleveland, for example, voted with the Republicans against a ruling by his committee chairman. Now, you might disagree on amendments but when it comes to backing the chair or the Speaker on a ruling, you always back your leader.

I told Ron there was no explanation for it. That's a cardinal sin. "How would you feel if you were chairing a committee and a member of your own party would vote not to sustain the chair?" He tried to explain and I cut him short: "I don't like it one bit."

In 1991 when he came up for reappointment as chairman of the Financial Institutions Committee, I didn't reappoint him. That one vote was the reason.

But in 1993 during my last term as Speaker, I personally called Ron and said, "I need a good chairman to head the Judiciary Committee, and I think you'd make a good one."

"You think I would? You're not still mad at me?" he asked.

"I was never mad at you, Ron. I was disappointed in you. You knew what I had to do, and why I had to do it."

"Well, yes, I understand," he said.

And I'll tell you, before I left, Ron made one of the best chairmen of Judiciary I ever had.

If you're a strong leader, I think you've always got to keep that door open. Jim Rhodes taught me that. He said, "Don't ever get so mad, Vern, that you can't bring people back in." To say you made a mistake and you're going to suffer forever for it won't work because sooner or later you won't have a working majority. If I ever thought somebody was really trying to hurt me or the caucus, that's a different story. But if they just made a mistake, well, we all make mistakes. I was always willing to try and work it out and bring them back into the fold.

Take David Hartley of Springfield, for example. When I made him chairman of the Agriculture and Natural Resources Committee back in 1983, I said, "Dave, I've got confidence that you'll do a good job. The only thing I want you to understand is that you've got to be loyal to me now." He said he had no problem with that because I helped him in his campaigns when he really needed the help, even though he cast some votes I didn't agree with.

Then in 1986 when I needed his vote on workers' compensation and insurance reform legislation, he wasn't there. Come reappointment time in 1987, I didn't make him chairman. But in 1991, when I needed a chairman of the Civil and Commercial Law Committee, I appointed Dave Hartley. I didn't hold a grudge.

Taking a chairmanship away is about the worst punishment that you could give. It meant a loss of $10,000 to a member over the course of two years, not to mention the loss of the title and responsibility.

There were other ways to discipline members, such as refusing to send them on trips or holding up their bills in the Rules Committee or other committees. I didn't enjoy doing those things, but I did them if it was necessary to maintain caucus loyalty.

If a member was supporting the caucus and doing what was in the best interests of the people, I pushed legislation for them. You never heard about all the bills I put on the floor for members of my caucus that I didn't particularly like myself. I did that many, many times because I felt very strongly that loyalty goes both ways.

One bill I really didn't have much use for was the mandatory seat belt bill. I thought the government didn't have any business telling people to wear seat belts if they didn't want to, and I believed it was probably unconstitutional. The federal government was threatening to withhold funds from states that did not pass a mandatory seat belt law, and even the big car companies were for it as an alternative to tougher auto safety standards. Nevertheless, it wasn't a done deal in Ohio as far as I was concerned.

Art Bowers wanted a mandatory seat belt law badly as chairman of the Highways and Highway Safety Committee. He also was very loyal to me. The Senate, with some difficulty, had sent a mandatory seat belt bill over to the House, and Art said all he would like is for the bill to get a fair shake if it passed his committee.

"If you work on this bill the way I know you will and it comes out of committee, I won't hold it in Rules Committee. I'll put it on the floor. You're too good a member of mine," I said.

Art's committee recommended it for passage, and, just to make sure, he asked me if I still felt the same way about the bill.

"I made a commitment, and it will go to the floor. But when it does, I will vote 'no,'" I told him.

When Art thought he had the votes, it was brought to a vote on the floor of the House and fell short of the required majority on a vote of 48-43. Art had it held on a motion to reconsider in the hopes that he could change some minds or get some more supporters to the floor.

Following the first vote, I never tried to change anybody's vote one way or the other. There was no caucus position on this issue, and if I were to start asking members to oppose the bill, it would be unfair to Art.

The following Wednesday, Art asked that the seat belt bill be reconsidered. He had done a head count and felt he had the votes this time. Just before the vote, Jeff Jacobs, a Republican member from Cuyahoga County who said he had been opposed to the bill, recounted the scene of an accident he had passed on State Route 315 the night before. Emergency medics had evacuated a woman who had been thrown through her car windshield. It was a bloody scene. Prior to that, Jeff said he opposed the bill on the grounds that it violated individual freedom.

Now he said he believed that "our greatest liberty, our greatest freedom is life itself." A short time later, the bill passed on a 52-41 vote.

That's just one example, but there are many other bills that went before the House out of respect for my caucus members. To me, it was just a matter of being fair and giving your members an opportunity to achieve some of their goals.

I don't like the terms "ironfisted" and "dictator." I always thought those were unfair. When the movie *Star Wars* was first popular, the name "Darth Vernal" was making the rounds at the Statehouse. There's no doubt about it, I was very strict. I've always said, when you're a strong leader, everybody benefits; when you're a weak leader, everybody loses.

I just thought that the House should be run like a business. To me, the House floor was not going to be a place where everybody could do what they wanted to do and say what they wanted to say. I didn't think the session was there to run itself. To me, you're not doing your job as a leader if you let that happen. Not too many people have challenged my authority on the floor and gotten away with it, although many have tried. My old friend Art Wilkowski of Toledo is one.

Art was always an independent sort, and one time he was mad about a bill of his that had been sitting in the Rules Committee for some time. I can't even remember what it was anymore, but he had spoken to me about it. Art knew that as chairman of the Rules Committee I could move the bill but chose not to do so.

He was more knowledgeable than most about the rules of procedure that we used in the House. These particular rules were contained in a very old volume that was locked away in the House clerk's office—the only copy available. Somehow Art managed to borrow that book from the clerk's office long enough to come up with a strategy for prying loose his bill.

The next day, Art stood up to be recognized and, naturally, I called on him as a member of my caucus. Then he made a motion to convene the House as a Committee of the Whole. If his motion was successful, the entire House could act on the bill and bypass the Rules Committee in order to get it to the floor. Right away, I knew he was up to something, but I wasn't sure what, so I quickly called a recess and got together Tom Winters, the house clerk, and Bill Mallory, the majority floor leader. We consulted the book and determined that the only motion that took precedence over Art's was a motion to adjourn. Then we reconvened.

"Representative Mallory," I said.

"Speaker, motion to adjourn," he said.

I took a voice vote and just like that, it was over in the blink of an eye. There was no point in him trying it again another day because he knew I wouldn't recognize him until I was sure he had dropped the issue.

Another time Art tried to buck me was following the 1980 election when the caucus was preparing to elect our leadership for the 114th General Assembly. He came to me insisting that we replace Francine Panehal of Cuyahoga County as our majority whip because he felt she was saying negative things about the leadership team behind our backs. He also questioned her loyalty and commitment to the caucus. I took it under advisement but wasn't ready to remove her from the team. I had heard some of the same talk, but I didn't feel threatened by it.

Unbeknownst to me, Art rented a room at the Neil House next to one where the caucus was gathering the night before our meeting, which was to take place the following morning. While we were in there, a band started up and it was making quite a racket. It consisted of a violin, accordion, and guitar, and it was playing lively ethnic music. Some of the caucus members were slipping out of our meeting to see what was going on, and it turns out that Wilkowski was over there serving refreshments and throwing a regular party. On the wall was a banner that read, "Wilkowski for Whip."

Art was up to his old tricks again, and this was yet another case where he wouldn't take no for an answer. Art was at his best when he was trying to outmaneuver somebody. In this case, however, the election of a majority whip was a bigger deal to him than it was to me.

The next morning during our caucus meeting, Joe Vukovich of Mahoning County nominated Art, and Tommy Bell of Cuyahoga County seconded the nomination. Then someone moved to hold a secret ballot, and the motion prevailed. When the votes were counted, Art won, 31-30, much to his surprise. Only five months into the legislative session, he resigned. He simply didn't want the job. The caucus replaced him with Ken Rocco of Cuyahoga County. Since Francine was not reelected, I suppose you could say Art succeeded at what he set out to do. I'll tell you this: If it had been somebody other than Art, I might have used some discipline, but he was a straight shooter and too good a friend for that.

Each leader has his own style. I've had some Republicans in the

House tell me that they'd like to go back to the old days when the process wasn't so wide-open as it is today. I have tremendous respect for the job Jo Ann Davidson is doing as Speaker, but in my opinion she might adopt a different style if she were in that position for a longer time. Term limits won't give her that opportunity.

The news media always focused too much on the power of the Speaker and the few times I disciplined someone. Discipline is what you use when loyalty breaks down. It doesn't make people loyal in the first place.

A leader who has the loyalty of his members has to work at it day and night. Bottom line: It means helping to get them elected and helping them to do their job as a House member so that they can stay elected.

One way I used to keep track of who needed help was to have charts made up after each election. I'd list how much we won this district by and how much we won that district by. I had four or five categories, and the districts where our margin of victory was less than one thousand votes was a special category.

I paid attention to those charts. When I'd see that something had to be done, I'd get the member in and we'd sit down and go over it. I would then make sure we'd move on something that they could use back home in a campaign, whether it was legislation or some important capital improvements.

If you were a freshman, you'd need some help; that was a given. You also had to keep an eye on the second-termers. Once you've been elected to your second term you're in a much better position to be reelected, but you still need to pay attention to the first and second term.

Of course if I felt one of my members was not loyal, that was a different matter. I'll never forget the time one of my members didn't support the caucus on a tort reform bill during the 117th General Assembly (1987–88). It was that individual's choice to oppose the bill, and it was my choice not to put any money into that person's reelection campaign. During the campaign, a local reporter asked what the representative was going to do without any money from the caucus.

"The Speaker can take his money and shove it where the sun doesn't shine," was the answer.

I'll have to admit, I thought that was cute. I liked spunk in a person. This individual was reelected without my help and became a valued and loyal member of the caucus. Some years later a county chairman was mad over something and asked me to withhold funds from the same person's campaign again.

"I had a chance once to get him and didn't. Not again," I told him. "First time, shame on you. Second time, shame on me."

Never did I lose sight of what it took to keep the majority, although I did take my eye off the ball once in 1980. I had come off the House floor and gone back to my Statehouse office when my secretary said, "The president wants you to call him."

I didn't know if she meant the president of the Senate or what, so I said, "President who?"

"President Carter."

"Is that right? Well, get him on the phone," I said.

It must have been a direct line because President Carter answered the phone, and my secretary about fainted. She managed to put him through to me.

"Mr. Speaker," he said with that Georgia drawl, "when are you going to be in Washington next? I'd like to spend some time with you."

"Whenever you want me there, Mr. President," I said. We arranged to meet later that week at the White House. He said one of the things he wanted to talk about was coal, which was of concern to Ohio because of the environmental problems associated with burning our high-sulfur coal.

When we met, it was just the president and me in the Oval Office. He committed to do whatever he could to help with our coal situation. I knew his commitment was good. I was indebted to the president and Vice President Fritz Mondale for coming through on a promise to expand the uranium enrichment plant in Piketon in my legislative district, an expansion that was later cut short by the Reagan administration. Naturally, when we got business out of the way, talk turned to politics. This was at the time when Ted Kennedy was giving the president a rough go of it.

"Mr. Speaker, would you have any problem endorsing me for re-election?" he asked.

Without hesitation, I said, "None whatsoever, Mr. President." Shortly after I got back, I issued a press release to that effect. It didn't end there. On many occasions I voiced my support for President Carter to the point where my dad became concerned.

"Son, I know you had to do what you had to do. The president kept a commitment to you. I understand commitments," Dad said. "But I want to tell you something: Don't focus so much on helping Mr. Carter get elected that you forget about your House races. I don't want you to let things go and maybe lose the House. Let the House be your top commitment."

That's when I learned I had problems in the House. Dad was the first to give me the warning. I went right to work making sure our candidates had the resources they needed and were doing what needed to be done. Thank goodness I did. We lost six seats that election, dropping from 62 to 56. President Carter lost to Ronald Reagan by nearly half a million votes.

In terms of creating loyalty, nothing was more important than being there for the members during election time. Another part of being a good leader, however, is getting to know your members by being around them and socializing with them. Over the years, the Galleria, the Neil House, and the Press Club were all places where you could get close to members and they could get close to you. You got a lot accomplished that way. If they had something on their minds, they were free to come out with it. I never underestimated the importance of this, both as an access issue and also for information gathering.

As Speaker, I probably spent more time after hours at the Galleria Tavern across Third Street from the Statehouse Annex than anywhere else. When the legislature was not in session, that's where the action was. I had a regular seat at the bar near a side exit, so I could slip out easily if I had to. My good friend Mike DelBane of Youngstown used to tell the waitress, "As soon as the Speaker hits the door, you tell him I want to see him before anybody else does. I know how busy he gets. Everybody wants to talk to him." A lot of unofficial business was conducted there, and it was good for members and for me. Mike used the seat next to me until he passed away. Then my good friend Ed Hinton, who represented the United Auto Workers, used the same seat until he passed away. After that, I just couldn't sit back there anymore. Too many memories.

I always tried to keep my members informed and spend as much time with them as I could. I did a pretty good job of it until I began to have health problems in 1992. It wasn't long after I stopped going to the Galleria in 1992 that it closed down. Not many legislators, executive branch people, and lobbyists went there anymore. Before that everybody went to the Red Lion at the Neil House at Broad and High streets. Those kinds of gathering places are gone today. With the financial disclosure law we passed in 1994, lobbyists can't buy drinks or dinner for members much anymore, and members are afraid to accept them anyway.

The more you socialize with members, the more you learn about their personal lives. As Speaker, I looked at members like a father would look at his family. If there was a problem in the family, then I wanted to help with it. You don't do it for politics. You do it because you respect them and you care about them. If I could help a member with a personal matter that had nothing to do with legislation, I did it. I've made loans to members and signed notes for them. If a member, his wife, or his child was in the hospital, I'd call and check on them, and if they were in the area, I'd stop to see them.

There was not a more honest and loyal member than C. J. McLin of Dayton. We had our disagreements over the years, but we could always work them out honorably.

C. J. was one of the first black members elected in the 1960s after the "one man, one vote" case decided by the U.S. Supreme Court forced us to go to single-member districts. I first really became acquainted with C. J. when I was trying to get A. G. Lancione elected House minority leader in 1967.

After we took over the majority in the 1972 election, C. J. called and asked if he and Casey Jones could come in and talk with me. They wanted to have a certain percentage of black House employees; I believe 10 percent is the figure they used. I was in charge of personnel, and I said, "Hey, fellows, let's not put any percentage on it. You send me some good applications and qualified people, and I'll see that they get all the consideration in the world. The day you think I'm not being fair, then you come back and talk to me about it."

I didn't want to put a percentage on it because I didn't think it was fair to them. If they were qualified people, I didn't want to have a per-centage I had to follow. If they were qualified, we'd put them on—and we did. C. J. and I had an understanding that if I ever had any prob-lems with any of the applications or with the black delegation at that time, he would like to know about it and he'd take care of it. He was a man of his word, and that's the way we operated.

Not too long after that, C. J. and the black delegation wanted to make Martin Luther King's birthday a state holiday. A lot of members were not too keen on the idea and I don't think that bill would have moved if I hadn't given a commitment to C. J. that I would push to get the bill out of the Rules Committee and onto the House floor for a vote. I was Speaker Pro Tem at the time and presided the day it passed.

A few years later when I became Speaker, some members in the black delegation began to think of themselves as a separate caucus and started to make demands.

It came to a head in 1977, when the black delegation got upset about the proposed budget appropriation to Central State contained in the Conference Committee report. The committee increased the appro-priation by $3 million over the $6.6 million Governor Rhodes had recommended but made the last $3 million contingent upon approval of the Controlling Board. They felt the additional money was needed, and the Conference Committee proposal was giving undue influence over Central State to the Controlling Board.

Myrl Shoemaker was Finance Committee chairman and our lead ne-gotiator on the budget. "What are we going to do?" he asked, upset.

"We're going to vote," I said, believing we had the votes to pass it.

It was one of the few times in my career as a leader that I had mis-calculated. While a majority of those present voted in favor of the conference report, we fell one vote short of the fifty needed to have a constitutional majority. Immediately, I knew what I had to do, and that was to round up those members who were not in attendance in order to pass a conference report the next day.

After the first vote, I sent for the all the members of the black del-egation, sat them right around my conference table, and looked them right in the eyes.

"You guys are the most ungrateful people I ever worked with. You wouldn't have the Martin Luther King state holiday today if it wasn't for me. Even the Speaker back then didn't want to put that out for a vote on the floor. And I'm the guy who insisted it go, and it passed by one vote. If this is the way you're going to operate, I'm done with you. Do as you please."

When I got through, Jimmy Rankin realized they had made a big mistake and asked what they could do to rectify things. I told him they needed to explain themselves to the caucus the next day. One by one they apologized for what they'd done and said that I'd been fair and honest with them.

Later, Chuck Kurfess, who was minority leader at the time, offered his help, but I declined.

"Chuck, I appreciate it but I don't want you doing that. I'm the leader, and it's going to pass with the majority party," I said.

Some of my members were hot about the black delegation, but I told them to cool it. I didn't want that kind of talk because it could really cause a split.

The next morning, Ike Thompson asked to see me. He and I were close personal friends, and he was upset over the whole thing. "I made a big mistake and didn't realize it until it was too late. I feel so badly I'll resign my chairmanship if you want me to," he said. Ike also offered to change his vote when the bill came back up.

I said, "Ike, it's going to be on the floor, and I don't care how you vote. I have the votes." We passed it the second time, and every black member voted for it except Tommy Bell. Afterward Ike came back to my office.

"I just can't get this off my mind. If there's anybody I love, it's you. Is there anything I can do to straighten this out?" he asked.

"Ike, you told me how it happened and that you were sorry. As far as I'm concerned, it's done. It's gone," I said. He didn't try to make excuses. If he had tried to put the blame on somebody else that would have been a different matter entirely.

From that time on, if anybody ever said anything bad about me to him, they had Ike Thompson to whip.

Just before the second vote on the bill, I was having lunch at the Neil House when in came C. J. McLin. We walked back to the State-house together and stopped to talk in the underground garage. He said he was also sorry about the way things happened, that things got out of hand.

"C. J., I always thought that you were a leader, not of a black caucus but of the black members. Let me tell you this: I recognize one cau-cus, and that's the Democratic Caucus," I said.

I told him to vote however he wanted to, but we weren't changing the Central State appropriation, and I was removing the money that the black delegation wanted for shuttle service from Portsmouth to Lucasville for families visiting the state penitentiary.

For several weeks after the second vote, I ignored the black delega-tion. Eventually, C. J. asked if I would meet with them. "I know you won't meet with us at the Statehouse, but would you do me a big fa-vor and meet with us somewhere else. I'd like to get this ironed out," he said.

So one day after session, I met with the delegation at C. J.'s apartment at the Americana on South Fifth Street. When I arrived, C. J. started off talking, and then Les Brown from Columbus picked up from there. I said, "Fellows, let me just end this now. Nobody has been fairer to you than me. You guys screwed up and you know it. I never want that to hap-pen again. Now, as far as I'm concerned it's over." And I walked out.

C. J. remained the leader of the black delegation, and he and I got along until the day he passed away. He was loyal to me, and I did everything I could for him. Not too long before he died of cancer in 1987, he called for me to come to the hospital. I had visited him a number of times, but this time he knew he wouldn't survive much longer. He asked me if I would appoint his daughter, Rhine, to suc-ceed him when he was gone. I said I would.

Apparently there was something between C. J. and the county chairman, Joe Shump, because it got around that Joe wasn't too hot on Rhine. I went over to the hospital again and told C. J. not to worry. "I'll honor your request and nobody else's. If you want Rhine to suc-ceed you, I'll take her name to the caucus and no other," I said.

The following week, two or three days before he passed away, he sent for me. He said, "I just want you to know that I had Joe out here, and Rhine's got his blessing."

I told C. J. I appreciated it, but I would have honored my commitment. "I just didn't want you to go through all that," he said. And that's the way we did it. When Rhine became a member, I took her under my wing. She'd been through a whole lot and she was just not well. It was tough her first term, but that second term, even that second year of the first term, you could see her come into her own and become an effective member. She and I were always very close.

Later, just after my dad passed away in 1990, she had a fund-raiser that I was supposed to attend. It was very important to her, so I went to her fund-raiser immediately after Dad's funeral. Rhine never forgot that. It meant very much to her. I swore Rhine in her first term in the House in 1988 and again in 1994 when she became the first black woman to serve in the Ohio Senate.

The black delegation could have divided the Democratic Caucus, but it was just the opposite. Many of the black delegation were among my most loyal members. People like C. J. and Bill Mallory understood that compromise is a part of the legislative process. You get a lot more accomplished when you're a part of a team.

Not everyone understood teamwork so well. In the 1970s some of the young Democratic members thought they were going to change everything overnight. They would meet secretly, and people called them the "Rump Caucus." It included Dennis Eckart and Virginia Aveni of Cuyahoga County, Denny Wojtanowski of Geauga County, Sherrod Brown of Richland County, Larry Christman of Montgomery County, and John Begala of Portage County. I didn't pay a lot of attention to them because 90 percent of the time they were wrong in what they were trying to do and everybody knew it. That was why they didn't accomplish anything.

The truth is that when those guys were giving me a hard time, it was one of the best times of my life. I was much younger then and a little feisty myself. When they were trying to pull something, I'd always find out and put a stop to it. Sherrod described the relationship well once. He said they were like flies buzzing around a horse's head. Those flies can try to annoy that horse day and night, but when it's all said and done, they're still flies and the horse is still a horse.

There were three or four of them who were telling me everything that was going on within their group. They knew I'd find out, so they wanted to protect their rear ends.

I also had my own team that kept me informed of their activities. Mike DelBane headed it. It included, among others, Tom Carney of Youngstown and Art Wilkowski and Barney Quilter of Toledo. They'd watch that group and even follow them if necessary.

One time the rump group was meeting at the old Statehouse Annex. I was over at the Red Lion when one of my team came up to me and said, "You know what they're doing, Speaker? Those little sons of guns are over there in a meeting right now."

I decided to have some fun with it, so I went straight over there, knocked on the door, and caught them cold.

I said, "You can meet all you want to, but I'll tell you right now it isn't working. I know what you're doing. There's eight or ten of you here tonight. Do you think that eight or ten are going to keep their mouths shut when they walk out of here? I'll know within five or ten minutes what you said. I just want you to know that, fellows."

Since I had people inside the rump caucus telling me what was going on and I had people outside the rump caucus tracking them, I had things going both ways for me. They might have thought they were playing games with me, but I had my own game going.

Some of those people in the rump caucus were very young and just didn't know any better. They somehow got elected and grew a little too big for their britches. Sherrod Brown was one of them. I first met Sherrod when I was Speaker Pro Tem and we were trying to line up candidates for the election in 1974. His county chairman called and said, "I've got a good one for you." I said bring him down and we'll take a look.

So Sherrod came to Columbus and walked into my office one day. I couldn't believe what I saw. He wore hair down to his shoulders, tennis shoes, and an old pair of jeans. His jacket was torn. He looked like he'd just gotten out of a boxcar on the freight line.

After I interviewed him for about fifteen or twenty minutes, I went into the other office and told A. G. Lancione, "If that's the best he's got to offer, we'll never win that district." Joan Douglass was the Republican incumbent, and I thought we'd never beat her. Never.

Well, that son of a gun went out and hit those doors, I mean *hit* them, and he won! Not by a whole lot, but he won.

I respected Sherrod Brown's ability as a campaigner. He just didn't know how to get things done legislatively in those days. I remember one time when my Reference Committee chairman, Jim Baumann, was running for Congress in Franklin County, Sherrod stopped by to talk about a bill I was trying to move.

"You know, I can get you some votes for this if you'll give me a commitment to make me Reference Committee chairman next session when Baumann's gone," he said.

He did it with a straight face, so I guess he was serious. I said, "You see that door? Get your butt out of here. I'm not making any commitment to you or anybody else. You get out of here and do as you please." It was one thing for Tony Russo to propose a deal when I desperately needed votes to elect A. G. Lancione minority leader, but I didn't need Sherrod's vote, and he didn't have enough sense to know he was in no position to bargain with me.

Denny Wojtanowski was a lot like Sherrod. Denny didn't pull any punches either. He was a straight shooter.

It wasn't but a few months after he left the House that I hired him as a consultant for our House campaigns. I always recognized that Denny had some knowledge about campaigns. And later, when he wanted to go into business, I helped him get started.

I never would make him a chairman, but I still liked Denny.

Dennis Eckart was another one who learned the hard way. One time I had made a commitment to Oliver Ocasek to move some legislation for the city of Cleveland. Well, Dennis Eckart and some others got up in caucus and argued against it.

I remember coming out at the end of caucus, and there he was bragging that I didn't have the votes. He had his back to me and didn't know I was coming through. After I heard what he said, I went up and patted him on the shoulder. He turned around and his face got beet red. I said, "You know what? You might have won the battle, but you just lost the war. I'll tell you that right now. You remember this day."

We passed the bill, but I had to do some maneuvering and get Republican votes.

That next year after the 1978 election, I was going to split up the Insurance, Financial Institutions, and Utilities Committee. Dennis wanted to be a chairman, so he called and asked if I'd have dinner with him at the Neil House.

We met and he asked for a chairmanship. I just looked him in the eyes and said, no way, and told him why.

"I told you to remember a certain date. I've got to have loyalty when I appoint my chairmen. That's just the way it is," I told him. Man, he was hurt over it. He said it was going to look bad to the *Plain Dealer* because he had been in office for a while and still wasn't a chairman. Dennis was begging me to change my mind.

"You're going to have to decide how to handle the [Cleveland] *Plain Dealer*. I'm just telling you right now you're not going to be a chairman," I said.

The next election he ran for the congressional seat being vacated by Charles Vanik, who was a Democrat. Dennis had strong opposition in the primary from Tim McCormack, who was auditor in Cuyahoga County, and Tony Calabrese Jr., a judge. An endorsement from the *Plain Dealer* meant a whole lot to him.

Denny Wojtanowski was his campaign manager. He asked if I would intercede with the *Plain Dealer* on Dennis's behalf. Before I got a chance, Tom Vail, the *Plain Dealer* publisher, called and said he had to make a decision in the race. I first met Tom when he was a reporter covering the Statehouse in 1959.

"I know you've served with all three of them, and I know you'll give me a straight answer. I'd like to talk to you about it because I'm probably going to make a decision on that endorsement next week," Tom said.

It was common knowledge that I had had some problems with Dennis over that Cleveland bill. I told Tom that was why I didn't appoint Dennis to a chairmanship.

"But I'll tell you this: If I was making the endorsement out of the three, Dennis would be my choice because he's hardworking and he knows what he's doing. Nothing against the other two at all, but if you're asking me who would be my choice, it would be Dennis," I said.

Again, I didn't hold a grudge. He had paid his price. Dennis was young and sharp and he knew it. When you're like that, you're going to make some mistakes if you don't watch out. The good part is that if you make mistakes, you can learn from them, and Dennis did.

The *Plain Dealer* endorsed Dennis. It was short and to the point, noting that "Eckart has compiled a fine record through three terms in the Ohio House of Representatives where he was well respected by his peers." Dennis won the primary handily with 47.4 percent of the vote. McCormack and Calabrese split most of the rest.

In the general election, Dennis faced Joseph Nahra, who had resigned his seat as a probate court judge to run for Congress. Nahra had a Harvard education, and the Republicans brought big names like George Bush, Henry Kissinger, and Republican National Committee Chairman Bill Brock into the district to campaign on his behalf. Dennis wanted help again, so I called Tom Vail. Dennis got the endorsement and won the election with 55 percent of the vote.

Throughout my career, most of my caucus members were team players. Sherrod, the two Dennys, and the rest of the rump group were the exception. Even those fellows would probably tell you they learned a lot from me.

Holding a caucus together in tough times will be even harder in the future with term limits in effect. With the clock running, everybody is going to get what they can while they can. Teamwork will fall victim to individual ambition. My old friend Barney Quilter was right: We served during the best of times, when things like loyalty, friendship, and teamwork were valued.

For me, one of the real keys to holding a caucus together and making it work was having a good leadership team, and I was fortunate to have one of the best. My top two people were with me from the day I became Speaker Pro Tem in 1973 until the day I retired twenty-two years later. That's unheard of for that number of years. I owe Barney Quilter and Bill Mallory a lot.

I was already in the House when Barney was elected in 1966. In fact, I had met him earlier that year at one of our candidate seminars, and we became good friends. From day one, Barney was friendly and honest, and when he told you something, that was it. Barney was loyal.

He would have made a great Speaker. When I was considering running for governor in 1990, we agreed Barney would be Speaker if I decided to run and the Democrats maintained the majority, which we surely would have. Eventually, I decided not to run. We were at a national legislative conference in Tulsa, and I called Barney up to my hotel room to talk to him about it.

"I'm not ready to make the announcement yet, but I've thought about it very seriously and I'm not going to run for governor. But I'll tell you what: I won't run for reelection, so you can become Speaker," I said.

Barney looked me right in the eyes and said, "No, no. If you're not the governor, I don't want to be Speaker. I don't want to talk you out of a decision you've already made, but I think you'd have made a good governor. Since that's your decision, I want you to run for reelection."

When I decided to retire, Barney never even considered staying on to run for Speaker.

Barney, Bill Mallory, and I all went out together. Bill would have retired in 1990 but I wouldn't let him. In fact, he even made an announcement that he wasn't going to run for reelection and I said, "Wait a minute. No. You can't do that." I called his wife, Fannie, and told her how important Bill was to me and to the caucus. After we spoke, she told Bill he better listen to me. Afterward, I put out a press release that said I needed Bill, and that he would run again after all because I asked him to.

I could not have done what I did as Speaker without Bill and Barney. The same goes for the rest of my leadership team, including the committee chairmen. When people wonder how the Democrats could have held the majority in the House of Representatives for twenty-two consecutive years under all kinds of conditions, it's largely because we always had a leadership team pulling in the same direction.

To read the newspapers, you'd think I constantly told members what to do, ordered them around every day. The news media formed their own opinion of what type of leader I was without ever seeming to understand that the vast majority of the time my caucus members were on their own. My members could do what they pleased as long as they were working for the good of the caucus.

If I did nothing but hand out orders, I wouldn't have lasted as Speaker. Your caucus members are like your constituents. They need to be satisfied with the job that you are doing. In my case, I'd say they were satisfied—not that there weren't a few complainers, but they were usually people who were more concerned with their own priorities than with being a part of a team. A leader also needs good staff people who are loyal to the cause, and I had some great ones, people like Rick Pfeiffer, Ty Marsh, Aris Hutras, and Tom Winters. Like Ohio State football coach Woody Hayes used to say, "You win with people," and I sure found that to be true.

Another reason caucus members were loyal to me is because they knew that anyone who tried to pick a fight with them would have to take on me too. That not only included our traditional adversaries but also some of our friends. For instance, organized labor was one of our biggest supporters, but more than once I had to stand up to them to protect my members.

During the 111th General Assembly, labor strongly supported collective bargaining for public employees. Bill Hinig of Tuscarawas County had voted twice in favor of collective bargaining that session. But when Governor Rhodes vetoed the bill, Bill was under a lot of pressure in his district not to vote to override.

Bill said, "My Democratic county chairman is on me, and the Democratic officeholders in my district are on my back. It's going to kill me if I vote to override. I can't do that." Many of those local officials didn't want it because that meant their employees would have bargaining power.

Rep. Harry Mallot of Brown County also came to me and said that if he had to vote to override, he would resign afterward because that vote would kill him in his district. Art Bowers was having a problem with it as well, and Art was a strong labor man.

So I told them, "We're not going to hang anybody out. You guys have supported that bill. If it's going to cause you problems on the veto, fine. I understand." Meanwhile, labor was still working on getting the number of votes to override because I told them that when the votes were there I'd bring it up.

When it came filing time for the next election, labor got someone to run against Bill Hinig in the primary. One night over at the Neil House, I laid it on the line with John Hall of the Ohio Education Association, Warren Smith and Milan Marsh of the Ohio AFL-CIO, and Ed Hinton of the United Auto Workers.

"Now fellows, if you take on Bill Hinig, I will use every resource I've got to get him renominated. If you want to take on somebody, take on somebody like John Wargo." Wargo, from Columbiana County, had gotten up on the floor of the House and tore into labor in the debate on collective bargaining.

They filed somebody against Bill Hinig anyway. It was a heck of a battle. There was much more at stake than Bill's race. It was a test of who was going to control the caucus—labor or me. If I had lost that district, I wouldn't have been Speaker all those years; labor would have gotten me for sure. But I took them on, and Bill won the election. In the process, I showed the caucus that loyalty goes both ways. If they were loyal to me, then I was going to be loyal to them.

❦ 4 ❧

Fund-raising

I f someone said in 1959 that I would raise more than $20 million for Democrats, I wouldn't have believed it. No one would have believed that it would take more than $5 million for a caucus to win the Ohio House in one election or $400,000 to win a single House district, but by the time I retired, it did.

Today a lot of people think of me as a fund-raiser, first and foremost. As far as I was concerned, fund-raising was just a means to an end, which was to keep control of the House in Democratic hands so that we could better serve the people of Ohio. I didn't hold the first caucus fund-raising event until I was fifteen years into my legislative career. Big-time fund-raising was something I got into out of necessity. It was just one of the many responsibilities I had as a leader; no more, no less.

Raising money for my own campaigns was never a big deal. In eighteen campaigns, I had opposition in the primary only once, and I was never seriously challenged in the general election. I raised money for each of my campaigns because, just like shaking hands at the fair all day, I took nothing for granted. But rather than hold fund-raisers, I got most of my money one on one.

The very first contribution I ever got was a twenty-dollar bill from Bill Konyha in 1958. Bill was the business agent for the carpenters union when the atomic plant in Piketon was being built, and we were introduced by Jim Buchanan, the local carpenters' business agent and a mutual friend. Not only did I get my first contribution from the carpenters but the first endorsement I ever received before the 1958 primary was from my carpenters local. Little did I realize then that years later Bill Konyha would help me revolutionize the way money was raised for legislators in Ohio.

The fact of the matter is that I never actually held a fund-raiser of any kind until 1962, and it wasn't even for me. Jim Lantz, the former Speaker and our minority leader at the time, was running for lieutenant governor while Gov. Mike DiSalle was running for reelection. (This was in the days when the lieutenant governor and the governor ran separately.)

Though there were five people in the race, it wasn't a sure thing for Jim. He asked me if I would be in charge of a fund-raiser, so I organized a sit-down dinner at the Deshler Hilton Hotel in Columbus and charged ten dollars a ticket. Jim did most of the talking, and that's about all there was to it as far as the program went. We netted one thousand dollars or so, which was a lot of money in those days.

Unfortunately, Jim finished a strong second to John Gallagher. That was the end of politics for Jim, but I was just getting warmed up. It would be more than ten years before I organized another big fund-raiser, and already I had learned that if you worked hard, paid attention to the details, and used your connections, there was a whole lot of money to be raised.

The next ten years were long ones because the Republicans had a grip on the majority and weren't about to let go. I put the time to good use by learning everything I could about state government and politics. One thing became clear to me as time went on: there was no such thing as a caucus organization when it came to campaigns. There were no caucus fund-raisers, Democratic or Republican. It just wasn't done. Candidates were mostly on their own, which was particularly rough on Democrats because the plain truth of it—then and now—is that when you're in the majority, it's easy to raise money; when you're in the minority, it is not.

I knew we couldn't keep doing things the same old way in campaigns because it didn't work. You could look at history and see that whenever we won the majority, the Republicans would always win it right back. Democrats won the House in 1948 on Harry Truman's coattails, ten years before I first took office, and that was just for one term. Thanks to the ill-fated right-to-work issue in 1958, we got it back for one term from 1959–60 and then were in the minority again. Granted, Democrats benefited some from changes in the way legislative districts were apportioned due to U.S. Supreme Court rulings, but all that did was give us a fighting chance to win the majority. The rest would be up to us.

The state Republican Party looked more seriously at the legislature. It always has. They controlled the House for years and years, and their contributors—mostly businesspeople—understood that the legislature had a direct impact on them and they would do well to put their resources there.

The Democratic Party, however, didn't have much money to give. Labor put resources directly into some campaigns, but not very much by later standards. Labor concentrated mostly on presidential, congressional, and U.S. Senate races.

Early on I saw that the Democratic Party would never be a serious fund-raising mechanism for members of the legislature. If we were ever going to raise the money we needed, the caucus would have to do it.

I also saw that labor had to be persuaded to put more money in Ohio House races, not just for our sake but for theirs. They may have whipped Billy O'Neill and the right-to-work issue in 1958, but business was kicking labor's butt when it came to controlling the legislature, and it's the legislature that makes the laws. We were the best friend labor had in state government, and I thought it was about time they recognized it.

In the mid-1960s, some things started to go our way. The U.S. Supreme Court's "one man, one vote" decision in 1964 forced all states to change the way they drew legislative districts and, in Ohio, that would give Democrats a shot at winning some districts we couldn't win before.

By the late 1960s, I took it upon myself to start raising money for the caucus. The Supreme Court decision changed the political landscape, and Governor Rhodes would not be able to run for reelection in 1970 because the state's constitution prohibited more than two consecutive gubernatorial terms. With a strong Democratic candidate at the top of the ticket, there was the potential of drawing larger numbers of Democrats to the polls, and that would make us more competitive in the legislative races.

You make a lot of contacts with a decade of experience in the legislature under your belt, and I used every one of them. I hit the road, made my pitch, and wasn't bashful about where the money came from. It didn't matter to me whether it was business, labor, lobbyists, or anyone else so long as they wanted to contribute to the cause. There was no where to go but up.

The money I raised was peanuts by today's standards. All I was able to do was give a few hundred dollars here and there to some of our candidates. If someone needed three hundred dollars to pay a printing bill, for example, I'd write the check on the spot. But in those days, a few thousand dollars could win a race, so contributions like that meant the world to a candidate.

I continued raising money, still not in large amounts, to help caucus members in the 1970 election. As it turned out, that was a tremendous year for Democrats. We picked up ten seats, Jack Gilligan won the governor's office, and the Democrats won control of the state Apportionment Board, so we would be drawing legislative district lines the following year.

Soon after the election, I engineered A. G. Lancione's one-vote victory as House minority leader. While I can't say the money I raised for the caucus was a major factor in that vote, it definitely helped because the caucus saw A. G. and me as a team. Nobody else was trying to raise money for the caucus.

Jack Gilligan predicted then that we would take over the House in 1972, and there was plenty of reason to be optimistic. With a Democratic governor, we were able to do some things for our incumbents (such as get capital improvements in their districts) that would come in handy during the campaign.

I could also build on my experience in raising funds for the caucus, only this time we would be running under lines drawn by Democrats. That would help with fund-raising, since there were always contributors who wanted to hedge their bets if the outcome of an election was hanging in the balance.

In 1972 Richard Nixon beat George McGovern in Ohio by more than a million votes, but when the legislative races were counted, we had bucked the trend. Democrats won a majority in the House by a margin of 58-41! We were back in the saddle after twelve long years.

The new lines were largely responsible for Democrats getting the majority in 1972. I knew that. But fund-raising, candidate recruitment, and a strong caucus organization are what would keep us there. History would not repeat itself if I had anything to do with it. All those years of serving in the minority, all those years of studying the process, making friends, and watching how leaders worked would soon begin to pay off.

Some big changes needed to be made though, and we had precious little time to make them. The more I studied the situation, the more convinced I became that raising money was a key to staying in office. It really hit me during a meeting at state Democratic Party headquarters with some of Jack Gilligan's people. They had retained an outfit from Minnesota that provided voter-targeting information on a statewide basis, and representatives from the company were explaining how it worked. I did voter targeting in my first election in 1958. I knew how important it was not to waste time and resources in precincts that wouldn't support a Democrat. It was one thing to put voter-targeting information together for one legislative district, but to do it for the entire state was a very expensive proposition.

That cinched it with me.

"I'm going to put together an organization so strong the Republicans are going to have a hard time ever getting the majority back," I told A. G. At the time, I wasn't exactly sure how I was going to do it. I just knew it had to be done.

I wish I could take credit for all the good ideas that I put into practice. That wouldn't be honest though. One day I was talking to Bill Konyha about the money situation. Bill, who was moving up through the ranks of the Carpenter's International, was as sharp as ever. He suggested something that would revolutionize the way legislative candidates financed their campaigns.

Up until then, legislative leaders had little control over how contributors spent their money. Bill knew that as well as anyone, because the labor unions had always made their own decisions about which campaigns to spend money on and how much. But he had a lot of faith in me and recognized that I was going places. Bill also knew that I was a strong leader and totally dedicated to keeping a Democratic majority in the House. Bill knew that I could make it happen with more control over contributions.

First, he said, hold a dinner to raise funds for the Democratic Caucus. Second, deposit those funds into a caucus committee account. Then it would simply be up to the House leadership to decide how to allocate those funds.

It was a beautiful idea because as the majority caucus, we could be sure of a strong turnout. Bill was willing to serve as the cochair of the dinner, so there was little doubt that labor contributions would be sizable.

Fund-raising dinners for individual candidates weren't new, but a legislative caucus in Ohio had never held a fund-raising event like that for a caucus as a whole. My entire career had prepared me for that moment—the Jim Lantz fund-raiser, my ability to work with other people, my reputation as someone who was fair and honest, and the fund-raising trips of the preceding three elections. Now that we were in the majority, I believed our caucus was finally in a position to raise the kind of money necessary to keep it there.

The first thing I did was sit down with a legal pad and start putting a list of contributors together. Next I started contacting contributors one by one. I made nearly all the initial contacts myself, and that didn't change until some years went by and the list got so big that it was impossible for me to make all the calls. Contributors knew when they got a call from one of my people about a fund-raiser that it was no different from talking to me. The first computer I ever bought was to keep track of our contributions because eventually it became too complicated to manage on index cards.

The ticket price for that first dinner was one hundred dollars, and we were selling tables of ten. When I called someone, I wouldn't ask for a specific amount.

"Do the very best you can do, and if I think you're not, I'll tell you," I'd say. Rarely did I ever feel people were not contributing enough. In fact, as the years went by and our majority became more secure, the opposite would happen. I might be thinking someone should buy three tables and instead they'd get five. I'd never let on that they exceeded my expectations.

"If that's the best you can do, I understand," I'd tell them.

I'd try to make it as easy as possible for people to participate in my fund-raisers. I wouldn't give them a deadline; they could pay in installments as far as I was concerned, as long as they told me. I always asked them to get the money to me as soon as possible because I wanted to earn the interest on it.

The Neil House was a natural choice for a caucus dinner because I had long ago developed a friendship with John W. Wolfe, the owner. The Wolfe family was, and is, influential in Columbus. Even though they were strong Republicans, it never mattered to John or me that we belonged to different parties. He always told his people, "I want Vern Riffe to have the best we've got, the best service and the best price."

I put on that first-ever caucus fund-raising dinner on December 12, 1973. The big, L-shaped ballroom at the Neil House was so full we had to set up tables outside the room and in the lobby on the second floor to accommodate everyone. We served up nice, big T-bone steaks, sides, dessert, the works, and people loved it. From then on, I stuck with T-bone steaks at the caucus dinner because Dad always said when something works, don't change it.

When it came to seating, I made all the decisions down to the last person. I had seating charts made up to make sure that contributors were treated properly and I certainly didn't want big contributors being seated in the back of the room. If this dinner was going to be successful, I wanted to take care of every detail.

Jack Gilligan was there, and at his suggestion we invited Gov. Philip Noel of Rhode Island to be the main speaker. "He'd like to give a speech in Ohio, and he doesn't want any money," Governor

Gilligan said. That was fine with me, since it meant that much more money would stay in the caucus.

That dinner grossed $85,000, making it one of the most successful political fund-raisers ever held in Columbus and one of the largest held in Ohio outside the two major party organizations up until that time. I made my mark that evening and for the first time ever, the House Democratic Caucus was standing on its own two feet in terms of financing its campaigns. Next election, Republican efforts to take the majority away from us would be met with stiff opposition and the resources to back it up.

The secret of my success was really no secret at all. I worked hard to develop a broad base of contributors. People representing interests across the board were comfortable with me because they knew I would deal straight up with them. If I could do something for them, I did it; if not, I'd tell them so. I more or less had an open-door policy to people or groups that wanted to see me, so they knew they could always get a hearing on an issue.

It wasn't difficult, for example, to get the bankers, the utilities, and the insurance companies to contribute, even though people might not consider them traditional Democratic supporters. They knew they'd get a fair shake from me. I was consistent. I built those relationships over a long period of time. People would say, "He might not tell you what you want to hear, but he's going to be fair." Believe it or not, in all my years of fund-raising for the caucus, I cannot remember a single instance where anybody turned us down for a contribution.

Naturally, as the years went by and we continued to hold onto the majority, our base of contributors got bigger and the size of the contributions got larger. But the key was always that I could get along with just about anybody or any group. They were comfortable with that, and they showed their appreciation when it came time to raise money.

Before we won the majority, I thought labor should contribute more to Ohio House races. With Bill Konyha's help, the 1973 dinner was a key turning point. We began to increase substantially the amount of money labor was giving and we were directing it to races where it was needed.

In the early going, some labor people couldn't see that we spent their campaign contributions to our caucus more effectively than they could. The year labor went after Bill Hinig because he wouldn't vote to override Governor Rhodes's veto of the collective bargaining bill—even though Bill had supported labor twice leading up to the vote—I told some of the top labor leaders in Ohio I would use every resource at my disposal to get Bill reelected.

"You mean you're going to use our money against us!" one of them said in disbelief.

"Look, mister, the minute you gave that money to the caucus, it was no longer yours. It belongs to the caucus, and I'll use it any way I want to," I said.

They got over it, and as time went on most of the labor leaders came to understand that giving to the caucus was a good investment. The caucus was putting together winning campaigns—from candidate recruitment and campaign strategy to work in the field, polling, direct mail, and radio and TV buys. Labor couldn't do that. The party couldn't do that. And the governor's office, which had helped in House campaigns before, couldn't do it as effectively.

I've stood up to contributors many times and sent their money back when I thought they were out of line. Years ago a utility company bought tickets to the caucus dinner. Then about January or February, a piece of legislation came along, and I took a position opposite of what the utility wanted. I got some letters from a couple of their managers, including my own in Portsmouth, saying they had become really disappointed in my position since they had bought tickets to the dinner. I got Rick Pfeiffer, who was on our leadership staff, and said, "You give every one of them their money back. You write the checks and I'll sign them." I've also returned money to the Ohio Education Association and the American Federation of State, County, and Municipal Employees. One advantage of raising a lot of money is that you don't have to be dependent on any one individual or group.

Some of the news media people think legislators are bought and paid for by contributors. That's nonsense. I never concerned myself much with those charges. If I had any power, I created it with a strong organization and hard work.

The news media rarely look into the cost of advertising, consultants, and the like. These are the main expenses driving up the cost of campaigns. It's not the candidates' fault. It's not the fault of labor, the Ohio Manufacturers Association, the Ohio Chamber of Commerce, or any of the special interest groups. It's TV, radio, and newspaper advertising, consultants, mail houses, and the whole industry that feeds off campaigns. Without some kind of curb put on what they can charge, there's no limit to how much candidates will raise and spend.

For someone who was supposed to be the king of fund-raising in Ohio, I sure spent a lot of time working on campaign finance reform bills. Just a few months before I held that first caucus fund-raiser in December of 1973, Governor Gilligan called a special session on campaign finance reform. This was right in the middle of the Watergate period, and the governor, being a reformer, was eager to move on it. But the Senate, being Republican, passed a bill that restricted what labor could give to candidates because labor didn't give to Republicans. After three weeks of haggling, it all fell apart and we adjourned the session with nothing to show for it.

The basic disagreement was the same that would plague efforts to reform campaign finance reform for the next twenty-two years: Republicans were trying to put a dent in labor contributions to Democrats, and Democrats were trying to cut down the amount of money that business gave to Republicans. The truth is, business has always given many times over what labor does—in Ohio and nationally.

We tried again to enact a limit on campaign spending in 1974, Jack Gilligan's last year as governor. It had bipartisan support ranging from Sen. Thomas Van Meter, a conservative Republican from Richland County, to Dick Celeste, then in the House. In House races, the limits were 15¢ times the average population of a House district, which at about 100,000 people per district worked out to about $15,000. For Senate races, it was 12¢ times the average population of a district for about $35,000 to $40,000. In the governor's race, the bill called for 10¢ times the population of the state for about $1 million. We figured these limits provided enough to run a decent campaign while putting a lid on excessive spending.

Then in 1976, the U.S. Supreme Court issued its decision in *Buckley v. Valeo*. That decision invalidated federal campaign expenditure limits as a violation of freedom of speech protections in the First Amendment to the U.S. Constitution. Anyone could see that Ohio's campaign limits would not stand the test of law, and the General Assembly removed the limits that same year.

The only way we could legally restrict what candidates spent is if they voluntarily gave up that right by, for example, accepting public funds. But every poll showed that huge majorities of taxpayers were opposed to using public funds for campaigns. There was no way on earth something like that could pass the General Assembly.

As our caucus fund-raising operation grew strong, I also was helping to raise money for the state Democratic Party. People forget that from 1963 through 1982, the Republicans dominated the executive branch for 16 years, the Senate for 14 years, and the House for 10 of those years. It was slim pickings for the Democratic Party. There were times when the party headquarters couldn't pay rent or utility bills. Many a time I'd loan them money, sign notes, or raise money for the party; otherwise, someone might have padlocked the door. From the time I got into leadership until the time Dick Celeste became governor in 1983, no individual did more to raise money for the state party than I did.

Even though the party had never done a great deal to help Democrats running for the House, and even though the caucus always came first with me, I was a loyal Democrat. To me, that meant doing what you could to help the party. The first eight years I was Speaker, Paul Tipps served as chairman of the state Democratic Party. Democrats didn't have the governorship during that time, so Paul developed a very close working relationship with people like Secretary of State Tony Celebrezze, State Treasurer Gertrude Donahey, Auditor Tom Ferguson, and me. It was a real team effort, and as the top Democratic officeholders in the state, we felt obliged to keep the party afloat by doing what we could to raise money.

When Dick Celeste became governor in 1983, he took the lead in party fund-raising. He put his own person, Jim Ruvolo of Toledo, in as state party chairman and Paul Tipps stepped aside. The party didn't have to rely on me to be its chief fund-raiser. That was fine with me because I had plenty to keep me busy. The only problem I had with Jim Ruvolo was during election time. Paul would meet with all the Democratic state officials, and you'd have a say in what was going on. When Dick was elected, he called the shots and Jim carried them out. The rest of us weren't nearly as involved in party decision making. I understand why that was, but I'm not convinced it was for the best insofar as the party was concerned.

Just prior to Dick's election, some of my members and friends decided to put on a dinner around the theme "A Salute to Leadership." Stark County Democratic Chairman John Meeks helped organize it, along with a former caucus member, Harry Lehman of Cleveland, and House Executive Secretary Joe Sommers of Canton. It took place on June 24, 1981, and little did I realize that it would serve as a model for what was to become a signature annual event.

That spring, Tip O'Neill was in town to help with a fund-raiser for Congressman Bob Shamansky of Columbus. This is when Tip was still Speaker of the U.S. House of Representatives. During the event, we got to talking.

"I understand you put on a pretty good fund-raiser."

"I try to do my best, Mr. Speaker. I have to raise money, you know," I said.

"I know you do. When's your birthday?" he asked.

This was in May, and I told him my birthday was on June 26.

"Well, it's probably too late for this year, but let me tell you what I'd do. Every year in Washington, I hold a Speaker's Birthday Party. I charge $1,000 a head. You ought to give serious consideration to that. June's a good month."

I got to thinking about it and realized this was a pretty good idea. Truth is, I had been thinking about ways to raise more money for the caucus, such as making the biennial caucus dinner an annual event. Even though it was too late to hold a birthday party that year, the Salute to Leadership dinner was scheduled for June and it would be easy enough to simply continue to hold a June birthday party instead in following years.

June was a good month, not just because it was my birthday. It's in the middle of the year, so it falls between lots of other events. And, as many people have pointed out over the years, it comes at the same time as the end of the state's fiscal year. That means just about everybody who has anything to do with state government is around when the legislature is trying to wrap up the budget.

By holding an annual birthday party, we would be going from one big fund-raising event every two years to three big events. That was good enough for me, but there was another advantage to the birthday party idea.

There were a lot of Republicans who liked what I was doing, but they could not bring themselves to make out checks to the Ohio House Democratic Caucus. Some of those same Republicans, however, had no problem whatsoever giving money—big money—when it went to the Riffe Election Committee.

John W. Wolfe is a perfect example, although there are others. Aside from the fact that we were longtime friends, Columbus was a second home to me, I had been very supportive of many projects that benefited Columbus, and John appreciated that. After I became Speaker, he didn't call me Vern anymore; it was always "Mr. Speaker." I often relied on him for good advice, and he never hesitated to help. John was a natural leader, and we had mutual respect for each other.

John Wolfe was as interested in me being reelected Speaker as any person in this state. Rather than sign a check payable to the House Democratic Caucus, he would make it out to the Riffe Election Committee. Beyond our personal friendship, John knew that I would be fair and honest with him whether it concerned Columbus or anything else.

The first five birthday parties were held at the Sheraton Hotel in downtown Columbus. After the 1986 dinner the hotel closed, but we had outgrown it anyway and moved the 1987 dinner to the huge ballroom at the Aladdin Shrine Temple on the northeast side of town.

Tip O'Neill had told me I'd be surprised at how many people would want to attend. Was he ever right about that! It took on a life of its own to the point where people would say, "I've got to be there." Some groups would charter buses, others would fly into town. The birthday party didn't have the same partisan tone that the caucus dinner had. When Jim Rhodes first came to my birthday party, people talked about it. And when George Voinovich became governor, he came to the party. Senate leaders such as Stan Aronoff loved to come. John Wolfe, Les Wexner of The Limited, John Fisher of Nationwide Insurance, and John McCoy of Bank One—people of that caliber—wanted to be there. When folks like that showed up, it became respectable for other Republicans to attend.

Corwin Nixon, God bless him, always bought tickets and attended. He wasn't concerned with how his caucus might react, even though the dollars were going to the Riffe Election Committee and most of that ended up being used against his candidates.

"This is your birthday and I want to be a part of that," he'd say.

It was a first-class affair and probably the top social event of the year for people in politics. The whole thing was set up to create a partylike atmosphere. We'd sell tickets by the table because it was much easier that way, but there were no tables. They would only get in the way. My good friend Ed Hinton of the United Auto Workers, God rest his soul, used to holler, "By God, where are those tables you sell?" So, one year we got a little table, I mean a small one, put a sign with his name on it, attached some balloons to it, and that was Ed's table. Every year thereafter, the only tables in the entire joint would be two for my family and one for Ed—a tradition we continued even after his death in Ed's memory.

You would think that there might be complaints about holding an annual birthday party fund-raiser in addition to the caucus dinner, but I can't remember any. The only complaints I can ever recall are things like, "Where's the shrimp cocktail?" or "Where's the dessert?" It got to where we had to hold off putting out the food so the early birds wouldn't gobble it all up. One thing for sure, we didn't cut corners. People won't come back every year if they don't enjoy themselves.

Ohio House campaigns were becoming more sophisticated at the same time that we were raising more money. In the early 1980s, TV was not a dominant factor in House races. But each year it was growing, and I could see that. That's one reason I was looking for another way to raise money. I knew that we wouldn't be able to raise what I thought we should on the biennial dinner alone.

I resisted using polling until we started raising a lot more money, and then polling became a regular part of House campaigns. You just had to do it. We didn't use direct mail at nearly the level we used in later years until we started raising more money.

If we had not gotten into TV, polling, and large-scale direct mail, I don't think we would have kept the majority as long as we did. You've got to keep in mind that historically Republicans could always raise more money than Democrats for House and Senate seats. Always, that is, until we put together the organization that we did. It was our organization that enabled us to afford and effectively use TV, polling, direct mail, and the rest.

Our fund-raising really started to roll after the birthday parties started in 1981. In the mid-1980s to 1990, the Ohio House Democratic Caucus became the kind of organization I dreamed about when we were still in the minority. Outside of the Apportionment Board, which had a direct bearing on House races because it drew legislative district lines, we were self-sustaining and independent of the party, the governor's office, or any other individual or group.

Probably the height of our fund-raising was the campaign of 1992. By all rights, we should have lost the majority. Two years prior, Republicans took over the Apportionment Board with the election of George Voinovich as governor and Bob Taft as secretary of state. To make matters worse, I became very ill, was hospitalized for nearly two weeks, and there was a time when the doctors weren't sure what was wrong with me.

We had a fund-raising strategy that was about as simple as you can get: raise as much as we could and dry up as much Republican money as possible. We ended the 1990 campaign with about $1.2 million in the bank, so we had a good start on the first part. As for the second part, as long as I was running for reelection with every intention of being Speaker again, many potential big-time Republican contributors were reluctant to count us out, even though we were running in districts that were favorable to the Republicans.

The public never knew just how sick I was in 1992. If that had been known, I'm not sure how much it would have affected fund-raising but it wouldn't have helped. In my view, it was critical that people believed I would be there just as I always had been in the past. When I announced in early 1994 that I would retire, we could no longer dry up Republican money, and it became much harder for the Democratic Caucus to raise funds. This was no reflection on my good friend Patrick Sweeney or the rest of the caucus—because they did their best to raise money—but a lot of our past contributors believed the majority would change hands since I wasn't running for reelection in 1994, and they wanted to place their money on the winner.

But 1992 was a different story. We had good campaigns, good candidates, and good consultants for the most part. Make no mistake about it though: money made the difference. In addition to the $1.2 million we had in the bank after the 1990 election, we raised more by the end of 1991 from the caucus dinner and birthday party. Then, in 1992, I had my most successful birthday party to that point, grossing $1.7 million. Still, as we got past Labor Day, it was evident to me that we needed another $500,000 or so.

By this time, I was out of the hospital and determined to raise that money. My plan was to go to major Ohio cities and tell some of the top money people who had supported me over the years what I needed. In Columbus, for instance, the first call I made was to John W. Wolfe. Now John already had put in $25,000 earlier, but I told him I'd like to raise another $50,000 in Franklin County.

"Let me get a hold of John Fisher [president of Nationwide Insurance] and we'll have it to you within a week," he said. And sure enough, they came through with their commitments for the money.

I went to Cleveland to raise another $100,000. John Climaco hosted a lunch in his office, and when it was over, we had commitments for about $125,000.

It was the same story in Youngstown, Dayton, and elsewhere. A lifetime of hard work, relationships, and trust all came down to this moment. There were so many people who would do whatever I asked because they had confidence in me.

One day in 1992, I had lunch in Columbus with Wayne and Mitch Boice, good friends who were in the coal business. The coal industry employs a lot of people in eastern Ohio, and I've supported many efforts over the years to help keep the coal industry strong. Wayne and Mitch liked my position on that and other issues and always gave me and the caucus strong support.

I'd say those two fellows had contributed or helped raise between $100,000 and $150,000 during 1991 and 1992 through the caucus dinner and birthday party.

"Fellas, we're going to have a battle this year," I told them. Naturally, they asked what they could do.

"If you could come up with $100,000, I'd greatly appreciate it," I said.

They didn't ask any questions. They didn't ask for anything. They just said, "Consider it done." Within a week or less, they brought me ten $10,000 checks from different people they knew.

If we were going to defy history and keep the majority under Republican-drawn lines, it would take every cent we could raise. I never thought I'd live to see the day we approached spending a half million dollars on a House race, but when one of my most loyal members, Wayne Jones, got drawn into the same district with Tom Watkins, a member of the Republican caucus, I knew we were in for a doozy. Two incumbents paired against each other is bad enough, because any caucus worth its salt has to do everything it can to support a loyal member. But to make matters worse, this district was in the Akron area, so we would have to spend big money on TV in a major media market.

Our direct mail costs were exceptionally high because Wayne sent out upwards of ten direct mail pieces to large portions of the district. The printing and mailing costs were sizable.

When it was all said and done, Wayne spent nearly $500,000 and won the race by 5,374 votes. Watkins spent almost as much. Up until that time, it was a record amount for an Ohio House race. I have to say this: Wayne worked very hard to raise as much money as he could on his own and did a good job at it too. But more than half the money he spent came from the caucus.

All in all, we spent more than $6 million on Democratic House campaigns in 1992 and won the majority again by a margin of 53-46—a decrease of eight seats. Still, it was the first time since "one man, one vote" and the creation of the Apportionment Board that one party had maintained a majority in the House under lines drawn by the opposition.

Our operation had to be firing on all cylinders to pull that off, and that took money. We may have raised that $6 million over a couple of years, but the way I see it, that fund-raising effort was thirty years in the making. I never bothered to figure out how much the cost of House campaigns had increased over the years, but Mike Curtin of the *Columbus Dispatch* did. He reported that in 1974 the average campaign cost of a House seat in Franklin County was $4,564, but by 1992 it had risen to $84,207—an increase of 600 percent, even after being adjusted for inflation. I'm not sure even I would have guessed that it had increased that much.

For three consecutive sessions before I retired in 1995, the House passed campaign finance reform bills. We tried to come up with a way to get candidates for state offices to voluntarily limit spending in order to avoid court restrictions against spending limits. Basically, our proposal allowed unlimited contributions to candidates who voluntarily agreed to spending limits, and contribution limits for candidates who did not.

In 1990 and 1991 our caucus initiated the bill, which passed the House both times, but in the former year died in the Senate due to inaction, and in the latter year never emerged from the Conference Committee. In 1993 the Senate passed campaign finance reform first, we amended it and sent it back, but again, it died in Conference. Some people thought I wasn't serious about those bills because I had done so well in fund-raising under the existing laws. I was dead serious though. If I didn't think a bill had merit or was against it, it never would have gotten to the Conference Committee much less out of the House. Anybody who knows me knows that.

I tried like the devil early in 1994 to get a compromise on the campaign finance reform bill in the Conference Committee and, in fact, got the Republicans to agree to one, but labor wouldn't go along. One of their biggest gripes was that the bill all but shut down large-scale in-kind contributions from labor, which was the one real advantage it had over business. Labor dug in and wouldn't budge. Then in late September or early October the labor folks (including Bill Burga, president of the Ohio AFL-CIO) asked me to meet with them. They wanted to know if I could get negotiations reopened with the Senate and the governor's office. They had changed their minds and were ready to agree to the proposal they had rejected earlier.

"I think it's too late, but I'll find out," I said. Stan Aronoff in the Senate might have gone along with it, but the governor's chief of staff, Paul Mifsud, said "nothing doing" after checking with his people.

It was a missed opportunity for labor because we lost the majority in 1994. The following year Republicans controlled everything from the governor's office on down, and labor got saddled with a new campaign finance law that was far worse than what they could have had. Now labor can't give nearly what it used to because of a $2,500 limit on contributions by political action committees, tight restrictions on in-kind contributions, and the way in which unions can solicit their members for campaign contributions. If I had been running again myself, I might have taken the bull by the horns and agreed to the compromise without worrying what labor thought as I had done on occasion in the past. But I told labor I wouldn't agree to anything unless they signed off on it, and I kept that commitment.

I didn't enjoy fund-raising. I didn't enjoy putting together the dinners. If we'd had a law that put everybody on the same level playing field, I'd have no objections to that. But I always said that until something was passed that gave us that level playing field, it was my responsibility as a leader to raise money and get my people elected. That's exactly what I did, but I was always for a strong campaign finance reform bill, and the record will show that I went to great lengths to enact them.

⊙ 5 ⊙

Reapportionment

Both Mother and Dad did their share of farming while growing up, but I never touched a plow in my life except maybe at the county fair to rustle up a few votes. I can tell you which end of a hog is up, and that's about it. Just the same, I guess you could say I became a member in good standing of the "Cornstalk Brigade" soon after joining the Ohio House in 1959.

In those days rural Ohio had more clout in the General Assembly than it does now. The makeup of the House was a lot different, with 139 representatives compared to today's 99. That wasn't the half of it. Due to the "Hanna Amendment" to the Ohio Constitution passed in 1903, every county, no matter how small, was entitled to at least one representative of its own. If the rural counties stuck together, they could really influence votes in the House on issues that affected them directly, such as school legislation.

In my own mind, I never really considered Scioto County to be rural because Portsmouth was an industry town. Any place that had a steel plant employing 4,000 people could hardly be considered rural, in my opinion. But based on the law we had only one state representative, so we were lumped in with other "rural" counties. The fact that I was a moderate-to-conservative Democrat helped me fit in nicely with the Cornstalk Brigade. In the early years, I cosponsored quite a few bills with my rural Republican colleagues. Like Dad always said, what's good for the people is good for the party, so I didn't have any problem voting with the Cornstalk Brigade when it benefited my constituents. Besides, it made good political sense because rural counties tended to be Republican, and they controlled the process most of the time.

I accepted the system just like everybody else, but anyone could see that there were some problems with it. Scioto County, for instance, had roughly eighty thousand people while Vinton County had only ten thousand people, but each had one representative.

On the flip side of the coin were big metropolitan counties like Cuyahoga, where hundreds of people ran at large in the primaries for eighteen or so state representative districts on what they called a "bedsheet ballot." The first year I ran for the House, there were 116 Democrats running in the primary for eighteen seats.

Having always been one to make the best of any situation I was in, I managed to represent my constituents pretty well under that system and was elected four times. Then it all got turned upside down by the U.S. Supreme Court's "one man, one vote" decision in 1964. There is no way I could have realized it at the time, but the consequences of that decision would have a tremendous impact on my career. It not only helped set the stage for Democrats to win the majority in the House but also enabled us keep the House for a record number of years.

Under the court's ruling, House districts had to have nearly the same population because, otherwise, some would be overrepresented and some would be underrepresented. In other words, small counties, such as Vinton or Scioto, would no longer get a break—not that I ever thought I was getting an easy ride. Whether there were 10,000 or 100,000 people in a district, it's hard work if you do your job right.

Somebody had to draw the district lines, and it was up to the Republican majority in the House and Senate to put a plan before the voters of the state. Ultimately, there was strong bipartisan support for an apportionment plan based on legislative districts with near equal populations, but not before some political jockeying.

In December 1964 the Republicans tried to push through a proposed constitutional amendment during a special session. Their majority in the House was whittled down in the 1964 election from 88-49 to 75-62, so naturally they wanted to act from the position of greater strength. Our caucus opposed that tactic to no avail, but the proposed amendment was soundly defeated on the May 1965 ballot with help from Democrats and organized labor.

The legislature tried until September 1965 to pass something that would satisfy the standards laid down by the U.S. Supreme Court. Every attempt at breaking the logjam proved unsuccessful until a federal three-judge panel imposed a temporary plan for the 1966 elections. That plan was the very first to permanently set the House membership at ninety-nine seats and the Senate at thirty-three.

All House districts would have nearly equal populations, as would all Senate districts, and in the case of the House, rural counties would no longer be assured of having one representative to themselves. Instead, most rural counties were combined in some way to create individual House districts. The "one man, one vote" decision was the end of the Cornstalk Brigade. Fewer rural legislators meant less political power for rural Ohio.

Roger Cloud was Speaker at the time and, of course, he was calling the shots insofar as the House lines were concerned. Roger and I used to shoot the bull after sessions on Thursdays, and I already had told him my preferences, since I was sure to have some territory added to my district. One day when I was at home down in the district, he called at about 8:30 in the morning to talk about my district lines.

"What was that county you told me you wanted to see go with Scioto?" he asked.

I told him Pike, a strong Democratic county.

"That's your county. That's your district," he said, just like that.

Roger always liked me, and that's the reason he did it. There wasn't anything more to it than that. But people always accused us of having a deal because I had supported the Fair Bus Bill in 1965 before the district lines had been redrawn. As Speaker, Roger was under the gun from Governor Rhodes to pass the bill, and my vote ended up being the key to getting it passed. The fact is I voted my conscience on the

Fair Bus Bill. Did Roger and I get along? Yes. Could we work together? Yes. There was no deal though. Even if the Republicans had been out to get me, I don't know that they could have done any real damage because Scioto County was my home county and it would have been the largest county in the district under any circumstances.

Despite the impact of apportionment on rural areas, as a Democrat I could see that there would be some advantages to the new arrangement. What the rural areas of Ohio lost in representation would be gained by the big cities and metropolitan areas. And those places had a lot more Democrats, except for Franklin and Hamilton counties. Take Cuyahoga County, practically all Democrats; Summit County, 80 percent Democratic; Montgomery, Lucas, and Mahoning counties, more Democrats. That shift was a plus for us, no doubt.

Finally, in August 1967, a bipartisan majority of the legislature agreed to a proposed constitutional amendment (subsequently approved by voters) that made permanent a ninety-nine-member House and thirty-three-member Senate. It also added two members—a House and Senate member representing the two political parties—to the state Apportionment Board which had heretofore consisted of the governor, secretary of state, and auditor. The House vote was 80-9, and I had no problem voting with the majority.

Heading into the election of 1970, there weren't too many Democrats betting we'd take control of the Apportionment Board. We had to win the governor's office, and even though Jim Rhodes could not run for reelection, Jack Gilligan, the Democratic nominee, had been defeated for the U.S. Senate two years prior by Bill Saxbe. He was liberal by Ohio standards, and we just didn't think he had a chance to win.

No one expected lightening to strike. It sure as heck did though, when the Crofters loan scandal broke. Crofters Inc. in Columbus was a loan company and a major contributor to the state Republican Party and Republican candidates. In 1970 it came out that Crofters had helped two companies get $12 million in loans from the state treasury. The companies went belly up not long after getting the money, and it threw the Republican ticket into a tailspin. The Republican state chairman, John Andrews, tried to get State Treasurer John Herbert, who was running for attorney general, and Robin Turner, who was running for treasurer, to resign in favor of other candidates because they accepted contributions from Crofters. They wouldn't do it, which ensured that there would be controversy surrounding the Republican ticket for the remainder of the campaign.

It was clear by Labor Day that Jack Gilligan was in pretty good shape because of the scandal. We realized that the Apportionment Board was within our grasp, but we needed to pick up one other seat on that board to get a majority. That's when a poll was taken and we discovered that old Joe Ferguson, who had come out of retirement to run and was nearly eighty years old, was right on the heels of the Republican nominee, Roger Tracy Jr. In the last four or five days of the campaign, Democrats at the state level, the state party, the county chairmen, everyone pitched in to put a bundle of money—every dime we could raise—into the auditor's race.

On election day the Republican ticket took a big hit. Jack Gilligan took the governor's office over Roger Cloud, Bill Brown won the attorney general's office, and Gertrude Donahey won the treasurer's office. Most importantly, we took control of the Apportionment Board when Joe Ferguson upset Roger Tracy to become state auditor. The only Republicans elected statewide to survive were Lt. Gov. John Brown and Secretary of State Ted W. Brown.

The night those results came in, I was the happiest person in Ohio. The day I had waited for came a lot sooner than I expected. Without that board, you couldn't win the majority in the House. You had to have that board.

As I look back on it now, there were any number of critical events that, if things had gone the other way, might have prevented me from becoming Speaker. The elections of Jack Gilligan and Joe Ferguson against the odds were two such things; the election of A. G. Lancione as minority leader of our caucus right after the 1970 election was a third. One of our first orders of business would be to redraw the district lines for the next election, and as A. G.'s right-hand man, I was involved in every decision that was made by the Democrats right from the start. If members had a problem or wanted something done, they came to me.

Fortunately we had worked hard on behalf of Democratic candidates for the House that election, and I reminded caucus members of this as I lined up votes on A. G.'s behalf. I also convinced them that A. G., with me at his side, was the one to take us the rest of the way to the majority. Members knew I was the only one in the caucus totally dedicated to moving us into the majority, and I was committed to A. G. He needed a majority of the caucus to win, and he took it by one vote on a secret ballot in a three-way race.

Since this was the first time Democrats had controlled the process, it was all new to us. The arithmetic part was easy. The hard part was dividing up a county like Cuyahoga. At one point, Harry Lehman and Lenny Ostrovsky got into a wrestling match in one of the Statehouse meeting rooms over who was going to get what in Cuyahoga County. The whole process got to A. G. so badly that he took sick and was hospitalized. What was going on just tore him apart, and I had to take over.

After we passed a reapportionment plan, everyone knew it would end up in court, so we did our best to get it into a court where Democrats would at least get a fair shake. The Republicans were getting ready to file in the Ohio Supreme Court, which had a majority of Republicans, but we outmaneuvered them and got it before federal Judge Frank Battisti first. The person who "challenged" our plan was a fellow named Sammy Jordon who owned a tavern named the Pink Elephant Lounge in Austintown Township near Youngstown. He had run unsuccessfully for the House in 1964 and 1968.

It was all planned and Marty Hughes, who was director of the Communications Workers of America at that time, was involved in it among others. Judge Battisti ordered that no court had jurisdiction over the case but him. He was a strong Democrat and tough. Boy, was he tough. When state Rep. Alan Norris of Westerville (later appointed a federal judge) and John McElroy, a former chief assistant to Governor Rhodes, tried to overturn our plan in the Ohio Supreme Court, Judge Battisti found them in contempt of court and fined them.

I would have done just about anything for Judge Battisti. He was first elected to the Common Pleas Court in Mahoning County in 1958, the same year I was first elected to the House. A couple of years later, I met him through the Youngstown delegation in the House. The Youngstown clan at that time was very close, not like today. And for some reason, I was very close to the Youngstown delegation, possibly because, like Youngstown, New Boston was a steel town. We had a lot in common.

Battisti was appointed a federal judge by President Kennedy in 1961. He never asked the party for a thing until after the 1992 election, when he wanted his nephew, Gino, to get a federal appointment as an administrative law judge. He had never had children, but he practically raised his nephew. I didn't think twice about heading up to Cleveland during an appearance there by Vice President Al Gore.

I told the vice president how Judge Battisti had stood up for the Democrats during reapportionment, how that contributed to Democratic control of the House, and what a good, personal friend he was to me. Gore said he would look into it and get back to me, but nothing happened. Finally, I called and talked to an assistant to ask what was going on. He said the administration couldn't get involved in it, or words to that effect. That was about the dumbest excuse I had ever heard, and I told him so.

What really galled me was that the vice president wouldn't give me a straight answer.

"It's strange that the Bush people were involved in it, the Reagan people were involved in it, and you say the Clinton administration can't get involved," I said. "You tell the vice president the next time he needs something from me not to call. When he wanted to run for president, I was one of the first to come out for him. If he can't handle one situation when there are thousands of judgeships all over this nation, that's pitiful."

With that, I said, "Thanks for your time," and hung up.

It wasn't fun drawing the districts and moving them through the courts, but it was all worth it when the results of the 1972 election were counted. We won the majority in the House 58-41, an increase of 13 seats for the Democrats. That's the power of the pencil.

Since A. G. was minority leader going into the election and I was his right-hand man, he was elected Speaker and I Speaker Pro Tem. For the first time in fifteen years, I was officially in leadership. Two years later I replaced A. G. as Speaker and began spending much of my time building a caucus organization to ensure we had the resources necessary to keep the majority for a good, long time.

Above: Vern Riffe being sworn in as state representative by his father, Vernal G. Riffe Sr., in 1967. Vernal G. Riffe II ("Skip") holds the Bible.

Right: Vernal G. Riffe Sr., mayor of New Boston

Above: "The Speaker" at nine months old

Right: Vern Riffe in the Army Air Corps, 1943–1944

Above: Vern Riffe and wife,
Thelma, in 1947

Right: During the railroad years
in the 1940s

Above: Being sworn in
as Speaker Pro Tem,
1972–1973

Right: Mr. Speaker with
John Glenn in the 1970s

Above: The new Speaker, Vern Riffe, in 1975

Below: The Speaker, Gov. Jim Rhodes, and Myrl Shoemaker in the 1980s

Facing page, top: Speaker Riffe and Governor Celeste celebrate at a 1980s birthday fund-raiser as Speaker Pro Tem Barney Quilter awaits his turn at the podium

Facing page, bottom: Speaker Riffe with Gov. Dick Celeste in the 1980s at a Civilian Conservation Corps Camp in his name

Above: Speaker Riffe in a classic pose while presiding over the Ohio House of Representatives in 1987

Left: Speaker Riffe swears in son, "Skip," as a Scioto County Commissioner in 1990. Grandchildren Micah and Nick assist.

Below: The Speaker thanks friends and family during the dedication of a bust in his honor at the Vern Riffe Center for Government and the Arts across from the Statehouse

By the time the 1978 election rolled around, we had increased our majority to sixty-two. During my career, we were able to reach that number three times, but for some reason we could never top it. It didn't really matter because as long as we were in the majority, we always had the numbers to get things done in the House.

For the first time in my experience, the caucus was raising significant money, doing serious candidate recruiting, and passing legislation that was good for our caucus members and good public policy. But all that would be for naught if the Apportionment Board changed hands. That's why, as we neared the 1978 election, I had one eye on the caucus and the other on the board.

Even today some people still don't understand that it doesn't matter what you're doing with your House campaigns if you don't control that board. Heading into the election year of 1978, I had some serious doubts about whether we could pull it off. Governor Rhodes was running for his fourth term against Dick Celeste. Dick was a hard worker and a great campaigner, but there's never been anybody like Jim Rhodes before or since. It would take an awful lot to beat him. Tom Ferguson, with his strong statewide name recognition, was a clear favorite over Donald Lukens of Cincinnati, so we figured we had that one locked up. In the secretary of state's race, Tony Celebrezze was taking on Ted Brown, who had held the office for nearly thirty years. That one would be difficult as well.

The way I saw it, our best chance to pick up that third seat was to get involved in the secretary of state's race. It wouldn't take as much money to win there as it would in the governor's race. I knew Rhodes would take nothing for granted when it came to his reelection, but I wasn't so sure about Ted Brown. The key in my mind was to have a good candidate with a strong name out of Cuyahoga County because northeast Ohio can make you or break you in a statewide race. We had someone who fit the bill in Tony Celebrezze.

First we had to convince Randall Sweeney to withdraw from the primary to clear the way for Tony. He was the son of Justice Asher Sweeney of the Ohio Supreme Court and a solid Democrat. Randy wanted something for pulling out, and what he wanted was a position as Tony's deputy if he won the election. It took some doing, but we got it done.

Tony was a hard campaigner and a loyal Democrat. He was log-
ging a lot of miles traveling the state, working with county chairmen,
making appearances he needed to make, and doing what he should
do as a first-time candidate for statewide office. The polls showed
that he was closing the gap on Ted Brown, but by Labor Day Tony
was flat broke.

That's when all of us went to work raising money for Tony, who
needed a two-week TV buy to win the election. I was heavily involved, put money in from the caucus fund, the Riffe Election Committee, you name it. The money just poured in. Tony made his TV
buy and he beat Ted Brown by less than 8,450 votes out of more than
two million. If Tony had not won that race, we would have been out
of business in the House.

It was so close that we were all concerned about the security of the
ballots. Ted Brown had ordered the ballots to be turned over to the
senior law enforcement officer in each county, but that was no good
because too many of those people were Republicans and it wouldn't
take too many votes to swing it the other way. I went to the secretary
of state's office with Tony and Paul Tipps, who was the state chairman, to try to work something out, and Tony got in Ted's face. We
had to get Tony out of there, and on the way out I told him, "It's bad
form to punch out a seventy-two-year-old man, Tony." Tony laughs
about it today, but he was hot.

There was little time to waste, so I got on the phone right away
and started making calls to Democratic county chairmen, trying to
anticipate where the Republicans could pick up four thousand or so
votes without being too conspicuous. As late as 2:30 in the morning
I was on the phone to people like Jim Ruvolo in Lucas County telling
him to seal those ballots.

Tony's lead held up, but after the election he and I disagreed over
whether a firm commitment had been made regarding Randy. I felt
it had, but Tony did not. That always bothered me afterward, and it
shook my confidence in him.

The Republicans were stuck with Democratic-drawn lines for another ten years, and that didn't set well with some people, who decided to do something about it. In 1981 a group called the Fair and

Impartial Redistricting Committee announced it would try to put an issue on the ballot to change the way state legislative and congressional district lines were drawn. Their pitch was to take the politics out of redistricting and reapportionment by using a formula focusing on population without regard to the party currently in power. Well, I didn't buy it. There's no way you can remove politics from the process. Besides, I liked the way the current system was working.

There was a time, shortly after we won the majority and before our caucus operation was in full gear, when we might not have had the wherewithal to fight something like that. But as we had shown in 1978 with Tony Celebrezze's race, I had the money and the organization to do a lot more than just win House races. I was fully prepared to do whatever it took to beat the proposal.

As it turned out, it didn't prove to be much of a fight. First I made it known where I stood on the matter by putting out press releases. This served notice that whoever got behind the proposal was crossing me. I also talked personally to people in the business community to let them know I didn't cotton to the plan one bit. That dried up a lot of the money that might have otherwise gone into the campaign to pass it. Finally, to show them I was willing to put my money where my mouth was, I sunk more than twenty thousand dollars into the campaign against the proposal. It was defeated easily on election day.

As far as reapportionment in 1981, it was smooth sailing for the most part. Any problems we had were so minor I don't even remember them. That was a big contrast with 1971, when we fought among ourselves and in the courts.

When it came to drawing congressional district lines, the legislature passed the plan. The whole time I was a leader, the House was controlled by the Democrats and the Senate by Republicans when it was redistricting time. That meant we would have to reach some compromise with the Senate. While congressional redistricting was not critical to my caucus or future as a leader, it was important nonetheless.

In late 1981 we were putting together the congressional redistricting plan at the same time I was considering running for governor. One day I was at the downtown Sheraton and ran into Congressman Bob Shamansky of Columbus, who had just finished a news conference in which he endorsed Bill Brown in the governor's race. I still hadn't made up my mind about running, and it didn't make a whole lot of sense to me that the congressman would be jumping the gun like that. I was none too happy about it.

"Did you have to do that? You know, I'm considering running for governor, too," I said.

The congressman said he owed Bill Brown for something and Bill was calling in his IOU. That wasn't good enough for me. The least he could have done was talked to me about it first.

"I don't appreciate that, Congressman. For you to do something like that when I haven't made up my mind and we're working on the congressional redistricting bill, I don't follow that," I said. "You remember this date."

I may wear a donkey label, but I have a memory like an elephant. When the congressional redistricting plan was passed, Bob's district was not as strong a Democratic one as it was before. His opponent in the general election was a young fellow named John Kasich, who was in the Ohio Senate at that time. I knew John was a smart young man who could give the congressman a run for his money under the right circumstances.

Like I said, there were always compromises when it came to congressional redistricting, and this was one compromise I had no problem making. Marty Hughes and the Communication Workers of America (CWA) challenged the plan in federal court. They could see what was going to happen. Opponents were alleging that the plan was intended to dilute black voting strength because some predominantly black wards in Columbus were carved out of Bob's district. Fact is, diluting black voting strength was the furthest thing from my mind. Ironically, once again I found myself on the other side of the fence from the former Democratic House minority leader, John McDonald, who had often been at odds with A. G. Lancione and me. John was one of the attorneys for the plaintiffs in the congressional redistricting case.

The plan was upheld in court and, to make matters worse for Bob Shamansky, he was targeted for defeat by the U.S. Chamber of Commerce. When the smoke cleared, Bob was the only incumbent Democratic member of the U.S. House to lose in 1982, and John Kasich became a star in the U.S. Congress.

As for how our state legislative districts worked, the 1980s passed easily enough. Our majority in the Ohio House went as high as 62 but no lower than 59. As we approached the 1990 election, we were in the fight of our lives—although we didn't realize how much so at the time.

Just like in 1978, we had to win two of three seats on the Apportionment Board. But unlike 1978, there was no incumbent in the governor's office since Dick Celeste could not run for reelection. George Voinovich would be a strong candidate but so would Tony Celebrezze, who had served one term as secretary of state and two as attorney general. He had a statewide base and the ability to compete with Voinovich in Cuyahoga County, being from there. Tony was bucking history by trying to win the governor's office. You had to go all the way back to the 1930s to find two such different Democratic governors elected consecutively, but you could never count out a candidate with Tony's base and resources.

Another big difference this time around was that we had the incumbent secretary of state, Sherrod Brown. The icing on the cake was that Tom Ferguson was practically a shoo-in to be reelected as state auditor.

All told, we could have been and should have been in a stronger position going into 1990 than we were in 1978. But right away things got off to a bad start.

In 1989, when it became clear that Tony Celebrezze would be the top Democratic contender, he asked to have a meeting with me. Tony's campaign manager, Bill Chavanne, and Paul Tipps, who was representing me, met first to identify the issues to be discussed. Tony, of course, was interested in what I could do for him politically and financially. As for me, I wanted some assurances from Tony that, if elected governor, he would consult me about his legislative initiatives before launching them and give me an opportunity to discuss cabinet appointments before he made them.

A short time later, the four of us met for a dinner meeting at Christopher's Restaurant on the top floor of the Vern Riffe Center for Government and the Performing Arts in downtown Columbus.

The meeting was in a very large private room with one table and four chairs. After several minutes of small talk, I began to talk business.

"When you're making decisions about your cabinet members, I want to discuss them with you," I began.

"I'm going to make those decisions. I'm not going to delegate that to anybody else. That's my prerogative as governor," said Tony, who seemed defensive about it.

If he had given me the opportunity, I would have explained that I was not asking for control of these decisions, just input as a legislative leader who would have to work with his administration. It was as though someone had primed him not to cooperate with me. I didn't take kindly to his attitude toward what I thought was a reasonable request of a Speaker or Senate president to a candidate for governor of their party seeking their endorsement. I started to give Tony a piece of my mind when Paul jumped in.

"Time out! Time out! What the heck is going on here? You two are talking like you don't know each other," said Paul, trying to get the conversation back on track. Both Paul and Bill looked stunned, like somebody smacked them in the head with a Louisville Slugger. For reasons that perhaps only Tony could understand, a meeting intended to create cooperation took a bad turn.

We finished dinner and were civilized enough, but there was no meeting of the minds that evening or for quite some time thereafter. Paul Tipps told me this was a major setback for Tony's campaign. My early endorsement would have dried up a lot of Republican money that went to Voinovich. Eventually, I got involved in a big way, but there's no denying that our attempt at working together suffered a significant setback that night.

That setback was compounded by other problems. At the start of that campaign, both George Voinovich and Tony opposed abortion. In fact in 1978, when George was a candidate for lieutenant governor and Tony was running for secretary of state, they even campaigned together in Catholic circles opposing abortion. If Tony had just stuck to that position in 1990, he would have taken the whole issue off the table. Then one day he called me to say he was scheduling a press conference to say he supported a woman's right to choose. He said people would withdraw their support and money if he continued to oppose abortion.

"Tony, it's a big mistake. You don't need that. Two or three months ago, you said you wouldn't change your mind on abortion. You just don't do things like that," I said. The way I saw it, he'd look weak and his credibility would be shot. "I'd tell anyone who's threatening you to just keep their money."

It was too late, though. He had committed himself, and I couldn't talk him out of it. The Republicans hammered him, and when Tony tried to go after George Voinovich on abortion he was just playing into their hands. From that time on, his campaign just never did gel. I did what I could to help elect him—put nearly $500,000 into his campaign from the Riffe Election Committee—but it was too much to overcome. Tony did himself in on the abortion issue. It was a self-inflicted wound as far as I was concerned.

The one that really gnaws at me, and still does today, is the secretary of state's race. Sherrod Brown should have won the election. He cut not only his own throat but also ours in the House.

It was always amazing to me that somebody as smart as Sherrod could make so many bad mistakes, but he did in the House and continued to as secretary of state. His biggest blunder was to consider taking a two-month fellowship in Japan when his job was to be here serving the people of Ohio. The way you get ahead in politics is by doing your job, and there was no way he was going to convince people that spending two months in Japan was doing his job. Nobody believed that Sherrod Brown was going to do any economic development work over there. A lot of people including myself told him it was a serious mistake to be thinking about it, much less talking about something like that. He'd lose the election for sure if he went through with it.

The press had a field day—stories, editorials, cartoons, the works. And of course the Republicans played it like a piano. Sherrod backed off and announced that he would not take the fellowship, but the damage was done. Bob Taft put a stake through Sherrod's heart with his "Sayonara Sherrod" ad on TV. Sherrod ended up losing by about 5 percent of the vote.

I put $350,000 directly into Sherrod's race. At one point he needed an additional $100,000 and came running to me. "I didn't give two bits for you when you were in the House, and I still don't," I told him. "The only thing I'm interested in is the seat you have on the Apportionment Board." He left and told everybody, "Boy, he sure tore my butt, but I got the check."

You might think I would regret not having spent more on his campaign, but, if anything, I'm sorry I spent as much as I did. He did himself in.

If I was the happiest man in Ohio on election night in 1970, I was the most disappointed person in the state twenty years later. We needed one of two seats on the Apportionment Board, and we lost both. We kept the majority that year, but it was all over. The pencil would be back in Republican hands, and sooner or later they would draw us back into the minority. It was only a matter of time.

Just the same, I was never one to lick my wounds. As far as I was concerned, the Republicans still would have to take it away from us. I was going to make it as hard as possible. We ended the 1990 campaign with $1.2 million in the bank. That was a good start. And as long as I was Speaker, there were a lot of potential contributors who would be reluctant to put big money into the Republican House Caucus. Since "one man, one vote," no caucus had won a majority of the House when the lines were drawn by the opposite party, but enough people figured if anyone could pull it off, I could. Frankly I believed it myself, although I knew it would be difficult—as hard as anything I had ever done.

My plan was to make the Republicans work for everything they got, and that included their reapportionment plan. As long as they had been in the minority, I figured they were likely to get greedy when it came down to drawing districts. This issue would be going to court, no question about it. I wanted to make sure we had the best legal team and the best legal strategy possible. At the very least, we could create some confusion during the election year, which would benefit us since we had more incumbents. It's like one person said in the newspapers, "What do you want, uncertainty or political death?" At most, we could minimize the damage in whatever plan went into effect.

I didn't waste any time calling together the people I knew who had been through the reapportionment battles of the past, folks like Mike DeAngelo, George Jenkins, John Climaco, Bob Dykes, Bill Gilliam, and Paul Tipps. Together, we had learned a lot about what happens when lines are redrawn and how to take advantage of it.

For instance, after taking over the Apportionment Board in 1970, one of the things we did was pair as many Republican incumbents into the same district as possible. That way, you were almost sure to eliminate some of their incumbents or at least force them to move from their home base. The Republicans were caught flat-footed by this tactic in 1972, and it really worked to our advantage. When you put as many as three incumbent Republicans into one district, something has to give, and in some cases Republican members retired rather than face a tough contest in a new district. We took the Ohio House by a landslide, and the lines we drew had a lot to do with it. Having been through that, I knew that the tables would be turned on us this time, and I wanted to make sure we were prepared, whether it meant asking an incumbent to move or bow out. The last thing we needed was to have our incumbents spend money and get bloodied up in a primary running against each other.

In Bob Dykes, we had someone who had drawn our districts in 1981. He knew the state, every nook and cranny, and he would allow us to get off to a quick start this time around.

It was critically important to find the right legal firm to handle our case. Many, if not most, of the big law firms had ties to state government and didn't want to risk future business. Some weren't interested in the case and, even if they were, I wasn't sold on going with a firm that might find itself compromised in taking on the governor, the secretary of state, and the president of the Senate—the three Republicans on the Apportionment Board. We needed a fighter, someone who would do anything it took to fight our case and not worry about the consequences. That's when Paul Tipps suggested Bill Gilliam and his firm from Dayton. Bill was a friend who had long known Paul and had ties to the Democratic Party. He was smart, tough, and not the least bit dependent on state government. I had confidence that Bill would do a good job for us.

Never in my experience had the opposition party stayed on top of the other side like we did. When the Republicans had public hearings about their plans, we hired court reporters to record everything that was said. (Some of those comments would be very useful in court.)

In October 1991 the Apportionment Board approved its plan, and the following week we challenged it in the U.S. District Court in Columbus. Through the appeals process it ended up in the U.S. Court of Appeals (Sixth Circuit) in Cincinnati. The chief judge was a Democrat named Gilbert Merritt, and we figured there was a decent chance he would appoint a fair panel of judges to handle our case. We couldn't have been more pleased when he named two Democrats, Nate Jones and John Peck of the appeals court, and one Republican, David Dowd of the U.S. District Court in Akron. Nate Jones was the former chief counsel of the NAACP at the national level, and we felt he would appreciate our concerns about the way minorities were handled in the Republican plan. So far things were breaking our way.

The Republicans tried their best to keep the case before the Ohio Supreme Court because they had a 4-3 majority there. They argued that it was a matter of state law and the Ohio Constitution. But just like Judge Battisti twenty years before, the federal judges didn't want to let loose of it. Jim Tilling himself said during the public hearings we recorded that consideration of the federal Voting Rights Act played an important part in the way they drew the districts. The way we saw it, that was plenty to give the federal courts jurisdiction. We went back and forth on it for a while, and the Ohio Supreme Court did uphold the plan at one point in a vote along party lines, but the case continued on in the federal courts anyway.

Initially our case focused on what we felt were violations of the guidelines for reapportionment that were approved by voters in a amendment to the Ohio Constitution, which was approved after the 1964 "one man, one vote" decision by the U.S. Supreme Court. The guidelines included provisions like not splitting counties when they didn't have to be split. As the case progressed, our focus changed. At the suggestion of Bill Mallory, who had been my majority floor leader in the House since 1975, we talked to Tom Atkins, a nationally recognized civil rights attorney who succeeded Nate Jones as chief counsel for the NAACP at the national level and now was in private practice in Brooklyn, New York. He had been involved in a successful lawsuit challenging at-large judicial elections in Cincinnati based on race, and Bill thought he could be of some help on reapportionment.

Once he looked at it, he thought we really had a strong case under the Voting Rights Act. Republicans had put too many minorities into eight urban districts to create suburban districts favorable to Republicans. Tom called it "packing" the districts and said it hurt blacks' voting strength. That line of attack became the focus of our case.

In the meantime we had a mess on our hands. Just as we expected, the Republicans paired as many of our incumbents as they could—ten in all. What's more, they crammed six more of our incumbents into just two districts, three in each. They even put two of my chairmen in Republican-leaning districts with their incumbents because they figured they could win them. Nearly one-third of my entire caucus was seriously affected, so we really had our work cut out for us. The Republicans even drew one of our incumbents, Mark Malone, into my district. Mark decided to move since I clearly wasn't going anywhere.

We did our best to work things out to avoid a bloodbath among ourselves. We succeeded to a large degree by persuading members to either move or not to run for reelection. In only two cases did we have our incumbents run against each other. In Cleveland, Jane Campbell, Judy Sheerer, and Sue Bergansky were thrown into one district. Judy chose not to run for reelection, and later won a seat in the state Senate. But instead of running against Jane, Sue decided to take on another of our incumbents, Frank Mahnic, and it was a bitter fight. Another ugly one was between Ron Gerberry, my Education Committee chairman, and Joe Vukovich, chairman of the Ethics and Standards Committee. All I could do was stay out of those districts until after the primary.

As we got into the spring of 1992, there was considerable doubt about when or if a primary would be held that year. The later the better, as far as we were concerned, since the confusion and uncertainty favored incumbents. It looked like that's the way it might go when the three-judge panel appointed a "special master" to redraw the plan and ordered a separate September primary for legislative candidates.

But the following month, the U.S. Supreme Court overruled them so that one primary could be held on June 2.

We continued to fight it tooth and nail, up to and past the general election. There is no way to measure how the litigation affected the elections, but in my mind it helped us. We also put on one heck of a campaign—spent more than $5 million if you count money from the caucus campaign committee, my campaign committee, and contributions directly to our candidates from other sources. There were about fifty people on our campaign payroll. Some Republicans had us dead and buried, but when the results were in on election night, we eked out one more term in the majority: 53-46.

It wasn't until more than a month after the election that our case was argued before the U.S. Supreme Court and months after that before the court issued a ruling. The Supreme Court was unanimous in upholding the Republican plan, but even that didn't end it. More than three years later, additional rulings by the U.S. Supreme Court regarding reapportionment and the Voting Rights Act kept it alive. More than $2 million was spent on attorneys alone.

People said I was always pretty good at keeping my eye on the ball. Yes, I could count to fifty insofar as the House of Representatives was concerned. I also could count to three on when it came to the Apportionment Board. And that, my friends, is where the majority begins.

The End of an Era

I've been disappointed or angry on many occasions in politics, but during my thirty-six years in office I can count the number of times I was truly upset on a single hand. One of those times was November 8, 1990.

It was two days after the election, and the Republicans had taken over the Apportionment Board with the election of George Voinovich as governor and Bob Taft as secretary of state. That meant they would be drawing legislative district lines for the first time in nearly twenty years. Believe it or not, I could accept that even though I didn't like it. If somebody beats you fair and square in politics, so be it. It's when the other side plays dirty that really sticks in my craw.

My son, Skip, had just been elected to office for the first time as a Scioto County commissioner. That, at least, should have been cause for celebration, but I had a few things to get off my chest.

With the Capitol Press Corps in attendance, I served notice that the Republicans would not get away with the dirty tricks and harassment that they used against my son but were really aimed at me.

They threw dead animals in his yard. They tailed Skip and his family, staked out their house, and harassed his wife, Patti.

"I come from hill country. We don't take things like that lightly down there. We don't get mad, we get even," I said.

My remarks at the postelection conference sponsored by Denny Wojtanowski's The Success Group were directed at the Republican state headquarters. Bob Bennett, the Republican state chairman, was there and heard what I said but slipped out before I was done with him. Bob always denied any knowledge of the dirty tricks, and I now suspect they were the work of some people under him, amateurs operating on their own who thought they knew what they were doing but didn't.

I was set to retire after the 1990 election if Democrats continued to control the Apportionment Board. Now it was out of the question. First of all, there was no way I could abandon my caucus under those circumstances. I was obliged to do everything in my power to prevent the Republicans from taking over the House in the 1992 election. Besides, I had a score to settle. If they were trying to distract me during the 1990 House campaigns by attacking my son and family, it didn't work. We picked up two seats and held the majority, 61-38. Now it was my turn to stick it to them at least one more time.

The 1992 election would be like no other in my experience. We had two years to put together the campaign of a lifetime with the best candidates, the best consultants, the best staff, and a boatload of money.

Money may have been the least of our worries. We had $1.2 million in the bank left from the 1990 campaign and had planned three major fund-raisers: two birthday parties and a caucus dinner.

Instead, the first thing I turned my attention to in 1991 was providing our incumbents with some legislative accomplishments to use in their campaigns. Normally the budget and capital bills would serve that purpose to a large extent. They're the most important bills we pass. When you're the majority party in the House or Senate, you use that budget to help your caucus members. Come election time, we'd go to great lengths to provide our candidates with information on how many tax dollars and projects had gone back to their districts. I'd stay on top of my members and campaign staff to make sure they used that information in the campaigns.

Because of the budget problems, trying to pass a capital improvements bill was out of the question for the foreseeable future. The public wouldn't understand how we could cut services on the one hand and borrow money to build on the other, and they'd be right. Besides, there was another way we could move on some capital improvements that was good public policy and good politics.

Previously the voters of Ohio had approved a program through which the state would provide matching funds to local governments for local infrastructure projects. Since the economy was struggling and state revenues were down, I saw this as an opportunity to put the program into high gear. I hadn't forgotten what Dad and Jim Rhodes had taught me about pumping money into the economy by putting people to work through capital improvements.

I worked out a deal with Stan Aronoff to pass a package of business incentives. Stan really wanted those bills because companies were leaving Cincinnati to take advantage of tax breaks in Kentucky across the Ohio River. In exchange, the Senate would consider our bill to spend $360 million in state funds on local infrastructure over a two-year period instead of three. When matched by local funds, an estimated $750 million would be spent all around Ohio on local infrastructure, and that's something for which our caucus could take credit. Everything went like clockwork and the governor signed the legislation.

Health care was a hot issue in 1992, so we decided to move on that too. Harris Wofford of Pennsylvania came out of nowhere to be elected to the U.S. Senate based, in large part, on the health-care issue, and Bill Clinton was also using that issue in his presidential campaign.

I decided to appoint a select committee on health care, and there was nobody better to head it than Wayne Jones. He had already put together a health-care reform bill and had expertise as a former deputy director of the Ohio Department of Insurance. Wayne's ability to handle a tough issue like that contrasted nicely with his election opponent, incumbent Republican Tom Watkins, who was a loyal, if not distinguished, member of the minority caucus. Even so, it would be a tough fight because the way the Republicans had drawn the district through reapportionment, voters supported Democrats slightly over 40 percent of the time.

The bill started out as a way to provide health-care coverage for more than a million Ohioans who didn't have any. While we never could get agreement on how to fund the children's health-care portion of it, we did some tremendous things for seniors and working people. For instance, we included health-care insurance "portability" language so that someone going from one job to another would not lose his or her health-care benefits. We required policies to cover preventative care for children, such as vaccinations. And we prohibited "balance billing" in Medicare, so that doctors could not charge patients for the difference between what Medicare covers and their usual total fee. Ohio was a leader in making health-care reforms, and we were way ahead of Congress.

In putting together some key election-year legislation, campaign finance reform also had to be a part of the mix. It was clear to me that we would spend more money this election than ever before, and both George Voinovich and Bob Taft had campaigned on the need for reform. It was equally clear that the Republicans could use it to their advantage, since we were sure to outspend them by a big margin. To take that issue off the table, I chose campaign finance reform as House Bill 1 and made Kate Walsh, one of our most vulnerable incumbents, the lead sponsor. You can bet that was no accident. Kate, a fairly outspoken liberal, was in her second term and had won comfortably against a weak opponent. The Republicans would be gunning for her, so it wouldn't hurt to be out front on something with popular appeal.

Taking the lead on campaign finance reform is a good example of something I always tried to do: take issues away from the Republicans. People made a big deal of it later when President Clinton took issues like welfare reform away from the Republicans during his 1996 reelection campaign, but I'd been doing that sort of thing for nearly twenty years. Whether it was property-tax reform in the 1970s, tort reform in the 1980s, or workers' compensation reform in the 1990s, my goal was to keep controversial issues from getting out of hand by beating the opposition to the punch in dealing with them.

Once we got our key legislation moving in the House, it was time to start thinking seriously about hiring campaign consultants, and one name stuck in my mind—James Carville. Carville had become known nationally when he helped Harris Wofford upset two-term governor and former U.S. attorney general Dick Thornburgh in the Pennsylvania U.S. Senate race.

I had met Carville two years prior over breakfast in Washington when I was considering running for governor. Paul Tipps, who kept up with his contacts in the Democratic Party around the country, heard some good things about Carville and suggested the meeting. I was impressed; Carville knew politics, had good instincts, and was a fighter.

Right after Wofford's election, I contacted Carville about being the lead consultant for our House campaigns. He hadn't even closed up shop in Pennsylvania, but he was interested. Working with us would be a different experience for him, dealing with twenty or thirty candidates instead of one. It would also be good money. Regardless of whether it was the money or the challenge that was the appeal, Carville said he would make Columbus his next stop.

When he arrived, Carville said as a condition of his employment he wanted his own team in Ohio to produce the TV and radio ads and the direct mail. We had always chosen those people in the past, but I had no problem with it. They would be directly accountable to him, and Carville would be directly accountable to me. We shook hands on it in December 1991.

Almost immediately I began to have concerns about him. In January 1992 Bill Clinton brought Carville on board to help run his presidential campaign. I knew how much work it would be to stay on top of our House races, and unless Clinton got knocked out in the primaries, I had a hard time figuring out how Carville would give us the kind of attention we deserved. Then I came to learn that he also was helping John Glenn in his reelection against Mike DeWine. It looked to me like Carville was spreading himself too thin. John Glenn and I talked about it and we were both watching the situation very carefully.

For a while, it looked like Clinton might be finished when the story broke in late January about an affair he supposedly had with Gennifer Flowers, an Arkansas state employee. It didn't stick though, and Clinton was doing well in the primaries. Still, I wasn't prepared to cut Carville loose without giving him a chance to honor his commitment. He assured me that he would.

I will say this: Just the fact that we hired Carville threw a scare into some of the Republicans—there's no question about that. Anytime you bring in a top consultant it gets the opposition to worrying, and Carville had become a celebrity. It's like what someone said after the Wofford race, that people spend a lot of time and energy trying to figure out what Carville's cooking up, when a lot of times it's all in their heads.

By and large, everything was falling into place nicely until April 23, 1992. Before that day was over, however, my life would never be the same. What was already going to be a tough campaign was about to become even more difficult.

I had two important political functions to attend that day. First, I was to introduce Indiana governor Evan Bayh at a reception. After that, I had to attend a fund-raiser at Denny Wojtanowski's house.

Although I had never met Evan Bayh, I knew his father, Birch Bayh, the former U.S. senator, and I was more than happy to introduce him even though I didn't feel well. Truth is, I hadn't really felt good since the start of 1991, but beginning around late December of that year all the nagging health problems I'd been having got worse. The day of the Bayh reception was particularly bad. I managed to get through the introduction okay in spite of the tightness in my chest, pain, and a fever.

By the time I got to Denny's house I felt terrible. At this point, I had a pretty good pain in my right side too. I didn't have but three or four bites of food the whole evening. When I couldn't stand it any longer, I had someone take me home, figuring a nice, warm bath might do some good. Instead, I continued to feel worse. At first I couldn't even get out of the tub, so I rolled over, got on my knees, put my hands on the side of the tub, and pushed myself up. I managed to get in the bed but didn't sleep a wink all night.

First thing the next morning, I called my doctor, Manny Tzagournis, who was also dean of the OSU College of Medicine and vice president for health services. Manny chewed me out a little bit for not calling him sooner and said get to the emergency room at the Ohio State University Medical Center right away. I called the now-late Dick Fickenworth, my House sergeant at arms, to take me there.

For three or four hours, they ran all kinds of tests on me. Finally

Dr. Tzagournis said he wanted me to stay overnight to be on the safe side while they continued to work on a diagnosis. I didn't leave the hospital for ten days.

At first they thought I had pneumonia because of the problems with my chest, the fever, and so on, but they couldn't pin it down. One day some of the people on my case were talking about it, and a young intern said my symptoms sounded like "vasculitis" to her. I didn't think anything of it at the time.

I felt about as bad as I ever had in my life, but not a day went by in the hospital that I didn't have my staff reporting to me about the campaigns. I may not have been at the top of my game—that's hard to do when you're in a hospital bed—but I was still making decisions and signing checks.

When they allowed me to leave, I was nothing like when I went in. I could barely walk. There was no feeling in my lower legs and my muscles were weak. It was difficult to breathe. I hadn't been home any time at all before I got a call to get back to the hospital.

That's when the doctors confirmed that I had a rare form of vasculitis known as "Wegener's Granulomatosis." I had never heard of it before, but when I read the information the doctors gave me, I knew for the first time just how sick I really was. Fifteen or twenty years earlier it was a fatal illness. Wegener's is related to rheumatoid arthritis and affects various tissues, small veins, and arteries. It causes everything from chest pain, sinus and upper respiratory problems to hemorrhaging, fever, weight loss, and more. Dr. Ron Whisler at Ohio State said he'd only seen fifteen cases or so in the quarter century he'd practiced medicine.

As soon as I got out of the hospital, I did my best to get back into the old routine, which was no easy task. I was taking heavy medications, including steroids. There were side effects such as mood swings and water retention that caused me to appear puffy. I didn't look well and I knew it, but I had to put the best face on things. If people knew the full extent of my illness, it would be bad for the caucus. I didn't need any contributors hedging their bets or thinking I might have to step down due to illness, and I didn't want my members to worry about anything but their campaigns.

If I had felt unable to perform my duties as Speaker, I would have stepped aside and turned things over to Barney Quilter. There's no question the illness made my job more difficult. I remember times when I could barely stand at the podium to preside over the House, but I did it—even when it hurt.

Within weeks of leaving the hospital, I held my biggest birthday party fund-raiser ever. My doctors had ordered me to stay off my feet, and my staff tried to enforce their orders by shoving a stool under me as I stood shaking hands all evening. I know they had my welfare in mind, and I regret having snapped at them, but the only thing that would have been more uncomfortable than standing would have been to sit as if I were disabled. It took me weeks to recover from that evening, and it was after that that I learned to pace myself.

Meanwhile, we were under the impression that the primaries might not take place until sometime in the fall of 1992. But once the courts ruled the primaries would go forward on June 2, 1992, we had to figure out which districts were winnable and which were not.

The place to start was with the voting history of each district, including a "Democratic index" that showed the percentage of voters in each district who tended to side with Democrats. Since we were dealing with all new districts, it all had to be put together from scratch—precinct by precinct. That is the exact same thing dad and I did in 1958, to avoid wasting time and resources in places a Democrat couldn't win. Doing it on a statewide basis was a big job, particularly since candidates had only thirty days to file from the date of the court ruling, so we hired it out.

When we got the index information, it was clear that the Republicans had done their job well. There was a large swing in the number of Republican-leaning districts versus Democratic-leaning districts. According to Bob Dykes's calculations, the Democrats had gained an advantage in this area since the 1971 reapportionment. Because we did a better job of raising money, we also had the edge in winning marginal districts that didn't lean one way or the other. We now faced a much different situation. Using voting patterns in the 1990 statewide races, Bob found that 47 districts were either strongly or moderately Republican versus 34 on the Democratic side—a net deficit of 13 seats. The remaining seats were considered marginal.

The numbers didn't change my expectations or my strategy. I still thought we could keep the majority, but now we had a better idea of where to put our priorities. In years past, it wasn't necessary to get involved in more than seven or eight races in a big way. This time we were looking at more than thirty to start with. Eventually, we had to whittle it down to twenty or so races to avoid spreading our money too thin on TV, radio, and direct mail advertising.

The first priority, as always, was to protect our incumbents. Incumbents generally have a better chance of winning, so if you're in the majority and you protect that base, it is very difficult for the other party to take over. It also helped me tremendously after the election. One reason I remained Speaker for twenty years is because my caucus members knew I helped them get elected and helped them stay elected.

The next priority was to challenge the Republicans where we thought there was an outside chance of beating them, as with people like E. J. Thomas of Columbus, an incumbent, and Jim Mason, who was running for an open seat in the Columbus area. Even though those districts favored Republicans, we believed there was a chance to pull an upset. In both cases we had female candidates, and I could see that women all across the country were running strong. I knew that the Republicans in Ohio were recruiting women as candidates just as much as we were. Not only that, but these two particular candidates were officeholders as well, which meant they had some base of support. Lou Briggs, who was running against E. J., was a Worthington City Council member; Lori Shultz, who was taking on Mason, was a Whitehall City Council member and a longtime employee of mine, serving as journal clerk in the Ohio House.

The numbers weren't good in those districts, but I've always felt that an offensive strategy like that forces them to protect their base and helps keep them out of our hair a little bit more.

The campaign really doesn't begin until after Labor Day in my view. I've never been convinced voters pay attention to House races any sooner than that. Consultants, however, could spend all your money before Labor Day if you'd let them. I believe that any advertising you do before Labor Day is all but forgotten by the election. Same for direct mail. As for polling, most people make up their minds two or three weeks before the election, so I've always questioned how reliable early polls are.

The consultants were pushing to do polling on issues in August. They argued it would be difficult to make hundreds of commercials and direct mail pieces without knowing what people were concerned about. As long as I'd been in office, people had always been concerned with the same issues—education, jobs, crime, and taxes.

I had done pretty well without much polling for most of my career. What really sold me on it was a poll showing that my son Skip was in trouble late in his first campaign for county commissioner in 1990. Based on that, Skip worked doubly hard and won, but it was closer than expected. I have always credited that poll with helping us to make that extra effort in the end of the campaign that put Skip over the top.

What I wanted most out of polls was the horse race question, so as in Skip's race, we would know whether to step things up or shift resources somewhere else. We wouldn't need that information until closer to the election. Nevertheless, I figured there's no sense in getting top-notch consultants if you don't pay some attention to them, so I went along with polling earlier than usual.

We did our first polling in early August and didn't stop until the weekend before the election. All told, we spent well into the six figures on polling—too much in my opinion—in little more than three months, most of it with Hamilton & Staff out of Washington, D.C. As if it weren't difficult enough doing poll after poll in all these targeted districts, the head of the firm, Bill Hamilton, had open-heart surgery smack-dab in the middle of the campaign. (Bill had done that 1990 poll for Skip, and I was used to dealing with him personally.)

The period between the Democratic convention in late July and Labor Day was when we really started to put the whole campaign operation into high gear. It's also when I knew James Carville had gone AWOL.

Carville was still doing fairly well by us until the convention in New York, which I attended as a delegate and member of the Democratic

National Committee. While there, I wanted to spend about a half hour with him. I talked to him over the telephone, and we set up a time for him to come over. He never showed up. From that time on he didn't spend any time with us. I continued to pay him as we originally agreed, but I didn't like it. We had some problems with his team too and had to bring in others to help with TV, radio, and direct mail advertising.

The only regret I have over the whole thing is that he didn't keep his commitment to me. If he had offered to reduce his fee or even called and said he didn't have enough time for us because of the presidential campaign, I could have understood. Instead, he just kept collecting the fees without giving our campaigns the attention they deserved from him.

By election day, every penny we had raised—more than $5 million—was either spent or earmarked. We produced 100 TV and radio ads and designed 175 different direct mail pieces. Roughly one million direct mail pieces were printed and sent. We were paying about fifty people out of the campaign account when you include consultants, campaign staff, and field staff. And there were bookshelves full of polls and voter-targeting information, all of which carried a hefty price tag.

I had a figure in mind as to what I thought we could win: fifty-five seats. There was nothing magical about it. I just felt that fifty-five seats were winnable, and that number would give us enough breathing room to survive the next election. When the final results came in, we had fifty-three seats. It was a different time from 1980 when we lost six seats, because we ran the next time in Democratic-drawn districts and won six back. No way would we be able to make that kind of comeback in 1994 in Republican-drawn districts. What's more, the results in the 1992 election bothered me because I thought there were a couple of seats we should have won.

We put a substantial amount into Don Czarcinski's race, outspent the Republicans by nearly two to one, and lost it by almost eight thousand votes. I was unhappy about that. In fairness to Don, 80 percent of the district was new for him, but it was a Democratic district and he should have won it.

We also should have won Frank Mahnic's race in Cuyahoga County. Frank was a fast-talker who was always getting into a bind over one thing or another, and it all caught up with him in 1992. Someone filed a lawsuit against a doctor in Cuyahoga County, and in the lawsuit they claimed Frank used his influence with the state medical board to help the doctor keep his license. Almost $400,000 was spent on his race, most of it caucus money, and he outspent his opponent, Mike Wise, nearly three to one. Still, he lost by 7,600 votes.

Besides Frank Mahnic and Don Czarcinski, we lost another incumbent, Terry Tranter, in Cincinnati. We upset two of their incumbents when Kate Walsh beat Dick Rench in Huron County and Wayne Jones beat Tom Watkins in Summit County; we failed to beat E. J. Thomas and Jim Mason in Columbus, and we split with the Republicans on some open seats.

No race stands out in my mind more than the one between Wayne Jones and Tom Watkins. First, they were both incumbents, which meant it was particularly hard fought by both sides. Second, it was in the Akron area, which meant it cost a bundle, particularly with TV ads. And third, they were both good candidates. Wayne was smart as a whip, a fighter, and one of the hardest-working candidates you'll ever find. Tom was a friendly, good-looking guy who people liked. He had a tremendous voice, sang everywhere he went, and charmed the socks off of people.

The way the Republicans drew the district, Wayne was really in a hole. His choices were to stay where he was and run in a district with a 41 percent Democratic index, or move and run against another Democratic incumbent. Wayne never even considered the latter. The way I saw it, the Republicans figured the district was too Republican for Wayne to win.

If the Republicans knew anything at all about me, they should have known I would spend whatever it took to reelect Wayne. It didn't matter to me that it was an expensive media market. Wayne was one of my most loyal and capable members, and it was a matter of personal pride to keep that district.

I've seen a lot of negative campaigns in my day, but that was one of the worst I've ever witnessed. Tom Watkins stooped about as low as you could go by trying to smear Wayne because of his loyalty to me. The *Akron Beacon Journal* had been on an unsuccessful crusade to get me for years over one thing or another, and Watkins thought he could use that to his advantage. It all began in the late 1980s, when I supported reforming the tort laws involving product liability and the newspaper opposed it. After that, the *Beacon Journal* was like Don Quixote attacking the windmills; they thought that everything that happened in the House was driven by campaign contributions. They called it "pay to play."

The *Beacon Journal* was aggravating, like a fly buzzing around your head, but it never affected any decision I made. I did consider suing them for libel, just to show them that sometimes when they attack people unfairly those people attack back. I even went so far as to sit down with Bill Gilliam of Dayton to talk about it. Bill had represented Paul Tipps in an action against the *Dayton Daily News* when he was chairman of the Montgomery County Democratic Party, and Paul got some money out of it. But libel suits are very difficult to win if you are a public official, and I didn't want to give the *Beacon Journal* the satisfaction of seeing me spend my money trying to beat the Knight Ridder newspaper chain.

In one Watkins commercial, an actor playing Wayne was going around stuffing money into people's pockets. They made him out to be a crook. It was a sleazy, lowball commercial. One day I decided to discuss the whole situation with Wayne.

"If you need to draw some distance between us, do what you have to do. It's okay with me. I want you to win," I told Wayne.

"Mr. Speaker, if I had to disavow you to win, I wouldn't want the seat in the first place," he said.

That's the kind of guy Wayne is. He's got guts. He knows the meaning of loyalty. And most importantly, he was one heck of a state representative, real leadership material.

Wayne hit Watkins hard, but it was not negative. He focused on the fact that Watkins simply didn't produce for his constituents, missed a lot of votes, and was more or less a benchwarmer who didn't even stand out in his own caucus. It was a real good contrast because Wayne was a go-getter with some solid accomplishments based on hard work.

In the end, it was no contest; Wayne won by 10 percent. He was the only Democrat out of twenty-two on the ballot in Summit County during that election to win in the area that comprised Wayne's district. It didn't hurt that we outspent the opposition more than two to one with a total of more than $420,000, but Watkins hurt himself. There is no doubt in my mind that a significant number of swing voters supported Wayne over Watkins to reject negative advertising. I know negative advertising can be effective, but I've never liked it because people can sense that a candidate doesn't have much to offer when all he can do is attack his opponent.

We spent more on Wayne's race than any other, more than twice what we did on Mark Malone in Gallia, Jackson, and Lawrence counties. In the end though, Mark's seat counted just the same. Mark's Republican opponent, Frank Cremeans, gave him a real run for his money. It was tight going down to the wire, so we made a good-sized TV buy for the homestretch.

"That TV at the end of the campaign killed me," Frank told me later. Frank recovered two years later to defeat the incumbent Democrat, Ted Strickland, of the Sixth Congressional District in southern Ohio, only to lose it back to Ted in the 1996 election. From top to bottom, the 1992 campaign was the best we ever conducted. We beat the odds and kept the majority. I fulfilled the pledge I made to myself in the days after the 1990 campaign. I was tapped out, physically and financially, but there was no time to waste in getting ready for the 1994 campaign.

When we convened in 1993 for the 120th General Assembly, I was elected to my tenth term as Speaker, a record in Ohio, and my eleventh term in leadership. Barney Quilter was reelected to his tenth term as Speaker Pro Tem and a record twelfth term in House leadership, going back to majority floor leader in the 110th General Assembly. Also, Bill Mallory was elected majority floor leader for the tenth time and his eleventh term in leadership. In those respects, the 120th General Assembly was starting out the same way it had for twenty years. But in many other ways this would be unlike any other session I had experienced.

On the other side of the aisle, my old friend Corwin Nixon had retired and the Republican caucus chose Jo Ann Davidson as the new House minority leader. Much like A. G. Lancione in 1970, her election to that position put Jo Ann first in line for Speaker if the Republicans took over the House in 1994. In my view, they couldn't have made a better choice. Jo Ann was very capable, fair, and honest and got along with everyone.

Things just wouldn't be the same though without Corwin. I don't have any brothers, but over the years people like Corwin Nixon, Barry Quilter, and Myrl Shoemaker were like brothers to me.

There aren't too many like Corwin anymore. He's a remarkable person. Corwin is a moderate Republican, never a part of the right wing. Never. I don't know whether it was the time or place in which we were raised, but Corwin, like me, believed that you help people regardless of what party they belong to. One time years ago a former Democratic official in Warren County used to hang out at the local Elks Club and play cards. He was barely scraping by, probably living off Social Security. Corwin Nixon would take him out and buy him clothes, a new suit, shoes, and a topcoat. He's done many, many things like that during his lifetime. He can't identify with right-wing Republicans who think nobody should be on welfare. I've heard him say that many people have no other choice. There are just not enough jobs.

When the House minority leader's position opened up in 1978, I let it be known that Corwin was my choice. Chuck Kurfess gave up the position that year to run for governor, and Corwin and Alan Norris of Westerville went after it. Some of the Republican caucus members were interested in who I preferred. Well, that was easy. I had known Corwin since the day he arrived in the House; we had served on the Rules Committee together.

"I have nothing at all against Alan Norris, but I want you to know that Corwin Nixon and I are personal friends. I can definitely work with him," I told them. He held the position until he retired fourteen years later.

Early in his last term, there was a move among some of the conservatives in his caucus to oust him as minority leader. I heard about it because some of the moderates in the Republican caucus came to me. They were concerned that all the caucus needed to do was take another vote among themselves.

"Oh, no, no, no. Once a person has been elected by a resolution of this House, there are only two ways to get him out of there: either he resigns or the entire membership of the House has to vote on a new resolution," I told them. "Now you tell that bunch that there's no reason to put a resolution in because it will never see the light of day. I'll pocket that resolution in a minute. It will never go to the floor."

I never asked Corwin to go against his caucus. We had a good working relationship, and he understood that you're going to get more out of somebody if you work well with him. Countless times Corwin came to me with requests, proposals, and legislation. If I could do it, I did, and if I couldn't, I'd tell him. There's no question that he got more accomplished for his caucus that way.

Jo Ann Davidson also was a moderate, and I could see that she would have her hands full with conservatives like Bill Batchelder of Medina, Jim Buchy of Greenville, and Bob Netzley of Laura, to name a few. There was no doubt in my mind that she would be much more effective than those kind could ever hope to be. A legislative leader has to be able to deal with people all over the political map, inside and outside the House, and the conservatives in her caucus only cared about one agenda—their own. Some people called them the "Caveman Caucus."

Many things had changed from two years earlier. This time, we had no money left over from the campaigns; the Democratic majority in the House was at its lowest level since we took over in 1972; and term limits were the law, so neither incumbents nor candidates were looking at legislative service as a career anymore.

One thing had not changed: I was absolutely convinced we could hold the majority again. The Republicans smelled blood, no doubt, since they had chipped away at our majority, but I was very confident in my ability to raise money and dry up Republican contributions. We still had the majority, so, barring a disaster, it would all come down to who had better run campaigns. I was confident that we would prevail there too.

The budget process was smooth sailing this time around with the additional revenue from the tax increase we had passed. Other key pieces of legislation on my agenda were campaign finance reform, a strong anticrime bill, and a set of economic development bills to make Ohio businesses and workers more competitive. I was satisfied that we were putting together a good list of accomplishments to take to the voters in 1994. All in all, I was ready to do battle and win another election.

By the end of 1993, everything would be turned upside down. I can't point to any one incident or development that caused this to happen. It was just one thing on top of another. Soon, instead of operating from a position of strength and confidence, our caucus was fighting for its life.

The first big controversy of the session for us began when Paul Jones introduced a bill to force the merger of Ohio's three Blue Cross plans. It was a multibillion-dollar proposition involving thousands and thousands of policyholders. The careers of highly paid executives were in the balance. Lobbyists' reputations were on the line.

Blue Cross & Blue Shield of Ohio argued that only one large "Blue" would survive and prosper in the marketplace, and a merger would help ensure that policyholders were best served in the future. Community Mutual Insurance Company, the Cincinnati Blue, said it was nothing more than a power play by the Cleveland Blue to accomplish something it couldn't do in the marketplace and hurt policyholders in the process. Central Benefits Mutual Insurance, the Columbus Blue, was small by comparison, but it sided with Community Mutual.

I didn't have any strong feelings about the legislation, but Paul Tipps, who represented Blue Cross & Blue Shield of Ohio, was pushing it, and Paul Jones was the Health and Retirement Committee chairman. Both men had been very loyal to me. I felt the bill deserved a fair hearing before the Insurance Committee, but that was all. Committee members were free to vote as they saw fit.

Soon things got out of hand. Lobbyists from opposing sides were getting downright hostile toward each other. Meanwhile, the news media were giving the issue heavy coverage. They had plenty to cover too, because both sides were taking shots at one another daily in the newspapers. Of course, the Republicans were all over it, trying to make it a partisan issue, even though a similar bill was introduced in the Senate by Bob Ney, a Republican and chairman of the Senate's Financial Institutions and Insurance Committee.

Before long, it started to reflect badly on the caucus, so I told Mike Stinziano, chairman of the Insurance Committee, to stop hearings on the bill. Then in June of 1993 I met separately with Paul Tipps and Tom Winters, my former chief of staff who lobbied for Community Mutual.

"This is hurting the caucus. It has got to stop. It's over," I told each of them. There's no way I could have had them in the room at the same time; they would have torn each other apart. That's how strong the feelings were. The bill never came up for a vote in committee, but to this day the wounds haven't healed between the two sides.

Then in September the *Cleveland Plain Dealer* reported that Paul Jones was soliciting honorariums from health-care concerns in the Toledo area. The day that story broke, I was mad—mad at Paul and mad at myself. I had heard in August that Paul was planning a fund-raiser in Toledo in conjunction with a public hearing before a subcommittee of health and retirement. I told him that the place for committee meetings was in Columbus, and the place for fund-raisers was either in his district or Columbus. Paul was inviting trouble by doing something like that. I had Wayne Jones chair the meetings instead.

Paul didn't follow my advice and arranged to attend some private events in Toledo, involving health-care concerns, for honorariums. He had hired someone to set them up, and Paul's office instructed this individual to keep the honorariums under five hundred dollars so that they would not have to be itemized on his financial disclosure form.

After the story broke on September 16, 1992, the nonprofit citizens' organization Common Cause soon filed a complaint with the House Ethics Committee, which would have no choice but to investigate. Meanwhile, the press was all over it, and unless we did something to calm everybody, it would only get worse. I told Paul that he should step down from his chairmanship until the issue was resolved.

"Do it yourself. It looks better for you to voluntarily step down than for me to force you," I said. Paul really resisted; he felt he had done nothing wrong. But he got hammered every day he remained a chairman, and after a week or ten days, he finally stepped aside. Paul asked me whether he could have his chairmanship back if he was exonerated, and I said, "Yes, if you are exonerated, you should have it back." There are those who wanted me to take Paul's chairmanship away permanently, right then and there.

This would be a real test of character for the caucus. The fact of the matter is that there were a lot of people who didn't care for Paul before any of this happened. Paul was the kind of guy people either liked or disliked; there wasn't a lot of in-between. Some members were jealous of him because he was a nice-looking young man, well dressed, very bright, and ambitious. He knew the health-care industry backward and forward, and he ran the Health and Retirement Committee with authority. Paul also could be very pushy, the type of person who, if he had his sights set on something, went after it and could go too far if nobody put the brakes on him.

There was a perception that I favored Paul Jones over other members and other chairmen. I did not; but, no member of my caucus was more loyal to me than Paul. There's no question I appreciated that.

An effective caucus, however, has to be able to stick together in good times and bad. I knew from experience that a caucus could survive a lot if members put personal feelings aside and did what was best for the group as a whole. If we did what had to be done and let the process work, things would be fine. If caucus members turned on Paul, it would rip the caucus apart and destroy any chance of keeping the majority.

While Paul's case was being investigated, we had to do something to tighten up the ethics and financial disclosure laws or the Republicans would beat us over the head with them until election day. We needed to get that debate behind us as soon as possible, so I had my staff work with Kate Walsh, chairman of the Ethics Committee, to draft a reform bill. Before the month of September was even over, cosponsors Kate Walsh and Randy Weston introduced the Comprehensive Lobbyist, Ethics, and Notification Bill, which we called the CLEAN Bill for short. It banned honorariums, but, even more significant than that, it required full disclosure of lobbyist expenditures on public officials and disclosure of public officials' income by source and amount.

You should have heard the private complaining from both sides of the aisle over that bill. Many, if not most members, didn't like it one bit, thinking it was overkill. The Republicans, however, had thrown down the gauntlet, and even though a lot of them were talking out of both sides of their mouths, they would now have to live with the consequences of ethics legislation. If I had to do it over again, I would have gone with a simple ban on honorariums and appointed a special committee to look at what other changes, if any, should have been made down the road.

I happen to agree with those who say you can't legislate ethical behavior or morality. No matter how the law is written, there are people who will exploit loopholes or break the law. You can either write the laws assuming the worst about people, or you can reach some reasonable middle ground and trust that most legislators will not be corrupted by a dinner or the acceptance of a speaking fee for one's time and expenses. I'd always supported the latter until now.

When it got to the floor of the House, that bill took on a life of its own. The House Republicans resented that we assumed the lead on the ethics legislation, so they began throwing out all kinds of amendments. The Republicans got so carried away they ended up passing amendments they didn't even like. One in particular from Lou Blessing of Cincinnati would have prohibited legislators from voting on any bill lobbied by a group that contributed more than two thousand dollars to their campaign during the preceding two years. After we passed the bill 96-0, the focus shifted to the Senate, and public and news media pressure on the House eased up somewhat. Nevertheless, the resentment toward Paul Jones remained so thick within our caucus that you could cut it with a knife. Paul had not only given the Republicans an issue but many of those members who were lucky enough to get reelected would likely have to live under a new set of ethics and disclosure laws that would change life as they knew it in Columbus. The new law would virtually shut down free drinks and meals. Legislators would be almost totally on their own, since under our state constitution they can't be reimbursed for expenses. If the Senate had not taken out Lou Blessing's amendment, a majority of legislators would have been barred from voting on the state budget and a lot of other major legislation as well.

Some members of my caucus were team players who would place the caucus first and do whatever was required to put the issue behind us. Wayne Jones was one of them. Wayne even had the intestinal fortitude to stand up during closing statements on the CLEAN Bill and tell everybody how hypocritical the media were being.

But instead of coming together and fighting through this thing, too many of my caucus members were cutting each other, and the fight had gone out of many of them. In the old days, when we did battle we usually won. But now, if members of my caucus were giving up, what was the use of me battling it? That's when I started thinking about hanging it up.

During the Thanksgiving holiday of 1993, I discussed retirement with my family. There were more arguments for it than against it. It boiled down to three things: first, I'd had a long career, and a good one; second, I could see how the caucus would no longer stick together; and third, I was tired and ill.

For much of 1993, I was in excruciating pain due to my back. During the early part of the year, I couldn't sleep at times, couldn't even lie down. For months, the only way I could rest was to sit in a reclining chair or stand with my back against the wall. After pleading from friends, primarily John W. Wolfe, I went to the Mayo Clinic during the spring and they discovered that the drugs I had been taking for vasculitis had eroded two disks in my back. They made adjustments in my drug therapy, and eventually the pain went away, but it made for a very difficult year.

I continued to mull retirement over until about the first of the year in 1994, when I made up my mind not to run for reelection. It was one of the hardest decisions I ever had to make.

I announced my decision in January to give the party enough time to find a candidate by the filing deadline in February. Skip had already indicated he was not interested. He loved his job as a county commissioner, was doing well, and was getting a lot accomplished. I respect him for making up his own mind and not feeling pressured into following in my footsteps.

The minute my plan to retire became public, I knew it would be harder to raise money for the campaign from there on out. To make matters worse, I had little leverage to dry up Republican funds since contributors knew I wouldn't be around after the election to run the House. Fortunately, we had our most successful birthday party ever in June 1993 and raised more than $1.2 million. We also had a good biennial caucus dinner in December 1993, which put us at a total of about $2 million, before I announced I would not run for reelection.

There was no way on earth we could match the 1992 election; we spent $5 million to $6 million and still lost eight seats. As difficult as it looked, I was not going to abandon ship. I would still head up the caucus campaign operation and do what I could to help the cause. As time went on, however, it was clear that someone in the caucus had to take a leadership role so that our supporters could see that the torch was being passed.

Nothing seemed to be working in our favor this time, including the statewide ticket. The way things were shaping up, the Democrats would have a very weak ticket at the top. Tom Ferguson was retiring as state auditor, Lee Fisher was running for reelection as attorney general with stiff competition from state Senator Betty Montgomery of Toledo, and state Senator Rob Burch of New Philadelphia already had locked up the state AFL-CIO endorsement for governor in the Democratic primary—a fatal error on labor's part. Rob came out early and had a strong labor-voting record, so they endorsed him without fully considering his electability.

Rob had no chance as far as I could see, and I had very serious doubts as to whether he could even put on a good showing—and that could spell trouble for Democrats running for the House later on down the line. Unlike Dick Celeste and Jack Gilligan before him, Rob Burch had no statewide political base, no organization, and no money. He was driving himself form county to county. It was a disaster from the very start.

I could see it coming a mile away, and I suggested to Jane Campbell that if she was interested in running for governor, now was the time to be thinking about it. If the Democrats had any hope of unseating George Voinovich, our candidate had to do well in Cuyahoga County, and Jane had represented the House from Cuyahoga for ten years. The fact that she was a woman would also help bring out the vote.

I didn't encourage her to run, although she might have interpreted it that way. In fact, I told Jane I didn't want to see her get into something if she didn't think she could win it. But I said if she was interested in running, she should put some feelers out, and did she ever. Jane hired a consultant out of Washington and unofficially began running for governor; she got some good press, in fact, but the money wasn't coming in.

By the time the Ohio Democratic Party was ready to make endorsements, it was a done deal since labor had a controlling interest on the party central committee. I had pushed successfully for my old friend, Harry Meshel, to replace Gene Branstool as the state party chairman when Gene went to Washington to work for the Clinton administration in the Department of Agriculture. There was nothing Harry could do at that point.

When I announced my intention to retire, Harry said that "everything would fall apart" for the Democrats in the next election. While he may have been overstating my influence, had I been running for reelection, I would have gotten involved in the party endorsement process and done everything I could to come up with a stronger candidate than Rob Burch. Since I was retiring, however, I pretty much stayed out of it. Now Harry was stuck with Rob Burch, and all he could do was put the best face possible on it.

It killed Jane when the party endorsed Rob Burch. She soon pulled out (wise, I think) and that was the end of it. She would have made the campaign interesting, but George Voinovich was too strong and had too much money. Even so, I think the brief time she considered running raised her stock as a future statewide candidate. With a good head start and the right people advising her, Jane could go places.

To make matters worse, some people in organized labor were going after the members of my caucus who voted for a workers' compensation reform bill. They went so far as to put up opponents against some of my incumbents in the primary. There were clearheaded labor people who understood that it was either compromise on workers' compensation or get something worse. For some reason, there were always those in labor who forgot who their real friends were.

I've heard people say, "Vern Riffe never belonged to a labor union. How does he know anything about it?" Well, I belonged to labor unions long before most of them ever did. I was in a union on the railroad; I was in a union as a fireman; and I saw my dad lose his job as a watchman at the steel mill because they wanted him to be anti-union and he refused.

I will say this, labor did the best it could when it came to campaign funds. I can't complain about that. Frankly, we could have used more help in 1994, but AFL-CIO President Bill Burga said they had done all that they could do, which was significant. I don't fault Bill because it was his first election as AFL-CIO president and he had his own problems to tackle. But I know what his predecessor, John Hodges, would have done. John would have borrowed whatever it took to help us and figured out how to pay it back after the election. I can't say enough about the way John came through in 1992.

Things weren't getting any easier in the caucus either. As we moved into 1994, the Ethics Committee continued its deliberations, and in February the committee finally issued a ruling: "It is . . . the committee's opinion that the behavior in the case before the committee was unwise and imprudent. It is also the opinion of the committee that actively soliciting and receiving honoraria from entities which may be regulated by or have matters pending before a board on which the member serves shows at a minimum the appearance of impropriety that reflects adversely upon the House of Representatives."

The committee recommended that Paul Jones issue a public apology and return the honoraria in question, which he did.

Now the committee had three Republicans and three Democrats on it, so the decision was about as bipartisan as you could get. That would have been the end of it if our caucus had stuck together.

The following week Paul came by and wanted his chairmanship back. Since the Ethics Committee ruled that the worst thing Paul had done was show bad judgment, I saw no reason not to honor my commitment and return the chairmanship to him. So, in early March I restored his chairmanship. Paul's staff immediately got into it with Otto Beatty of Columbus, whom I had named interim chair of the Health and Retirement Committee. Paul wanted his committee files back and Otto didn't want to give them up.

The Republicans saw an opportunity to stir things up some more. They introduced a resolution to strip Paul of his chairmanship while at the same time complimenting Otto on his handling of the Health and Retirement Committee. They were playing hardball, and some members of my caucus disliked Paul so much that they were willing to go along with it.

It was apparent to me that if Paul didn't step down from his chairmanship, he would probably be ousted. Unlike our caucus, the Republicans would stick together, and they only needed a handful of votes from our side to pass their resolution. I wasn't about to let that happen. Part of having success in politics is recognizing the inevitable and making the best of it, even if that means merely controlling the damage. I told Paul to give up his chairmanship voluntarily, get out of the newspapers, and try to save his election. Paul had a big ego and nothing happened right away, but I sent word to him that either he'd do it by letter to me the following week or I would.

Since the Republicans had seen fit to use a resolution for political purposes, I had one drawn up stripping one of their members, Dale Van Vyven, of his title as ranking minority member of the Health and Retirement Committee. A former secretary had filed a sexual harassment lawsuit against Dale that included some pretty embarrassing and graphic love letters he allegedly had written.

As far as I was concerned, this would show whether the caucus could stand up and fight, or whether it would turn on itself. I figured I knew the answer since some of our caucus was ready to support the Republicans on their resolution. I was pretty disgusted with the whole turn of events. I don't like using resolutions that way, but it was clear that the Republicans were going to do whatever it took to win the majority. Since neither Paul nor Dale had any findings of wrongdoing against them, I saw absolutely no difference between the Republican resolution and the one I was proposing.

There were members of the caucus who wanted no part of the Van Vyven resolution. These members tended to be the ones who were not team players, and they vented their frustrations by helping to bring down Paul Jones. They weren't looking out for the caucus; they were looking out for themselves.

That's when I knew I had made the right decision about retirement. I thought that if this is the way the caucus is going to be, it's definitely time to leave because I want no part of it. I was so disappointed, I actually thought about retiring immediately.

Let me set the record straight on a few things. Paul Jones did some dumb things, some incredibly dumb things. He made me furious on more than one occasion—the honorarium controversy included. But if arrogance, stupidity, or bad judgment was a crime, nobody would be innocent. Paul was cleared of any illegalities by the Ethics Committee, and later, when a charge that he altered a campaign contribution check to benefit himself was referred to the prosecutor, that charge was dismissed. There was a right way and a wrong way to handle the charges against Paul. Like it or not, I followed the proper procedures—the same procedures that would be used for any member, regardless of who it was or what party he belonged to.

I could have dismissed Paul from his chairmanship, but when I had dismissed a chairman in the past, it was because the person—as a member of leadership—had failed to support a caucus position on a key vote. That standard was well established from my first days as Speaker. Paul's case was another situation entirely.

By late spring, I couldn't say that the ethics controversies were entirely behind us because not all the complaints and investigations had been concluded. To a large degree, however, the remainder of the year could be devoted to wrapping up legislative business and getting on with the campaigns.

Ever since I announced my intention to retire, I had been thinking about what role I wanted to play with respect to the caucus from there on out. My first choice as a successor would have been Barney Quilter, but he, Bill Mallory, and a number of other veterans were going out with me. That left one person as the clear front-runner in terms of seniority and leadership experience, and that was Pat Sweeney.

Pat was always very loyal to me. He recognized early on how I was organizing the caucus and doing what needed to be done politically. Pat was one of the first to back me as Speaker in 1974; he did it at a news conference in Cleveland.

While I never had any trouble with him, he often marched to a different drummer. A lot of times Pat would be the lone dissenting vote on a bill, whether it was in committee or in the full House. He'd do it out of principle sometimes and other times just because he felt ornery. Pat also liked to have a good time, an Irishman in the truest sense of the word. He didn't get married and start a family until he was forty-four. (Let's just say Pat lived life to the fullest.)

He definitely had the talent and brains to be a leader; it was just the follow-through that was sometimes a problem. That's one reason why I always thought Pat would make a better Speaker than a minority leader. As Speaker, he could put people in charge of things, preside, and get all the glory. But as minority leader, people look to you to get the work done.

Outside the caucus, Pat faced another problem. Because he was unpredictable and sometimes shot from the hip, many important individuals and organizations that worked with the legislature were wary of him. For instance, the Ohio Education Association traditionally was a big supporter of our caucus, but they were concerned about Pat because he openly supported school vouchers. They were very reluctant to give Pat the same kind of support they had given me.

When I got into leadership, I kept a low profile on legislation unless the caucus had taken a position on it. I knew that being unnecessarily outspoken on issues could cause problems for a leader, and oftentimes people were investing in consistency and stability more than the party labels. By being fair and honest with people and keeping my commitments, I was able to get support from traditional and nontraditional sources. With Pat, they weren't so sure what kind of leadership they were investing in.

Another problem we had to deal with was what to do about fundraising in 1994. I had announced that I would not hold a birthday party fund-raiser in 1994; I didn't feel it would be right since that money had always gone into the Riffe Election Committee and I wasn't running for reelection. If any more fund-raisers were to be held, it was up to those who would be around to carry on after me.

Sometime in the spring Pat Sweeney stepped up to the plate and decided to organize a tribute to me as a fund-raiser for the caucus. He was accepting a big responsibility, and all eyes would be on him.

It was set for August because you really don't want to go much later than that with a major fund-raiser when every candidate is scrambling for money. There was a lot of phone work and travel involved in lining up commitments, and Pat worked hard at it. When it was all said and done, the fund-raiser brought in about $300,000, not bad considering the uncertainty over the election and the change in caucus leadership.

Until this point, I had gone out of my way to avoid endorsing someone to succeed me as caucus leader. The members needed to make their own decision because they would have to live with it, not me. But as time went on I could see that the uncertainty was creating problems within the caucus and among supporters, who didn't know for sure who the next caucus leader would be. When people like Mike Shoemaker and Dave Hartley began to challenge Pat in the caucus, I decided I owed it to Pat to announce my support for him and let everybody know where I was coming from. In late August I told the Ohio Democratic Party at the convention in Cleveland that Pat was the person I would like to follow me as Speaker in 1995, and I closed ranks behind him for the most part.

We did everything we could to be competitive in terms of fund-raising. There was no way we were going to outspend the Republicans by anything near the nine to one we did in 1992 because I was in no position as a lame duck to dry up Republican money. But it wouldn't be lopsided in their favor either. I knew they couldn't do that until they were in the majority.

Our strategy was basically the same as it had always been—protect your incumbents, and go after their incumbents or open seats where you think you have a shot at winning. There was no money to waste and no margin for error. Let's say I wasn't as comfortable about our prospects as I was in 1992, but I truly believed we could win in 1994.

What I wasn't counting on was such a pitiful top of the ticket for Democrats. Rob Burch was going absolutely nowhere; the press wasn't paying much attention to him, and George Voinovich didn't have to pay much attention to him because he was riding high with the public and had fifteen to twenty times more money than Rob. To make matters worse, President Clinton's popularity was at a low, and Congress was wracked by scandal and gridlock. There was no question in my mind that all the bad feelings out there would hurt us.

In short, there was very little reason for Democratic voters to go to the polls. That would be bad because I knew that big turnouts favored Democrats and low turnouts favored Republicans. Republican voters are just more disciplined about voting.

This would affect other races significantly, including the U.S. Senate seat from which Howard Metzenbaum was retiring. Running to replace him was his son-in-law Joel Hyatt, who owned and operated a national chain of law offices called Hyatt Legal Services. He had never run for office before, but he had a good mentor in Howard and he began making the rounds among Democrats long before Howard announced his retirement. The other contender was Mary Boyle, one of my former House members—and a good one—from Cleveland who subsequently served on the Cuyahoga County Commission.

Normally I would have endorsed Mary, as she was a former member, but Howard called me and said it would mean a lot to him if I endorsed Joel. Even though Howard's political philosophy was considerably more liberal than mine, I've got to share this about him: Anytime I'd call him about a matter, he was there to help. He'd always been very good to me. There's a federal judge who would not be here today if Howard had not honored my request. I just thought I owed it to Howard. It was nothing against Mary or for Joel, it was for Howard.

As we neared election day, it looked less and less likely that we would beat any of the Republican incumbents in the Ohio House. We had worked hard in about four or five of those races, but our candidates and money were coming up short. My greater concern was losing our incumbents. We were fighting for our lives in races where we should have had the election well in hand.

In Huron County, for instance, Kate Walsh was running against William Taylor, a dentist by trade who was in his seventies and hardly campaigning at all. The Republicans ran the whole campaign by advertisements and direct mail. Kate had the advantage of incumbency and the opportunity to build a record, but she never worked the district year in and year out like I thought she should. The fact that she was liberal didn't help either because she opened herself up to attacks, such as being a free-spending liberal by cosponsoring a multibillion-dollar "universal" health-care bill that neither the taxpayers nor the legislature would ever support.

Judy Carr of Alliance, whom the caucus had appointed to replace her deceased husband Francis, was being hammered by a conservative who did nothing but attack. Her opponent, Ron Hood, had no political experience. As far as we could tell, the only job he had ever had was as an Amway salesman, and we couldn't even confirm that. Judy also had made the mistake of cosponsoring the universal healthcare bill and the Republicans jumped on it with a big TV buy. All this happened at a time when Clinton had just gotten destroyed in Congress for overreaching on health care. Representative Bobby Hagan was the genius who persuaded Judy and Kate to sign onto that bill.

Then there was Mike Stinziano, who had been in the House for more than twenty years and should have been a shoo-in but was in trouble. Mike's troubles began in 1992, when he angered the gay community by using a direct mail piece that stated his opponent, Jerry Neal, was gay. Neal was no threat to Mike. I told him it was a bad idea. But he went ahead with it anyway, had it mailed through the Franklin County Democratic Party, and ended up getting himself and the party in trouble. There was a very large gay community in Mike's district, and it never forgave him.

Then in 1994 the newspapers reported that Mike, among others, had accepted honorariums for making a presentation to some companies and organizations following dinner at Paul Tipps's house. Capitalizing on all the controversy surrounding Paul Jones and honorariums, the Republicans cut some negative TV ads against Mike, even making him into a cartoon character clutching wads of cash. They ran it heavily at the end of the campaign, and it hurt.

By the time election day arrived, I knew it was over. I didn't say so because we still had a job to do until the polls were closed and the votes were counted. When I arrived at headquarters on election night, I gathered the campaign staff into a small room, closed the door, and told them how much I appreciated their hard work. They never gave up, worked long hours away from their families, and did whatever they were asked to do. It's tough, physically and mentally, to go through a campaign. There are not many endeavors where you put your heart and soul into something and when it's all said and done, there's a clear winner and a clear loser.

There was still some time before we could begin checking the county boards of election for vote counts, so one of the staff asked, "What do you think we ought to do?"

"Say a prayer," I told them. And then I did.

When the results were in, the Republicans had a 53-46 majority and our twenty-two-year reign as the majority party in the Ohio House was over. The final results confirmed what I had feared: voter turnout killed us. Were it not for a horribly weak top of the ticket for Democrats—Burch got less than 30 percent—I remain convinced that the race for majority control of the House would have been much closer, and we very well may have won it.

There were six races in which the Democrats lost by an average of less than seven hundred votes. Among them were Kate Walsh, Judy Carr, and Paul Jones. There was some drama—at one point Kate Walsh and William Taylor were literally only a handful of votes apart with Kate trailing. It would be days before we knew that Kate had lost by only 12 votes out of more than 37,000 cast. Mike Stinziano lost by about 1,100 votes or 5 percent.

Wayne Jones had a closer race this time than he did against Tom Watkins in 1992, but he eked it out by 802 votes. On the whole, there wasn't much to celebrate that night. And while they didn't realize it fully, life wouldn't be the same for our incumbents who won re-election. No longer would they be able to see their bills move in the House; no longer would they be able to raise campaign funds—as individuals or as a caucus—like before; and no longer would they have committee chairmanships from which they could truly have a tremendous impact on legislation.

As for the U.S. Senate race, unfortunately for Howard it was not a good year to retire, because Joel Hyatt got crushed by former Congressman and Lt. Gov. Mike DeWine, who became the first Republican U.S. senator in Ohio since Howard Metzenbaum beat Robert Taft Jr. in 1976.

In December I convened the House to take care of some business, but largely to honor deceased past members and current members who would not be returning. It would be one of my final opportunities to address the House before the swearing in of new members in

January. I'd been through many difficult situations that put me to the test during my career, but that day nearly overwhelmed me. As I stood before my colleagues, it was all I could do to keep from getting choked up. I wanted to wish everyone good luck, my caucus and the Republicans alike. Most of all, I wanted to thank them for helping to make my career possible.

"No one in this state has had a better career than I have. I could not have achieved this without people. The people elected me eighteen times and my colleagues elected me ten times as Speaker. As I am fond of saying, I either did a pretty good job or I fooled a lot of people. One gentleman has suggested to me that it might be a little bit of both. Perhaps he is right.

"There is no one in this room—past, present, or new members— whom I would not help as long as they believe in this institution. When you spend half of your lifetime in government, you cannot forget the people who got you there.

"I have worked with Democratic governors, Republican governors, Republican leaders of the Senate, Democratic leaders of the Senate, Republican leaders of the House, and so on. It is called working with others. These are the things I will remember. These are the things that make democracy work."

A few minutes later, I adjourned the House and walked off the podium, soon to become "citizen Riffe." This was a day I always knew would come but tried not to think about. Now that it had arrived, it hardly seemed real.

✺ 7 ✺

The Governors

or years I had a couple of small signs on my desk, and anyone who came into my office couldn't help but notice them. The first, a replica of a plaque the great Harry Truman had, said, "The Buck Stops Here!" I sure enough believed in that. The second sign said, "Let's Compromise: We'll do it my way."

People got a real kick out of that second sign because more often than not, I got my way as a leader. The popular belief was that I forced my will on people most of the time to get what I wanted. I won't deny that I'd use my power when I had to; what good is it otherwise? But what many people never understood is that I was practical. I was a realist. I tried not to take unreasonable positions, and I worked with other leaders because that's the only way you get anything in our system of government.

During the time I was a leader, I worked with four very different governors and got along with each one of them. I can't imagine two people more different than Jack Gilligan and Jim Rhodes, one about as liberal as you get in Ohio and the other absolutely despised by liberals.

Dick Celeste and George Voinovich were just about as far apart. No matter, I found a way to work with all of them.

It didn't always come easily. In fact, sometimes those relationships got worse before they got better. But there's one thing I cannot take away from any of them: Jack Gilligan, Jim Rhodes, Dick Celeste, and George Voinovich were among the hardest working, committed individuals I've ever known. Whether I agreed with them or not, I couldn't help but respect that.

JOHN J. GILLIGAN

By the time I got into leadership as Speaker Pro Tem in 1973, there weren't many good politicians in Ohio who I didn't know when they reached the Statehouse. Jack Gilligan was one who crossed my path long before he became governor.

I first met Jack in the 1960s, when he served on Cincinnati City Council. I followed him in the newspapers too. He was a real leader on City Council—never shy about where he stood on an issue. You could see that he wasn't one to sit still. Being a liberal in a city full of conservatives had to be tough, but Jack took on all comers—including the county Democratic Party—and did well. He had political courage and principles. I admired that.

When he ran at large for Congress in 1962, I helped him in Scioto County. He was from a strong Democratic family, and he was working the state hard, doing the right things. He lost to a political unknown named Richard Kennedy—probably due to the popularity of the Kennedy name—who ended up being somewhat of a racist and an embarrassment to the party. Nevertheless, I felt then that Jack could go places.

I wasn't totally surprised when he beat U.S. senator Frank Lausche in the 1968 Democratic primary. Lausche underestimated both Jack and the power of organized labor, which despised the senator. Jack, by contrast, had an excellent labor voting record for the one term he served in Congress from the First Congressional District (1964–66).

Labor at the state and national levels targeted Lausche for defeat, and Jack was the guy they picked to do it.

Still, I didn't think Ohio was ready to elect anyone so liberal when he ran for governor in 1970. Jack probably also thought he'd have a tough time, since he had just lost that Senate race two years before. But timing is very important in politics, and his timing couldn't have been better.

Nobody was expecting a scandal, but when "Crofters" broke in 1970, it knocked the legs out from under the Republican ticket. Crofters put Jack Gilligan in the governor's office. Otherwise, I'd be talking about Governor Cloud. There's no telling how much that scandal changed Ohio political history. I wouldn't have become Speaker in 1975, if ever, because Democrats would not have taken over the Apportionment Board. If Roger Cloud had been elected governor, who knows if Jim Rhodes would have been elected governor another two terms, or whether George Voinovich would have ever become lieutenant governor and, later, governor.

To Jack's credit, he ran a great campaign, a modern campaign using TV, radio, direct mail, voter targeting, and the news media very effectively. His operation was hitting on all cylinders.

Roger was a different type of person entirely, more from the old school of politics. He was not the type to be holding news conferences or running a hard-hitting campaign. His campaign never really got into sync before the scandal, and after Crofters broke it only got worse.

I still think Roger Cloud would have been elected were it not for the scandal, because Roger was a middle-of-the-road Republican. His politics came closest to that of the average Ohioan.

Jim Rhodes strongly supported Roger. That was back in Jim Rhodes's heyday. Buzz Lukens and Paul Brown were in the primary, but Jim Rhodes came out for Roger and got him the nomination.

Nobody was happier than me on election night; Democrats now controlled the Apportionment Board and would redraw the legislative district lines for the 1972 election. Yet there was a part of me that felt bad for Roger. He was a dedicated public official, honest as the day is long. Roger wasn't out to make a big name for himself; he just wanted to go to the next level and do a good job. I always considered him a good friend. The governor's race was the first election he lost in thirty-six years of public life.

Jack Gilligan and I may not have been at the same place on the political spectrum, but we had a lot more in common than people realized. He, like I, understood the need for a strong state party, and I give him credit for working to build the party into an effective organization. Second, he wanted a Democratic House and Senate, and he used his position and his resources to help us win the House majority in the 1972 election and the Senate majority in 1974. And, third, I agreed with much if not most of what he fought for in the legislature, including the income tax.

The man had real foresight, always planning ahead while at the same time fighting battles. He had enough good sense, for instance, to give Joe Ferguson some big contributions late in the 1970 campaign in the hopes of winning the state auditor's office and controlling the Apportionment Board. "Jumping" Joe, as he was known, had been out of office for seven years and was seventy-eight years old. It was a huge comeback helped by Crofters, no doubt. Still, Jack's contribution to Joe's campaign made *a* difference if not *the* difference.

During the first two years of his term there was only so much I could do as a member of the minority, but I did whatever I could to help the administration. During the second two years, after we gained control of the House, I more or less ran the caucus for Speaker A. G. Lancione as Speaker Pro Tem and worked much more closely with the governor.

There's no question the governor and I were very different people. He had a privileged background; I grew up in a working-class family. He had graduate degrees; I never graduated from college. He was Catholic; I was Protestant. He learned politics in a big city, and I in a small town. None of that made a bit of difference to me.

I could see why some people found him difficult to get comfortable with. He's not the type of person you'd walk away from on the first meeting and say, "Boy, what a guy." You had to spend some time around Jack, and once you did you found that he was a person who stood for something. When he took a position, he stuck with it—no ifs, ands, or buts.

As the governor began his term in early 1971, we had just ended eight years under Jim Rhodes during which the state's share of primary and secondary education had decreased significantly. Local governments picked up the slack with increases in the property tax, but by the end of the Rhodes administration taxpayers in many school districts were fed up and voted down levies. As a result, there were a number of highly publicized school closings. That set the stage for Jack Gilligan to seek more taxes.

He made a strong case for why state government needed more money, particularly in areas such as education and mental health.

I had had some knowledge of mental institutions. Dad had a sister, Ruth, who was mentally handicapped and institutionalized in Kentucky. He and Uncle Ed used to visit her once a month, and sometimes I'd go along. I saw the conditions and the people. It's not something you forget—ever.

Later, as a legislator, I discovered that things weren't any better in Ohio. Once, as a member of the Public Improvements Inspection Committee, I had to excuse myself from a tour of the Apple Creek Hospital in Ashland because what I had seen made me sick to my stomach—the conditions, little children deformed and screaming. Oh my, it was just terrible! When I called home that night, I said to my wife, "Thelma, we ought to pray every day and thank the good Lord that we have four children who are all right." I never will forget it. After that, I wanted to do whatever I could do to improve that situation. We made some big improvements, and much of it began with the Gilligan administration.

There were so many needs in Ohio that weren't being met, but the revenue just wasn't there. Even though the governor campaigned on the issue, he never came right out and advocated a specific tax increase. Instead, once elected, he appointed the Citizens Task Force on Tax Reform, which was chaired by Jacob Davis, CEO of the Kroger Company. The task force, which included business and labor representation, recommended a personal income tax, property tax relief, homestead exemption, and a reduction in the tangible personal property tax. These were all things that I supported, and it was the basis for legislation that the governor introduced later.

As usual, the labor people were divided on the income tax. Some, including AFL-CIO President Frank King, thought business wasn't taxed enough. At the same time, a lot of Republicans and some Democrats in the legislature thought business would be taxed too much if incomes were included as a part of the corporate franchise tax. Even so, there were some powerful business groups falling behind the governor. The Ohio Council of Retail Merchants preferred the income tax to the sales tax. And the Ohio Farm Bureau saw the income tax as a way of holding down further increases in property taxes.

The responsibility for leading the effort among Democrats in the House fell to me, along with A. G. Lancione, our minority leader who was in poor health, and Barney Quilter, our Minority floor leader who was recuperating from back surgery. The income tax simply could not pass the House with Democratic votes alone. But a far tougher problem existed in the House Republican Caucus, which was split three ways. They were not only arguing over whether there should be an income tax at all but they were arguing over whether it should be a flat rate or a graduated rate. I preferred the flat rate, but labor would never go for that and the governor was against it as well.

Things were even worse in the Senate. Business and labor were fighting over it too, and the battle lasted most of the year. We had a number of interim budgets to keep state government running and four conference committees before the income tax was finally passed.

But Jack Gilligan deserves the credit, along with some Republicans like Chuck Kurfess, who wasn't afraid to stand up to pressure within his own party to do what he thought was right. I also remember that Stan Aronoff, nearly twenty years before he became Senate president, cast a crucial vote that broke a deadlock in the Senate to make the income tax possible. Enacting the income tax was a real test of character, and I'm proud to say that I stood with Jack Gilligan, Chuck Kurfess, and Stan Aronoff in supporting it.

That was a watershed year for Ohio. State government really began to change and grow after that. By the end of the Gilligan administration, the state had eight thousand more employees and the state budget was almost twice as big. Funding for primary and secondary education increased by nearly 60 percent, as did enrollment in vocational education. Staffing and conditions improved significantly at the state's mental institutions, and Ohio began to deal with its environmental problems.

Much of the labor-backed legislation became law. Significant increases in unemployment compensation were approved to the point where Ohio became a model for other states. Workers' compensation benefits improved tremendously as well, and we established a state minimum wage for the first time, which increased wages for half a million working people in Ohio. We had strong people carrying that legislation in the House, real veterans like Leonard Camera of Lorain County on workers' compensation and Vern Cook of Akron on unemployment compensation. They understood the issues. They understood labor and their contributions were recognized later when each had state facilities named in their honor.

When I think of Jack Gilligan, those are the things I remember. He was a good governor, and I was proud to be a part of what he accomplished. When conservatives looked at that agenda they saw "liberal" written all over it. That's why I've always laughed when people call me conservative, because I backed Jack Gilligan on most of his major programs. Even some of the governor's own people didn't think I'd work for his agenda because they didn't understand me.

Truth is, Jack Gilligan wanted me to be Speaker during his tenure. Had he been reelected, it would have happened for sure, but it almost came to pass during his first and only term.

In late 1973 President Nixon appointed Bill Saxbe to be his new U.S. attorney general after firing Elliot Richardson in the midst of the Watergate scandal. Bill Saxbe, one of our U.S. Senators, was stepping into a real mess, with the President carrying on the way he was. Back home, what it meant was that Gilligan would have to appoint a replacement.

The governor was in a bind because both Howard Metzenbaum and John Glenn desperately wanted to be in the Senate. Organized labor, inside and outside of Ohio, was putting heavy pressure on the governor to appoint Howard, but there was little doubt that John would run for the seat when it came up for election in 1974. As everyone knew, those two hadn't been too fond of each other since Howard beat John in the 1970 Democratic primary, only to lose to Robert Taft Jr. in the general election.

Early on, Jack wanted to appoint A. G. Lancione to fill Bill Saxbe's unexpired term so that I could be Speaker. During the income tax fight of 1971, I was the guy the administration worked with when it came to the House Democratic Caucus. After that, when Jack wanted something done, he came to me. He knew I was going to be honest and fair with him, and if I didn't agree with him, I would say so. It had become that kind of relationship. The governor told me privately that he was leaning toward A. G.; even his wife, Katie, said she thought that's who he would appoint.

I understand why Jack ended up appointing Howard; labor support would be critical to his reelection, and Howard already had shown that he could beat John in a primary. When A. G. didn't get the appointment, I know it hurt him a bit. It would have been a great honor for him, a tremendous way to end his career. The irony is that John Glenn went on to beat Howard in the 1974 Democratic primary and to win in November.

Another time Jack was prepared to appoint me to statewide office, probably because he respected me and thought I could hold it for the Democrats come election time.

In June 1973 Joe Ferguson became very ill with diabetes while still serving as state auditor. He was so sick that they called in a priest to give him the last rites. I was staying at the Sheraton Hotel at the time, and one morning about 8:30 I got a call from the governor's secretary. Well, I had been out late with the guys the night before, living it up, you might say. I didn't feel so hot and was still in bed when I answered the phone.

"The governor would like to see you as soon as possible. It's very, very important. Urgent," his secretary said.

That got me going. I jumped into the shower, half shaved, and got myself over there and, by gosh, he was waiting for me.

"Vern, you know how ill Joe Ferguson is. I've kept in close touch with his people, and there's a chance he might not make it. If that happens, I'll have to appoint someone to replace him. Vern, how would you like to be state auditor?" he asked.

It was not often that I got blindsided on a political matter, but that one came like a bolt out of the blue. It never crossed my mind that that's why the governor wanted to see me. I wasn't real comfortable talking about it because Joe was alive, but a governor needs to think about things like that because if a vacancy does occur, he has to fill it. Once I got my bearings, we discussed the pros and cons of it.

"I'd have to run in a couple of years and, you know, the name 'Riffe' isn't too well-known, particularly in the northern part of Ohio. I just don't know about it," I said.

"We'll make your name known. We'd start right away. Plus, you'll be signing every state check that's sent out. Your name will be going out all the time," the governor said. "I sure wish you'd consider it. I'd like you to be on the ticket with me."

I considered it because the governor asked me to, but I wasn't coming up with a lot of reasons to accept the position if it was ever offered. Now that we were in the majority in the House, I figured there was a good chance I could be Speaker someday. I knew that was something I could do and would enjoy. I wasn't so sure about state auditor.

It was a moot issue anyway because Joe, who was eighty-one at the time, recovered and served out his term. Tom, his son who was a deputy in the state auditor's office, ran the next election and served through 1995. I appreciated the governor considering me, but looking back I'd say my place was definitely in the House.

We broke a lot of new ground during those years, and I was in the forefront of much of it. Never in my wildest imagination would I have thought anyone would call me "Mr. Arts" someday, but the seed was planted during the Gilligan years.

One day while I was Speaker Pro Tem, the governor was telling me how Ohio was one of the biggest states in the nation and yet we spent practically nothing on the arts compared to other states. He asked me to put some money in the budget for the arts. I didn't have much of a background in the arts, but what he said made sense to me. The more I thought about it, the more I could see that it was bigger than just the arts; it was also a matter of economic development. When I was growing up back home we had nothing in the way of arts, but today we have people from at least three states coming to Portsmouth to see performing artists like the Julliard String Quartet at the Vern

Riffe Theater for the Arts at Shawnee State University. I saw the connection back then. Jack Gilligan was absolutely right.

I put $500,000 in for each of the two years of the budget. That was the very first significant appropriation for the arts in Ohio. Since then, we have given many millions of dollars to the arts, helped build numerous performance facilities, and established something tremendous for the people of Ohio. Along the way I've been a two-time recipient of the Governor's Award for the Arts and had two performing arts centers named after me. I earned the recognition through my efforts as a legislative leader, but it began with Jack.

It was also during the Gilligan administration that Ohio passed the Equal Rights Amendment, and I presided the day it passed the House. I may have grown up in a time and place where a woman's place was in the home, but I didn't waver one bit in supporting the ERA, which undoubtedly surprised some people. The ERA was a part of the national Democratic platform and the state Democratic platform. I was for it, no question. Not only was it a matter of policy, but it was the right thing to do.

What people don't understand is that my mother had a job during most of her adult life, long before that became the norm for women. I also recognized early in my leadership that women made not only good candidates but good legislators too, and I personally recruited many women to run for House seats who today are leaders in their own right.

The ERA debate was hot—real hot. My job was to get it passed and keep things from getting out of hand. When Joe Tully of Lake County asked to be recognized for an amendment, I saw it as an opportunity to establish my leadership or risk letting things run wild, which I was not about to tolerate. I ruled him out of order before he knew what hit him, and I gave some cock-and-bull story as to why. I didn't even know what I was talking about. The ERA passed by one vote, and the Republicans found out early that I wouldn't hesitate to rule them out of order.

People don't remember that. What they remember is the time in 1974 when, as Speaker Pro Tem and chair of the Personnel Committee, I required women on the House staff to wear dresses or skirts instead of pants. Eventually I relented, but I make no apologies. Whether people choose to believe it or not, it was a matter of professionalism to me.

There weren't too many issues after 1972 that passed when both the governor and I opposed them, but the lottery was one that did pass. While we were both against the lottery, we opposed it for different reasons. I don't mean that Jack Gilligan was fighting it the way George Voinovich fought casino gambling in 1996 as governor, actually putting together a statewide campaign against it. He just didn't think it would generate enough money to be worth the effort. However, where I come from and in other rural areas of the state, people wanted no part of it. Once the legislature put it on the ballot for a statewide vote, it was the big metropolitan counties that passed it.

There's no doubt in my mind, though, that the lottery has benefited education. The lottery has helped a lot of small businesses by bringing people into stores for tickets. When the lottery issue was before the legislature the first time in 1973, we didn't know how or where the tickets would be sold; that would be determined later through separate implementing legislation. But based on what I know today, there's no doubt in my mind that it has been good for the state and good for education. I told the higher education people that they ought to look at getting in on it, but they didn't pursue it.

Another area where we broke new ground was in ethics and campaign finance legislation. Before the Gilligan administration, officeholders had to report very little about their campaign finances and even less about their personal finances. When it was all said and done, we had to report all contributions and all sources of income. It was a tremendous change from the past. I remember when nobody wrote checks; it was all cash because you didn't get contributions in big amounts like five or ten thousand dollars.

I'd say a majority of legislators didn't care for those bills much, but I had no problem reporting my sources of income or the contributions I received.

These changes were inevitable because we had had the Crofters scandal in Ohio; the post-Watergate period reformers in the Democratic Party, like Jack Gilligan, were reacting to a national concern. Newspapers were calling for something to be done.

Typically Rep. Pat Sweeney of Cleveland coauthored and supported Jack's ethics bill but voted against many, if not most, of the ethics bills that came up in succeeding years. Pat was always one to shoot from the hip—liberal, conservative, you never knew where he might come out on an issue. (You still don't know today.) He was always there when you needed him to support the caucus, so I let him do what he wanted the other times.

Jack also served during a time when the Vietnam War was winding down. Ohio had gone through the worst of it in 1970, when the four students at Kent State University were killed by the Ohio National Guard and protests or riots were disrupting other universities. Those were some real tough days for the legislature, but in truth, there was little the legislature did or could do with respect to the Vietnam War. I sponsored a resolution to create a joint legislative committee to study campus disturbances.

"Something has to be done. We can't patrol every campus. We need to know the cause of the trouble and then act to get rid of it," I said at the time. "If university officials and teachers are not doing their jobs, then they ought to be fired. If the students are breaking the rules, then they ought to be expelled."

We held hearings at different universities around the state. Kent State was still on everyone's mind, and nobody wanted a tragedy like that again. One might think that we would feel threatened as representatives of the state going into these places. Quite the contrary. I remember after one hearing an attractive young woman, a student at one of the universities, approached a colleague and me.

"Hey, you guys want to smoke some marijuana with me?" she asked.

Whether she was sincere or somebody put her up to it, I don't know, but we declined and went on our way. The only illegal substance that ever passed my lips was distilled in the hills of southern Ohio, and I stopped doing that when I was a young man.

As for the war, Jack Gilligan made it clear before he was elected governor that he opposed U.S. involvement in Vietnam. It was felt at the time that his position hurt him in the 1968 U.S. Senate race against Bill Saxbe. Personally, I believe the war was one of the worst things to ever happen to our country. Still, once our government made the decision to get involved, I felt it was our obligation to be loyal. I will fault the government for not going in there to win from the start. We approached the Vietnam War in a piecemeal fashion, which is no way to win.

I appreciated the help our government gave me upon returning form World War II, and I wanted to do something like that for Ohio's Vietnam veterans. I therefore sponsored a proposed Vietnam Veterans Bonus constitutional amendment. Like the "52-20" money I received after World War II, the amendment called for a payment to returning veterans of up to twenty dollars per month of service in Vietnam, with a maximum of five hundred dollars. However, if the serviceman or woman died in action or was missing in action, the survivors would be entitled to one thousand dollars per month. Likewise, prisoners of war received a thousand dollars. Veterans could elect to take education assistance in lieu of a cash bonus in an amount twice that of the bonus. The amendment was approved by voters in the November 1973 election, and I am extremely proud to have had the opportunity to do something to recognize our young people who served.

For all his strengths, Jack Gilligan made some critical political errors, the kind that helped his opponent beat him in his reelection bid in 1974. My dad always said, "You can make mistakes in politics, but you can't make too many mistakes." Jack made one, maybe two, too many mistakes. But true to his character, he didn't make excuses or pass the blame even if he should have. I always thought that his biggest problems were a result of bad advice from some of the people around him.

The first critical mistake occurred in 1971 during the fight to enact a state income tax. Operating under interim budgets was taking its toll on the services of state government. Spending was exceeding revenues, the governor had to do something, and he did—a 10 percent across-the-board cut with few exceptions. Thousands of people were laid off. There was a good deal of pain all around.

He did what he had to do, which I respected, but there was a part of it that made no sense at all. The governor was led to believe by his people that if he closed all the state parks it would bring the Senate to its knees to pass the income tax bill. This was in September, mind you, the last big summer month for the parks. What I saw was a political disaster in the making. Myrl Shoemaker, A. G. Lancione, and I went to the governor and pleaded with him not to do it. It would anger the public and give his political enemies some heavy ammunition. But like I said, Jack Gilligan is as hard-nosed as anybody I've ever known. He wanted that income tax more than anything else, and his staff and advisers convinced him that closing the parks would pressure the Senate into action.

Shortly after that, the governor was scheduled to attend a retirement dinner for my dad in Scioto County. He was the main speaker and planned to bring half his cabinet there. But trouble was brewing down home. People were circulating a petition to give to the governor, and there were plans to picket the American Legion hall where the dinner was to be held. I got wind of it and started working the telephone.

"Now wait just one minute," I told them. "My dad had nothing to do with the closing of the parks. This event is for my dad."

"Well, we don't want any part of that redheaded SOB," one of them said. I saw that I had to get down there quick to keep things from getting out of hand. I met with a group of angry people at the Ramada Inn in Portsmouth.

"You can take it out on the governor if you want to, but this is Mayor Riffe's night," I said. "I'm telling you, cut this stuff out."

I finally managed to get through to them, and there was no protest that night. We had a big crowd, so big we had to set up loudspeakers outside. Dad had been the longest-serving mayor in the state of Ohio, and people respected that and were paying tribute to him.

But, oh, did Jim Rhodes use the park closings against the governor three years later. I don't remember the words, but I can still see those empty swings blowing in the wind in one of Jim Rhodes's campaign commercials in 1974. It was devastating.

Another key issue that hurt him badly, in my view, involved the state budget. As we approached the end of the fiscal year (June 30) in 1974, the Legislature Budget Office (LBO) predicted that there would be a significant surplus, upwards of $60 million. The governor, however, said there was no surplus, none. He was basing his statement on what his advisers were telling him.

We went back and reported to our caucus that there was no surplus, that the LBO figures weren't right. We figured the executive branch had more resources at its disposal in overseeing the budget, so their information must be correct.

The following day Myrl Shoemaker called me behind the rail in the House chamber during session. I could see from his face that he was upset about something.

"Vern, I don't want too many people to know this, but I got to double-checking on the budget, and I was told this morning that there is a surplus in the budget, and it's big—as much as $80 million," he said. "I know what you and A. G. said in caucus yesterday. I don't know where you got your information."

"I got it from the governor," I said.

"Well, why don't we keep this to ourselves until I can get this straightened out," he said.

The next day Myrl came to me with all the facts and figures. "Either they lied to you, Vern, or they don't know what they're talking about," Myrl said.

"I'll tell you one thing, they're not going to get away with it," I said. I went straight to A. G., and he was stomping and fuming about it. With A. G. and Myrl present, I got the governor on the telephone and laid it on the line.

"If we do have a surplus, and I believe we do, then we've got a serious problem here. We've got education people and other interests in this state tearing at us for that money if there is a surplus," I said. "I'm not saying you're not telling the truth. I'm just telling you what is happening."

Right away he called a meeting in his cabinet room, and he had his budget director, Jay Tepper, and other top staff there. Both the Democratic leadership in the House and Senate were there too. It didn't take long to establish that the LBO information was right, and the governor's people were wrong. It was mismanagement, pure and simple. To this day, it's hard for me to believe that they could make a mistake like that. I've always been suspicious of it. No doubt there were some people in the administration who would have liked to have carried over a surplus into the next term, assuming the governor would be reelected.

He adjourned the meeting, but before everybody left I asked the governor a question: "How could this happen to you as governor?"

"I don't know, Vern," he said.

"Well, if I had somebody on my staff put me in a position like that, they wouldn't be around for fifteen minutes. I'd fire them," I said.

Jack didn't say a word. I looked around, and Jay Tepper's face and the staff's faces were red. I had made my point and left.

Sometime in July the governor invited me to dinner at the Clarmont to pay off a bet. I can't remember what; we were always betting over something. I met him at his office for a couple of drinks there first. He always kept a bottle of Scotch for himself and a bottle of Canadian Club for me. Then we headed to the Clarmont, where he started ordering martinis. We talked about a lot of things, but the surplus episode was still on his mind.

"How strongly did you feel about what you said in that meeting, about firing whoever was responsible?" he asked.

"I felt very strongly about it. If you don't do something, it's going to come back to haunt you in the campaign. They're going to use it against you. If you don't do something with those people, you've got no excuse. They can accuse you of mismanagement," I said.

He said he was concerned about firing staff because they had families.

"Let me tell you what I'm going to do. I'm not going to fire them so that they won't have any jobs, but I'll find something else for them to do and let people know what was done—that you can't have mistakes like that and give out wrong information," the governor said.

"Well, governor, that could help," I said, thinking he would take care of things, but he never did. A long time later, when it was too late, he said he just got too busy with the campaign and never followed through.

Jim Rhodes broadcasted a masterful television ad, using a shell game as the theme. Somebody was moving the shells around, and the question was being asked, where was the $80 million? That and the parks ad probably turned the tide for Jim Rhodes.

There were plenty of people griping about "that redhead" in Scioto County. My dad could see that the governor was in trouble as far back as the spring, when a little-known Democrat named James Nolan made a better than expected showing in the primary by getting about 30 percent of the vote. This was the same James Nolan who was the lead plaintiff in the Ohio lawsuit that found the state in violation of the U.S. Supreme Court's "one man, one vote" ruling.

Even so, there wasn't a time during the entire 1974 campaign that the Gilligan people didn't think they would win. They should have won. Again, some of the people close to him were giving him bad advice.

About two or three weeks before the general election, I was leaving the Statehouse when Bill Chavanne of the governor's staff saw me and invited me in for a drink with the governor and some of his staff. When I walked in his office, there was the governor with Jack Hansen, his chief of staff at the time, and two or three others just shooting the bull.

"You know, Vern, the governor is going to be the strongest, most powerful elected official at the Democratic National Convention in 1976," said Hansen, pretty full of himself. Right away, I'm getting irritated because Jack Gilligan was not running unopposed—nor was he scared, but he should have been.

"No kidding. You feel that way?" I said.

"I'm telling you, he's going to be a strong candidate," Hansen replied.

I looked over at the governor, and said, "Governor, if you believe that, you'd believe about anything. I don't know what in the heck he's smoking in that pipe, but it can't be tobacco. This election isn't wrapped up."

The governor was taking in every word.

"If the governor is reelected by fifty thousand votes, I'll be satisfied. I'll be the happiest man in this room tonight," I said, looking at Hansen, who was predicting the governor would win by a quarter million votes. "I've been traveling this state for my members while you've been in this office. People are mad over the income tax, they're mad over closing the parks, they're just mad."

When I walked out, the governor followed me.

"Governor, don't let them snow you. This thing's going to be close," I said.

The following weekend he was down in Scioto County, and Dad and I took him around.

"Vern, I've been thinking about what you said."

"Governor, what do the polls show?" I asked.

"They show I'm going to win," he said.

"I hope that's true, but I've had many a Democrat tell me they're not going to vote for you. They're mad." I told him.

That White House talk was another thing that didn't help Jack Gilligan. Nothing good can come out of that kind of talk when you're running for reelection. It even caused some problems for me when Father Colby Grimes was standing in for his brother, Father Kenneth Grimes, as House chaplain one time.

Colby was giving the prayer to open session one day, and out of the blue he asks for divine intervention to put Jack Gilligan in the White House! Needless to say, the Republicans got their backs up about it. While Colby didn't mean any harm, Chuck was getting pressure from his caucus to do something about it, so he came to see me. The Republican Caucus was threatening not to go back to the floor the next day if Colby was giving the opening prayer again. I told Chuck I thought that would be a mistake, since neither I nor he, when he was Speaker, could control what a chaplain said. If they wanted to walk, it didn't matter to me.

That evening Father Colby called and asked to meet with me the next morning. We did, and he said he didn't want to open session anymore because of the commotion he had caused.

"Father, you're coming back. If they think for one minute that they are going to threaten us and get away with it, they've got another thing coming. If you don't show, I'm going to be really disappointed," I said.

"If that's what you say, then I'll be there," said Colby. He delivered a fine prayer, and in it he apologized for what he had said.

Father Kenneth Grimes was with me on election night, and we could have used some divine intervention then. We were watching the election results on television when the governor's office called asking me to come to the Neil House. The governor was getting ready to address the crowd, and I said I would join him. But before we did, I met privately with Jack in his room.

"This thing doesn't look good for me," he said.

"What are you talking about? Governor Rhodes just conceded about a half hour ago," I said. What I didn't know is that one of the networks had just projected Jim Rhodes as the winner. Jack wasn't doing nearly as well as he should have been in Cuyahoga County. The rule of thumb had always been that a Democratic candidate for governor must carry Cuyahoga by at least 100,000 votes to win; Jack took it by 55,000.

Naturally, the governor didn't go downstairs to the ballroom and say he might lose it. Jim Rhodes had already gone to bed thinking he was the loser. It wasn't until the wee hours of the morning that someone woke up Rhodes and told him he was governor again.

Jack took it hard. It just broke him. I never will forget it. After the election, when I was chosen Speaker, the governor congratulated me.

"If there's one thing I would have liked to have done, it would be to serve as governor while you were Speaker," Jack said.

He got beat by ten thousand votes, less than one vote per precinct statewide. That would be devastating to anybody.

Jack accomplished a lot for the state of Ohio, and I was proud to be a part of it. What we did for education, mental health, the environment, and so many other areas were very important because many times in the past these issues had been ignored. I think we would have worked well together as Speaker and governor. As it turned out, his public service career was ending just as mine was starting to take off.

JAMES A. RHODES

In the grand scheme of things, the so-called "Six-Day War" didn't amount to a hill of beans. Symbolically, however, it served notice that the General Assembly was not going to be a rubber stamp for Jim Rhodes's third term the way it was the first two.

As 1975 began, I was the new Speaker, and the legislature was sworn in about a week before Governor Rhodes. During the last week that Jack Gilligan was governor, the House and Senate passed six bills, things we knew Rhodes wouldn't sign. One involved congressional redistricting, and three others would have transferred certain powers, including income tax collections and appointments to boards of elections, from Republican-controlled offices to Democratic-controlled offices. The final two bills would have expanded unemployment compensation and made voter registration easier.

Normally those bills would have been signed by the lieutenant governor who, under the state constitution, was the presiding officer in the Senate. The lieutenant governor at the time was John Brown, a Republican, and everyone figured he would just pocket the bills until Governor Rhodes could veto them. To get around the problem, the Senate adopted rules authorizing either the lieutenant governor or the Senate president pro tem to sign bills.

A meeting was called in Oliver Ocasek's office about ten o'clock on Saturday morning the weekend before Rhodes was to take office. I took Art Wilkowski and Harry Lehman of Cleveland, who was the chairman of the House Judiciary Committee, over to Ocasek's office. Oliver was Senate president pro tem, and with him were Attorney General Bill Brown and Sen. Dave Headley of Akron.

Bill Brown and his people were telling Oliver that neither he nor the lieutenant governor had to sign the bills. My people argued that they did. Bill Brown was right there when I looked Oliver in the eyes and said, "I disagree with the attorney general, and I disagree with Dave. You've got to have a name on those bills." Harry and Art insisted a signature was necessary from both sides to verify proper procedures were followed in each chamber.

Meanwhile the Republicans got a court injunction stating Oliver could not sign the bills as long as the lieutenant governor was at the Statehouse to do it. John Brown just planted himself in his office and wouldn't budge, so nobody could say he was unavailable and unable to sign the bill. Once the bills were ready to be signed, he camped out in his office until Rhodes took the oath.

I put my name on them Saturday morning and sent the bills over to Oliver's office, but he wouldn't sign them. There was nothing left to do but take them to Governor Gilligan late on Saturday night, and he signed them.

When it got to the Franklin County Common Pleas Court about

my second or third week as Speaker, they called me in to testify. The first question I was asked was why I signed the bills. I said that under the state constitution the presiding officer of the House and Senate signed all bills to verify that proper procedures were followed. The judge agreed, ruled the bills unconstitutional, and they were thrown out. Both Oliver and Bill Brown were wrong on that one, and if Oliver had signed those bills they would have become law. I always had good leadership people advising me. This case was no exception.

I had mixed emotions about trying to force those bills through, but Democrats had just taken over the Senate, our Democratic governor was leaving office, and I was the new Speaker. I had to make a decision, and I made it. If there is one thing a strong leader does, it's make tough decisions—one way or the other.

No sooner did the "Six-Day War" end than we were fighting over the budget. That was the only time I can remember when we were dealing with three separate budget proposals instead of one.

Jack submitted one, even though he was going out of office. His administration didn't go quietly. No doubt about it, they were bitter. Rhodes, of course, submitted his budget as the new governor. I could see a fight brewing, so rather than be caught in the middle, I decided the House would draft a budget proposal of its own.

Even in the best of times, there's a lot of fighting over the budget. I've always said that when the governor's budget passes the House, the governor won't recognize it; and when it comes out of the Conference Committee, nobody recognizes it because of all the changes. That's compromise. But in 1975 Jim Rhodes wasn't in a compromising mood, and he issued more than seventy line-item vetoes.

I don't remember a more wild beginning to an administration than that one, but it would be wrong to say I did not get along with Jim Rhodes during my first term as Speaker. When it came to his economic development program in 1975, I supported the governor completely, even if the Senate did not.

Jim Rhodes always said the only way you bring the economy back naturally is by putting people to work. Maybe I got it from him, maybe from my dad, but I believed the same thing: If you put money into construction it helps the economy. People are working and spending.

By 1975 the economy was in bad shape and something needed to be done. Manufacturing plants were closing throughout Ohio and unemployment was the highest it had been in modern times.

Jim Rhodes picked up where he left off by proposing his "Blueprint for Ohio" plan. He asked for $4 billion in capital improvements, tax incentives for business, and a state housing finance authority to help working people buy houses.

It would have been easy for me to oppose them. Both organized labor and the Ohio Democratic Party were against the package, and Senate Majority Leader Oliver Ocasek was against two of them. If I had opposed the bond package as well, nobody would have thought anything of it except Jim Rhodes.

Sometimes people just don't understand me, as if every decision I made was based on politics. I was never one to fear any issue if I thought I was doing the right thing. Unemployment was high and construction in my district was practically nil. To me, it was crystal clear which way to go, so I met with labor people at the Neil House about the governor's bond issues.

"This is the right thing to do. This should be on the ballot for the people to decide. I'll tell you what is at stake: if these issues pass, you'll have more construction and that means more jobs. You can say anything you want, you can do anything you want, but you're not going to change my mind," I said.

"Do you think you're doing the right thing politically?" one of them asked.

"If it's right for the people, then I think I'm doing the right thing politically. Time will tell," I said.

Labor didn't come right out and denounce me, but they didn't like it much. They thought I was going to bed with the governor, so to speak, but fact is they just couldn't get past the 1974 election and Jack Gilligan's defeat. Jack was a real friend of labor in this state, and they weren't ready to give Jim Rhodes a darn thing.

That's not how I felt though, and the House passed all four bills and sent them to the Senate. Oliver would have done just about anything labor asked him to. He agreed to put the housing and transportation issues on the ballot, but labor was dead set against the other two. I called the governor about 9 P.M. one night and told him the best he would be able to get was two out of four.

"Vern, if I can't get all four on the ballot, I don't want it. Two won't work," he said.

That killed it insofar as the legislature went, but the governor gathered up the signatures to put all four on the ballot anyway. Before the election, Oliver came to my office to talk about the bond issues.

"Do you trust Jim Rhodes?" he asked.

"Yes, I trust him," I said

"Well, I don't," said Oliver

Later on, Oliver and Governor Rhodes became good friends, but that pretty much summed up the relationship between them that session.

Come election time, the bond issues went down in flames by a big margin. I do not believe that is any reflection on Jim Rhodes or the merit of the issues. I chalk it up to labor's opposition—the fact that the legislature did not put them on the ballot and that there was some improvement in unemployment as the election neared. Labor was more powerful then than it is today. They had more members. Were it not for labor's opposition, I think all four would have passed. Eventually much of what Governor Rhodes wanted came to pass anyway.

Confrontation continued in 1976 when Rhodes gave the General Assembly a tongue-lashing during his belated State of the State Address. I remember June 10, 1976, as if it were yesterday. I sat at the podium in the House chamber with Lt. Gov. Dick Celeste while the governor delivered a scathing attack on the legislature. He accused us of deliberately underfunding Medicaid. But I always felt he was getting a lot more off his chest. It was his second year back after sitting out the Gilligan term, the House and Senate were both controlled by Democrats, and things just weren't going his way. He was angry and frustrated.

"During the past several years, state spending has increased at a much faster rate than revenue growth. If this trend is to continue, we will face a deficit of at least $700 million in the next biennium," he said. "The majority leadership of the General Assembly has succumbed to the weakness of too many legislative bodies of increasing programs for constituents, but failing to make the more difficult decision of how to pay for them."

At one point he looked straight at me and Dick and said, "You've done nothing, nothing in the way of providing jobs and employment."

Then he pointed out to the members of the joint assembly and said, "Don't go back to your districts and say you've done everything you can. You've done nothing!"

Of course I wasn't happy about it, but I wasn't mad at him either. I guess the best word to describe my feelings at the time is "disappointment." Jim Rhodes became used to having a Republican legislature to rubber-stamp his proposals during his first eight years as governor. The first time he was elected governor, he carried 85 of 88 counties. The second time, he carried all but one county. He had about as much control as a governor could have. Now, the tables were turned; he had won a very narrow victory over Jack Gilligan, voters had rejected his four bond issue proposals the previous November, and he was smarting. I didn't appreciate it that he was pointing a finger at me, since I had supported many of his proposals, the bond issues included. I'd never experienced anything like that before or since.

When some weeks later he asked for another opportunity to address a joint session, Oliver Ocasek and I declined. I'd be darned if I was going to give him the chance to take another shot at me in the House chamber. He ended up giving his speech in the Statehouse Rotunda, but at least I didn't have to listen to it.

Jim Rhodes worked like the dickens to elect Republicans to the legislature in 1976. Early in the year, he had tried to put together an effort to redraw the legislative district lines that elected Democratic majorities in the House and Senate but dropped it after the filing deadline already had passed.

When the election results were in, Democrats picked up three seats in the House and the majority stayed the same in the Senate, 21-12. That's when I believe he realized that what he was trying to do wasn't working, that if he was going to get anything done, he had to work with us to iron things out.

A turning point in his relationship with the legislature came with the winter of 1977 and the resulting energy crisis. We still had our differences, but some of the hard feelings that had built up over the previous year were set aside to deal with the severe weather.

In reality, there wasn't a whole lot that anyone could do, even the governor. He mobilized the National Guard, shut down some state facilities, ordered thermostats to be turned down, pestered the federal government for help, and went after utilities, including Columbia Gas Company. He was a whirlwind, but he couldn't create energy where there wasn't any.

He even helped with a prayer service in the Statehouse Rotunda. One of my members, Phale Hale of Columbus, was a minister and he worded the prayer. We were praying for all Ohioans to get through this hardship. It was during this time that Oliver and the governor got back on track with each other like we hoped they would.

Those fights didn't mean much compared to the legacy that Jim Rhodes left and of which I was proud to be a part. When I think of him, I always will think of jobs and education, because those two things were more important to him and me than anything else.

One thing about Jim Rhodes is that when it came to "jobs and progress," he never quit. Our philosophies of economic development were very similar: Stimulate the state economy through necessary state construction, and make Ohio a good place to do business—but not at the expense of working people. That's it in a nutshell. I supported whatever it took to attract business so long as working people were not penalized. For business, that meant things like providing incentives, lessening the tax load, and fixing tort laws and workers' compensation. The way I saw it, businesses provide the jobs, so it was in the best interests of workers that Ohio have a favorable business climate.

The flip side was that businesses can't prosper without a productive workforce, and it was in this area that I more often parted company with Jim Rhodes. Many times I supported labor against the wishes of business when I thought it was in everyone's best interest to do so. Examples that come to mind are improvements we made in unemployment compensation, establishment of a state minimum wage, expansion of workers' compensation benefits, and support of a prevailing wage in the construction industry.

Overall, however, in my experience nobody did it better than Jim Rhodes when it came to job creation. He was an absolute master. I learned a lot from him.

I was with him in 1977 at a Columbus-area hotel when he brought in a big delegation of Japanese executives from Honda. Honda was looking to locate a motorcycle production plant in the United States, and the governor really wanted it in Ohio. The governor got some criticism, comments like, "Why is he fooling around with the Japanese," and so forth. But with Rhodes it was always "jobs, jobs, jobs" or "jobs and progress, jobs and progress." He was like a broken record, relentless, but he made things happen. Jim Rhodes didn't care because he knew that if Ohio could get this plant, we would have the inside track on getting an automobile production plant as well.

He had a lot of believers in the Ohio General Assembly, me included. We backed the administration in approving property tax abatements for up to fifteen years; $2.5 million in state funds for water, sewer, and rail improvements; and an $860,000 loan to Marysville to enlarge a sewer line that was to be connected to a state-financed line and pump station.

As a result of Honda locating in Ohio, thousands of construction jobs and some twelve thousand production and administrative jobs were created, and scores of other businesses have sprung up around Marysville. Much of what the man advocated came to pass in economic development.

Then there was the time Oliver Ocasek and I went to Detroit with Governor Rhodes in late 1977 to meet with Henry Ford II. Batavia in Clermont County was under consideration as a site for a new Ford auto transmission plant. The purpose of the Detroit meeting was to demonstrate to Henry Ford that the legislature would provide whatever was necessary in order for Ford to locate in Ohio, and the governor had it all figured out.

When we were ushered into the conference room, Governor Rhodes said, "Vern, I want you to sit at the end of the table."

"Wait a minute, Governor. That's where Henry Ford is going to sit," I said, assuming he would be at the head of the table.

"No sir, he's going to sit right there next to you. He never sits at the head of the table," the governor said. "He always sits to the right."

Sure enough, Henry Ford came in, sat to my right, chatted for a moment just like he had known us for years, and then proceeded to tell us what he thought was needed in terms of incentives to make the decision on the plant. Basically, what he wanted was a real-estate tax abatement, a break on corporate franchise taxes, and the development of the Batavia property on which they wanted to build.

I believe he already had made up his mind based on whether the necessary legislation passed. The governor looked at me and said, "Vern, can you take care of that?"

"Absolutely, Governor. I'll take care of it."

Then he looked at Oliver and said, "Do you have any problem with that?"

"No. I think we can handle it all right."

I sent that bill over to the Senate within days of our return. The Senate passed it and the governor quickly signed it into law. On December 14, 1977, Ford announced that the $500 million transmission plant and its projected 3,500 jobs would go to Batavia.

Another time we went to Detroit together to talk to the Jeep people about what we could do to help them expand production in Toledo, which would create an additional two thousand jobs for the area and help ensure that they'd stay in Ohio. I knew what I was going to do on the way up there—whatever had to be done. Same with Oliver, as well as with Speaker Pro Tem Barney Quilter and Sen. Marigene Valiquette, both of whom were from Toledo and had accompanied us.

Rhodes was successful in two ways. First, Jeep committed to the expansion after the state agreed to provide low-interest loans to the company. (Thank goodness we did because Jeep sales have soared and the plant is booming.) Second, the governor was getting great headlines less than a month before the 1978 general election. It couldn't have hurt him because Jim Rhodes won that election over Dick Celeste by less than fifty thousand votes.

The cases of Honda, Ford, and Jeep illustrate the very critical role of the legislature—that of working with the governor to quickly and effectively seize economic development opportunities. I had my differences over the years with Governor Rhodes, and Lord knows Oliver did too. But one of the responsibilities of a governor is to put together economic development strategies and use the position of chief executive to deal directly with business and industry. Nobody did it better than Rhodes in my experience.

I think his leadership in economic development is exceeded only by his leadership in education, particularly higher education. When I was first elected Ohio had a handful of universities, community colleges, and technical institutes; today there is an institution of higher learning within easy commuting distance of every citizen. When I began there was no system of vocational education in our public schools. Today Ohio is a model for the country. It is Jim Rhodes's vision that is responsible for much of that progress, of course with the cooperation of the legislature.

In spite of this he was criticized by people who thought he didn't do enough for education. Their criticism was based largely on the decreasing state share of funding for primary and secondary education, which dropped from 40 percent at the start of his administration to 29 percent at the end of his second term in 1970. There were also school closings under his watch.

I always thought the criticism of Governor Rhodes was unfair. Schools were getting more money from the state during his first two terms; it's just that the state percentage of total school funding was going down while the local contribution was going up. He was trying to do more with less before George Voinovich ever used the term, and that wasn't an easy thing to do.

Yes, Ohio had its share of school-funding problems during Jim Rhodes's second two terms, but state and local governments all over the country were in financial crisis during that time. This is not a defense of Jim Rhodes, just a statement of the facts.

Even though we enacted the income tax during the Gilligan administration to help fill the void created by fewer successful local levies, people still were angry about property taxes. For many years, industrial and commercial property had been assessed at a higher rate than residential and agricultural property. Litigation in the early 1970s changed that. The Ohio Supreme Court issued rulings forcing Ohio to equalize the assessment rates. Property owners already were seeing their property tax bills rise without an increase in millage rates, and plenty of them were hopping mad.

I could see that something had to be done about property taxes, and Jim Rhodes was a willing partner. There was the danger that if we didn't do something, the approval rate of tax levies would drop even further or, worse yet, there would be some kind of tax revolt like the one that produced Proposition 13 in California. Not only did Proposition 13 lower tax rates but it required a two-thirds majority in both the California House and Senate to enact any tax increase.

In 1975, Jim Rhodes's first year back in the governor's office after an absence of four years, the Senate took up what was called the "equal yield" school-funding formula while the House worked on the budget that would fund it. At this point every school district in Ohio was under some form of hold harmless guarantee that ensured a district the increases due to rising property values. Unlike the old property tax rollback law that it replaced, House Bill 920 applied only to real property, not personal property. This caused a shift in the total property tax burden to business and personal property taxpayers.

Other tax-relief efforts that were initiated by the legislature but supported by Jim Rhodes were a reduction in the unfair tangible personal property tax on businesses, a 10 percent property tax rollback for which the state agreed to reimburse local governments, and an additional 2.5 percent property tax rollback for residential and agricultural property.

As much as Jim Rhodes despised tax increases, they were becoming harder and harder to avoid. State government had grown tremendously during the four years he was out, and welfare was taking a bigger and bigger bite out of the budget every year. Neither Jack Gilligan nor Jim Rhodes could control welfare. To make matters worse, by the late 1970s Ohio schools were heading into one of the worst financial crises in history.

In 1977 scores of school districts all over the state were in danger of closing because of a lack of money. Cleveland was the biggest and worst off. To complicate things further, the federal courts ruled earlier in the year that the Cleveland and Columbus school districts had to be desegregated. That meant big money for busing on top of everything else.

Cleveland was in particular danger of closing. As a leader, I felt an obligation to make sure the state's largest school district didn't close. Jim Rhodes didn't like the looks of it any more than I did, although he was still loathe to increase taxes. It was clear that the Cleveland district couldn't manage itself out of this crisis, and under state law at the time there was nothing to prevent them from closing their doors and sending students home.

Not everyone shared our view. Many in the legislature whose own school districts had struggled year in and year out for adequate re-sources were opposed to bailing the Cleveland district out. Simply passing a separate appropriation for Cleveland was out of the ques-tion. People in other districts would say, "Forget it! We're not go-ing to take that." The challenge was to find a solution that would get enough votes to pass.

It seemed to me that allowing schools to borrow money to get through the rough times might be an answer. There was no law allow-ing schools to borrow money at the time, so they didn't have many options to prevent closing if voters wouldn't approve tax levies. I talked to Tom Ferguson, the state auditor, to see if it could be done, how best to do it, and whether he thought it was constitutional.

The result was legislation to create a state school loan fund pro-gram whereby a school district applied for money along with a plan for how to pay the money back. All this had to be approved by the State Board of Education and, after that, by the Controlling Board.

As it turned out, it wasn't a big fight. Politically, the bill was fair to everyone. It wasn't a Cleveland bailout; it was a way that any school district could stay open until it got back on its feet financially. It took effect in 1978 and in the years that have passed, that law has kept many school districts from shutting down. I hated to see schools go though financial troubles like that. The loan fund was not a solution to the funding problems that schools faced; it was a very important Band-Aid to help them through a crisis. Twenty years after my first experience with school-funding legislation, Ohio's long reliance on local property taxes to finance schools continued to cause enormous problems.

The following year Jim Rhodes took it one step further by proposing legislation, which was eventually enacted, that prohibited schools from closing.

The next three years were among the most difficult I had ever experienced in terms of funding schools. In 1980 Governor Rhodes cut the budget and asked us to raise taxes, including the sales tax by nearly $400 million, which we did. The following year we had to raise taxes again, upping the sales tax from 4 percent to 5.1 percent, and gave schools a 33 percent increase in funding.

No matter what we did, things only seemed to get worse. In 1982 we worked with the governor to come up with more than $400 million more in the budget cuts and a nearly $600 million tax increase package that included a temporary income tax surcharge. A year later one of Dick Celeste's first major initiatives would be to make the surcharge permanent and add to it, resulting in the infamous "90 percent income tax increase" that dogged him and the Democrats who supported it for years afterward.

I'm sure presiding over a school and budget crisis is not the way Jim Rhodes wanted to go out of office, but I respected him for what he was tying to do. He just didn't like to raise taxes. As I've said before, I've voted for nearly all the tax increases that passed during my thirty-six years in the legislature but only because I thought they were needed.

During that very difficult last term, Rhodes made another lasting contribution to higher education in which I played a crucial role.

Outside of Shawnee State, if there's a state university that's close to my heart it would be the Ohio State University. All our state universities are fine institutions, and I wouldn't put one over another. They all make a tremendous contribution to young people in Ohio, and I have many good friends at each. But being the largest university and being located in Columbus, where I spent most of my time for nearly four decades, I developed particularly close ties to Ohio State. If the people there could convince me that the university needed something, I'd generally get it done and cut through the red tape if I could. It didn't hurt either that Jim Rhodes was also a big supporter of Ohio State.

One day in 1980 the governor called me down to his Statehouse office as he often did. I walked in, not knowing what he wanted to talk about, and there standing with him was a gentleman I did not know at the time, Dr. Arthur James.

"Vern, I've got an amendment here to put $40 million in the capital improvements bill to build a new cancer research hospital at Ohio State," the governor said matter-of-factly. He then turned it over to Dr. James, who explained what it was all about.

This was all new to me, so I didn't really know if it was needed or not, but I figured Jim Rhodes's wouldn't ask me personally if it weren't important.

"Governor, have you got a copy of the amendment?"

"Yes, right here," he said and handed it to me.

I went upstairs to Myrl Shoemaker, who chaired the House Finance Committee that was holding hearings on the capital bill, and told him I wanted it in. I thought Myrl was going to drop. It wasn't that he opposed the cancer hospital; he just didn't know where the money was going to come from since the size of the bond issue was more or less fixed by agreement.

"Myrl, I want that in there," I said, and left it to him to figure out. Somehow he managed to work it in, and we passed it. Unfortunately, even though Democrats controlled the Senate, the Democratic leadership was fighting with the governor at the time and the capital bill was one of the casualties. It didn't pass that year.

Two years later I put money for the cancer hospital in again and increased the amount to about $50 million. This time the capital bill cleared the General Assembly with no problem, and that is how the world-renowned Arthur G. James Cancer Hospital and Research Institute came to be.

Finally, Jim Rhodes played a role in what is unquestionably my personal highlight in the area of education—the establishment of Shawnee State Community College in Portsmouth as Ohio's thirteenth state university.

Throughout my leadership career, I had gone out of my way to be fair and spread things around when it came to building up Ohio's system of higher education. Yet it had always been in the back of my mind that someday Shawnee State Community College should become a state university. Jim Rhodes and I had talked about it a number of times. I was just waiting for the right time.

Then in 1985, during Dick Celeste's first term as governor, Rhodes was giving a speech at Shawnee State Community College when right in the middle he turned to me and said, "Vern, this needs to be a four-year university." Then he turned to Bob Ewigleben, who was president of Shawnee at the time, and said, "Bob, when the Speaker proposes that, I expect you to be for it." It was there on that stage that I decided to go ahead and do it.

I might have pursued it sooner, but the state was having budget problems during the early 1980s, and it just wasn't the right time for it. By the mid-1980s, the state budget was in good shape, partly because of the income tax increase of 1983.

That bill went through the legislature with hardly a dissenting vote, not because I was powerful but because I had supported higher education projects in just about every legislative district in this state. Many members felt it was due to my district.

What Shawnee State University has done for Portsmouth and Scioto County is tremendous. First of all, southern Ohio has always had a lower number of high school graduates continue on to college. Shawnee State has opened the door to a new world of higher education for young people in my part of the state.

Not only that, it has been a boon to economic development. Outside of hospital and government employment, Shawnee State is one of the largest employers in the county. There are probably four hundred employees who wouldn't be there if it was still a community college. It has been a shot in the arm for businesses in the community, and it's brought many outstanding performers to our area to appear at the Vern Riffe Center for the Performing Arts. Wherever you go in this state that has a university, it's the same story. That link between education and economic development was something Jim Rhodes lived and breathed from the first day he was governor.

RICHARD F. CELESTE

I very well could have been a candidate for governor in 1982 if Dick Celeste had not run. In retrospect, I'm glad I didn't. Dad always said, "If you're not sure about something, don't do it." I loved my job as Speaker but I was unsure of my prospects for governor.

I had toyed with the idea of running along with my good friend Marvin Warner of Cincinnati. Marvin had not held elected office before, but he was the former ambassador to Switzerland under President Carter, he had chaired the Ohio Board of Regents, and he had always been a big financial supporter of Democrats. We even joked about whether he would run for governor and I for lieutenant governor or vice versa. My heart was never really in it though because Dick had positioned himself very nicely for a run in 1982 and I expected him to do it. His strong race against Jim Rhodes in 1978 gave him the statewide experience he needed, and Governor Rhodes could not run for reelection to a third consecutive term under our constitution.

Still, I didn't rule out a run myself. If I could get the party endorsement in the primary it would give me the statewide name identification I needed to go forward with a candidacy. Paul Tipps, the Democratic Party chairman, was a good friend, but Paul had to be neutral or risk causing a rift in the party. Dick thought the candidacy was due to him since he took on Rhodes in 1978. Bill Brown, the state attorney general, wanted to run and he wasn't about to hand it over to Dick. Frank Celebrezze, chief justice of the Ohio Supreme Court, also was considering a run, as was Cincinnati City Councilman Jerry Springer.

Frank and I were the only ones who wanted an endorsement, which was not enough. That's when I decided to stand pat and let whoever stayed in fight it out. At one point Frank had actually submitted a letter of resignation from the Supreme Court in order to run for governor but overnight had a change of mind and asked Governor Rhodes to return his letter.

I really had no intention of getting involved in the primary, but I was being pressured to make an endorsement not only from the other candidates but from some of my friends, such as Reps. C. J. McLin and Mike DelBane. They felt that since I was a leading Democratic officeholder, I should play a role in who would win the nomination. Many of them were withholding their support from any of the candidates and waiting to see what I would do. I began to think of it more as a leadership issue on my part.

All the prospective candidates were my friends, but the two I was most inclined to support were Dick Celeste and Bill Brown—Dick because I worked with him in the House and respected his ability, and Bill because he probably had the political philosophy closest to my own.

I really had not made up my mind when I received a call from the Brown people asking that I meet with the candidate, Paul Tipps, Marvin Warner, and Bill's consultant Bob Squires, among others at the Sheraton Hotel near the Columbus International Airport. Bill was ahead in the polls at the time, and I could see that they were angling for an endorsement to help lock it up.

We were in session that day, so I was not able to meet with them until early evening. They had had a few drinks and were loose and somewhat cocky. We made some small talk and then Bob Squires cut to the chase.

"Mr. Speaker, we'd like to have you aboard. We think we've got this thing won. I know we can win it if you come aboard," he said.

Then Duane Welsh, Billy's campaign manager, spoke up.

"If you come out and endorse Billy, you can name your own liaison with the governor's office," he said. I let him talk a little bit more before I cut him off.

"Let's go back to that liaison person. I don't need that. I don't need anybody between me and the governor. When I want to talk to the governor, I talk to the governor. When he wants to talk to me, he talks to me. Thanks a lot, but I don't need that," I said. Their arrogance was a little hard for me to stomach.

Bill was sitting there not saying a word. Then Squires made a big mistake.

"Well, you better get on the train because it's leaving the station. If you don't, you're going to be left off," he said.

That's all I needed to hear.

"Fellas, if you've got this wrapped up like you think you have, what in the hell am I doing here? I've got work to do," I said, grabbing my coat and starting to leave. Both Paul and Marvin asked me not to go, and then they asked everyone else to leave except Bill. Marvin wanted a commitment from us that if I endorsed Bill and he was elected and if John Glenn was successful in running for president in 1984, then Bill would appoint Marvin to the U.S. Senate. It wasn't my idea in the first place, but it was a fair question to ask since it would be a political appointment and Marvin had been a loyal Democrat.

"Speaker, I can't do that. That's against the law. I don't want to get myself in trouble," Bill said.

"Nobody's asking about the law. We're talking politics now," I said. "You mean to tell me you can't make a commitment that if you're governor you would appoint someone to the U.S. Senate?"

"No, I don't want to do that," he said.

"What are we doing here, folks?" I asked, and with that I was out the door.

The fact of the matter is, I had soured on Bill before Marvin asked about the appointment. He didn't seem to be in charge of his own operation when he let others do the talking for him. I could even understand if he did not want to make a commitment to Marvin right then and there. But to say that such a commitment was against the law was just plain nonsense. I just didn't have any confidence that Bill was someone I could work with.

Marvin told Paul as they left together, "If they ever had a chance of getting Vern's endorsement, they lost it tonight." That was exactly right.

Word soon got around that I wasn't going to endorse Bill, and my good friend Ed Hinton, who lobbied for the United Auto Workers and had a son working on Bill's campaign, wanted to talk to me about it.

"Could I talk to you about not making an endorsement? If you'd stay out of it, Bill will win," he said.

"Ed, that's going to be hard for me to do. There are other people who think I should get involved. I'll think about it."

I did, but I just couldn't get over my concerns about Bill. So the following week I found Ed over at the Galleria Tavern across from the Statehouse.

"Ed, I'm going to make an endorsement. I'm going to endorse Dick Celeste."

Ed knew that if I had made up my mind, there was no point in trying to change it.

"Well, if you're going to do it, you're going to do it. Dick will win if he gets your endorsement," he said.

The next think I know it turns up in the *Dayton Daily News* about a month before the primary that I'm going to endorse Dick. I was mad about that story, and I've always suspected that someone associated with the Celeste campaign leaked it, although I can't prove that. Both the Celeste and Brown campaigns wanted my endorsement very badly because they knew wherever I went Marvin Warner would go too. Between the two of us, we could direct a lot of support and financial resources in the candidate's direction. About the same time, the *Columbus Dispatch* conducted a poll that showed Bill Brown about four points ahead of Dick. Both sides knew my endorsement could make a difference.

I was sufficiently peeved about the news leak that I decided to make the Celeste campaign squirm a little, so I waited nearly another week without saying a word to anybody about it. Dick and his consultant, Jerry Austin, were just beside themselves.

"I don't like it a damn bit for somebody to go out and write about what I'm going to do when I haven't made up my own mind," I told them.

After I felt they had sweated it out long enough, I called Dick.

"I'm ready. Put it together, however you want to handle it. I'll do it tomorrow." It was less than one month before the primary election.

So the next day we started with a press conference at my Statehouse office, then to press conferences in Dayton, Toledo, and Cleveland. I never will forget that trip because I took Myrl Shoemaker with me. Myrl was Dick's running mate to be lieutenant governor, and it may have been the first and last time he ever flew. He didn't like it one bit. Dick offered the position to me but, naturally, I wanted to either stay where I was or run for governor. He had two or three other names in mind, and Myrl was one of them. Myrl was tops on my list because not only was he highly qualified but he balanced the ticket, Dick being from Cleveland and Myrl from Chillicothe. "Celeste and Shoe in '82" was the slogan.

The following day I chartered a plane and went to Canton, Youngstown, and Cleveland to raise about $250,000 for Dick. The following week Marvin and I put together a fund-raiser on Marvin's farm outside Cincinnati and raised another quarter of a million dollars. Whomever I endorsed, that's where Marvin was going—money and everything.

At the time I made that endorsement, Billy was ahead by about five points in the polls and had all the money. Dick didn't have any. So in a period of a week or ten days we raised about $750,000 and with that Dick was able to get quality TV and radio time. When the *Columbus Dispatch* did its next poll a week before the election, it was dead even at 38 percent each, with Jerry Springer getting the remaining 24 percent. Dick ended up winning the primary by about 5 percent.

In the general election against Congressman Clarence "Bud" Brown, everything was going Dick's way. First, Dick was tireless and just out campaigned Clarence. Second, it was a good year for Democrats because unemployment was high and President Reagan's popularity was low. Finally, Jim Rhodes was not enthusiastic about Clarence Brown. When he ran for the U.S. Senate in 1970 against Robert Taft Jr. and got beat in the primary, Clarence Brown had endorsed Taft. Jim Rhodes never forgot that.

It was a great victory for Dick, a great victory for the Democratic Party, and a great victory for me personally. Little did I realize that we would have a very short honeymoon before heading into two of the toughest years I ever spent as a legislative leader.

When Dick took the oath of office, he was facing a projected deficit of more than a half billion dollars. The temporary income tax surcharge that was in place was set to expire on March 31.

For the first time in my experience as a leader, Democrats controlled the House, the Senate, and the Governor's Office. Harry Meshel had replaced Oliver Ocasek as president of the Senate, and if Dick, Harry, and I could agree on something, we had the numbers to get it done. The tax issue was the biggest item on our plate, so we tackled it head-on. Together we decided to make the temporary surcharge permanent and increase it by 40 percent—all in one bill. Somehow I couldn't see at the time that we were setting ourselves up to take a big hit.

When the bill passed the House and the Senate, it did so on a partisan vote with Democrats voting for and Republicans voting against. We had taken the full brunt of passing what Republicans labeled "the 90 percent income tax increase." It was the dumbest mistake I ever made in my entire career in leadership. Politically, we survived the consequences of that vote and maintained our Democratic majority in the House the next election, but many believe that vote was the undoing of the Democratic majority in the Senate, which fell in the next election and has been held by Republicans ever since.

The answer seems so clear to me now. What we should have done was extend the temporary tax until June 30, and then include the tax increase in the budget bill. That would make it much harder for Republicans to vote against it, or they would have a lot of explaining to do back home as to why they opposed spending in their districts.

Perhaps Dick, Harry, and I were blinded to the political realities by our control over the process. I do not think I would have reached the same decision if the governor or the Senate were controlled by Republicans. That forces you to think differently and anticipate where the fallout would be. We could have accomplished the exact same thing in a much less harmful way by simply putting the tax increase in the budget, but we didn't do it.

In May 1983 the Republicans organized a group called Ohioans to Stop Excessive Taxation with the goal of putting an issue on the November ballot to repeal all the income tax increases. They succeeded in getting the signatures to do it, and many Democrats found themselves in the position of fighting the issue all over again. For me, it was not unlike explaining my support for the DiSalle tax increases to voters in 1960. The budget was out of balance, and Governor Rhodes had cut about all he could cut. He didn't want to cut education, of course, and at one point said he would not go along with any cuts in welfare because he was not going to have cuts in food and assistance to kids on his conscience. I think he surprised a lot of Republicans with that stand, but the state needed the money.

I did everything I could to defeat that issue—gave speeches, raised money, whatever was required. Dick, Harry, and I helped convince Howard Collier, Rhodes's former budget director, to come out and oppose the issue along with John Mahaney, the director of the Ohio Council of Retail Merchants. Symbolically, that was important. They knew something had to be done; it was just a matter of how.

In the end it was no contest. The repeal effort failed overwhelmingly. I'd like to think voters understood that the state needed the money. In any event, Republicans used that tax issue to try to scare voters for years afterward.

Just as the original enactment of the income tax was a shot in the arm for schools in the mid-1970s, the income tax increase helped stabilize public schools in Ohio during the 1980s. During fiscal years 1981 and 1982, fifty-five school districts had to borrow money from the state to keep operating. Over the next three to four years, state support for schools increased 11 percent a year, and the borrowing all but stopped.

Higher education had been taking it on the chin too. The state subsidy for public universities and colleges dropped by more than 20 percent per student from fiscal years 1979–83, forcing up the students' share of the cost by nearly 50 percent. That wasn't doing anything to help access to higher education, and the income tax restored much needed state support.

Some of Dick's finest work was in higher education. He promoted the Board of Regents' "Selective Excellence" programs, which were funding incentives to individual institutions to develop excellence in teaching, research, and service to the public. I enthusiastically supported nearly all of Dick's higher education initiatives, many of which received national recognition.

Even as we worked on the budget, we tackled another issue I had been fighting for years—collective bargaining for public employees. Twice during Jim Rhodes's third term we had passed collective bargaining legislation but I could never put together the votes to override his veto in the House. There was tremendous pressure on many of my members not to override each time, and I wasn't about to lose anyone in my caucus over the issue.

With control of the General Assembly and the governor's office, passing collective bargaining proved an easy task. I supported it for two reasons. First, I believe that labor unions serve a legitimate purpose in representing working people. Labor influence was strong where I grew up, and I knew firsthand what a difference they made in protecting and advancing the cause of workers. Second, I firmly believed that the number of strikes by public employees would decrease if we passed a collective bargaining law. The old Ferguson Act, which prohibited strikes by public employees, had never worked because walking off the job was the only recourse employees had when they were treated unfairly. By being about negotiating contracts and filing grievances instead, I believed that many of these issues would be resolved before things worsened to the point of a strike. In the years that followed the enactment of collective bargaining, strikes by public employees in Ohio have all but disappeared.

Enactment of the income tax increase improved education funding at all levels and collective bargaining alone would have made a successful term for Dick in my book. But his finest hour was yet to come.

The year 1985 started out innocently enough, but before the first week of March was over, Ohio would be plunged into the worst banking crisis in its history. What's worse, it involved Marvin Warner, which put Dick and me in the very awkward position of resolving a potential disaster that involved a good and loyal friend.

It all started with the collapse of a brokerage company called ESM Government Securities Inc. in Fort Lauderdale, Florida. ESM had ties to Home State Savings Bank, Ohio's largest privately insured thrift, owned by Marvin. The state regulated Ohio's savings and loans, commonly referred to as "thrifts," which were insured by the private Ohio Deposit Guarantee Fund. When ESM collapsed and the extent of its ties to Home State became known, depositors took out $150 million in just two days and wiped out the guarantee fund. If something wasn't done quickly, roughly $1 billion in savings belonging to nearly ninety thousand depositors were at risk. The run started to spread to the other sixty-nine state-chartered thrifts, threatening the deposits of a half million people.

Dick just took the bull by the horns. First, he closed the thrifts to prevent certain disaster. Then he set three goals: make sure no depositor lost money, reopen the thrifts as quickly as possible, and recover any tax dollars that might be necessary to solve the crisis.

The governor did an outstanding job in the way he handled it, getting Republicans and Democrats alike to work with him. Partisan feelings were put aside for the most part as we all worked together to meet his three goals. In a matter of days we passed legislation spelling out the conditions that thrifts would have to meet in order to reopen, and the following week fifty-nine of the sixty-nine thrifts were at least partially open for business.

Next, through an Ohio Department of Commerce loan and a $91 million bond issue, we shored up the thrifts so that they could obtain federal deposit insurance and sold off Home State. Within six weeks, almost all the depositors were given access to all their money.

As I look back on it, it seems amazing that none of the depositors lost a dime and that the state recovered all of its money. It was a cooperative effort on the part of the state, but it was a real shining moment for Dick Celeste, and I give him credit for showing true leadership in a crisis.

Watching what happened to Marvin was tough, tough on me and tough on Dick too. Marvin had been good to Democrats in this state, but his fate was out of our hands and in the courts. He was prosecuted in the Hamilton County Common Pleas Court and, along with several others, was convicted of misapplication of bank funds and securities violations. Marvin served about three years in the London Correctional Facility in Ohio. As an officeholder directly involved in dealing with the Home State crisis, I didn't feel it appropriate to call or visit during his incarceration, but I did keep up with him through his ex-wife, Jodi Piehowicz, a former legal counsel on my staff. After his release, I visited with him and Jodi in Florida and we remain friends today.

If Dick had a problem that first term, it was some of the people he had around him. His administration didn't do a good job of screening some of the cabinet level positions, and as a result he had some real embarrassments. James Rodgers, his head of the Department of Youth Services, hired ex-convicts to work with kids, and he was later convicted of felonies involving bribes, taking kickbacks, and theft in office prior to joining the governor. Minnie Fells Johnson resigned as head of the Department of Mental Health after reports of patient abuse in some of the state facilities. And they weren't the only ones who got into hot water. Dick's administration was being tainted by others' misdeeds in a way that unfairly detracted from the many good things he accomplished. He even got accused of cronyism for reappointing my friend Mike DelBane as chairman of the Public Utilities Commission, but Mike did an excellent job and there was never any hint of trouble when he was in charge.

Dick's wife generated a certain amount of controversy for him as well. Dagmar Celeste was very outspoken about issues of concern to women, world peace, gay rights, and the like. She wanted to be very much involved in the administration and was. I can remember times when I was going over issues with Dick and he'd say, "Let me think about it, and I'll get back with you." I knew what was going on. He had to go back and check with her. I just think it was a situation where he was governor and didn't want to get in any controversy or confrontation with her because she had a history of doing that. My dealings were always with the chief executive, whoever he might be, but it is fair to say that Dagmar's strong beliefs were one of the political realities with which Dick had to deal.

Much was made of those occasions when Dick and I were at odds. I won't kid you; those first two years particularly, when Democrats controlled the House, the Senate, and the governor's office, were two of the most difficult years in leadership that I endured. It was like a family feud at times. I was outspoken, and when I thought Dick was wrong, I told him. He did the same with me.

I remember one time when Ralph Nader was in Columbus, and Dick invited him to stay at the Governor's Residence. I wasn't too pleased about that because Ralph Nader had been lambasting me publicly over my support for some version of tort legislation. His position was that reforming tort laws in personal injury and medical malpractice cases was not necessary; if anything, he wanted the laws liberalized. While Nader was really no threat to me, he was trying to make a villain out of me. I thought the governor was showing poor judgment in putting up Ralph Nader when I was the one he needed to get along with.

When Dick vetoed a package of tort reform bills in 1986 and the Senate failed to override, I made no bones about the fact that I was not pleased. I got together with Dick, and he committed to me that if a new bill was introduced next session, he would work with the legislature to arrive at a bill he could support. A bill was introduced the next session and Alex Shumate of the governor's office was assigned to it. There were people working hard on the governor not to go with a compromise, not the least of which was Stan Chesley, a high-powered trial lawyer from Cincinnati and a major contributor to Democratic candidates. While this was going on, I was in Cincinnati giving a speech when Hamilton County Democratic Chairman John "Socko" Wiethe brought Stan Chesley along to discuss the matter with me. Stan said he had a commitment from the governor to oppose further tort legislation.

"Now let me tell you something, Stan. I don't know what the governor told you, but I have a commitment from him that this bill will be worked out to where everybody is in agreement and then he'll sign it. I just want you to know that," I said.

"Well, we'll see," he responded, and did we ever. A compromise was worked out. The governor kept his commitment to me and signed the bill. Alex Shumate was very, very helpful in working things out. But the experience was rough on Alex the first go-around.

"I hate this because I know the Speaker is mad at me, but I had to do what I had to do," he was telling people. When I heard that, I asked Alex to come to my office.

"Alex, I'm not mad at you. I'm really not mad at the governor. I'm just disappointed in the governor," I said. "You've got a job to do. You work for the man downstairs. If you worked for me and weren't loyal, I'd boot you out of my office. As long as you're there, you carry out his orders."

As Dick headed toward the last year of his first term, Jim Rhodes must have felt the governor was vulnerable. That worried several of Jim's former cabinet members who approached me during the summer of 1985. They were concerned about it because he was seventy-five and had already served for sixteen years. They were worried that another campaign would take a toll on him, and they wanted me to tell him so.

In September I was going to a 33rd Degree Mason ceremony in Grand Rapids, Michigan, with Jim Rhodes and Chuck Shipley, a former aide to the governor and later the director of the Department of Public Safety under Governor Voinovich. We charted an airplane, and on the way back I brought it up.

"Governor, I want you to understand one thing. I'm not talking to you about not running because of Dick Celeste. We've been friends a long time, and I wouldn't do anything to hurt you or give you bad advice," I said. "I'm talking to you about this because some of your friends are saying they don't think you should run. I just thought you ought to reconsider whether you want to run or not."

We talked about it a little more and then he'd had enough.

"Now, Vern, let me tell you something. First, I like being governor. Secondly, this governor has done a lousy job. And third, let's remain friends, but I intend to run and I intend to be governor again," he said. From that time on, I didn't mention it anymore.

Jim Rhodes was a man of his word. He ran in a three-way primary with Paul Gillmor, president of the Senate, and state Sen. Paul Pfeifer. When he won with only 48 percent of the vote, I could see he was going to have a tough time. Dick Celeste had built one heck of a campaign organization, was a tremendously hard worker, and had learned from his defeat in 1978. He also had addressed some of the problems in his administration and sold himself as the hardworking governor that he was. At this point, Dick really didn't need my help, which was just as well. Don't get me wrong, I wanted him to be reelected. Party comes first. But I did not relish being in the position of bringing down a friend in Jim Rhodes.

The low point in that campaign for Jim Rhodes was a televised debate in Cincinnati the Sunday before the election. It just tore me apart. I felt really sorry for him. The way it came across, it was a young man versus an old man. Many of his comments didn't make sense. The funny thing is, I don't think Dick wanted that debate; Jim Rhodes wanted it. If the opponent had been somebody like Paul Gillmor, Dick might have had some problems. Having Jim Rhodes as an opponent was probably the best thing that could have happened.

It was a landslide. Dick won by 650,000 votes, and that was the end of Jim Rhodes's political career. But being the person that he is, he got on with his life by making real-estate deals, patenting an air purification system, and getting involved in other various ventures.

Much of Dick's most important work came during his first term. He wanted to raise taxes again for education during his second term, but I didn't believe the votes were there for another big tax increase and it went nowhere.

Soon after his reelection, speculation began that Dick was interested in running for president in 1988. It was more than speculation. I received a call from his father, Frank, early in 1987 asking if I thought Dick should consider running for the presidency. I had known Frank for many years, and he was a good friend of my dad's when Dad was mayor of New Boston and he was mayor of Lakewood. In the 1950s Frank ran for attorney general and Dad was his campaign manager in Scioto County.

"The only thing I'm worried about, Frank, is whether he's waited too late because Michael Dukakis, Gary Hart, and others have been out there already," I said. "If there's not an early front-runner then, yes, I think he should consider it."

Then that summer the *Cleveland Plain Dealer* published some stories alleging that Dick had had extramarital affairs. Mary Anne Sharkey, whom I always respected, had written them. By this time, Gary Hart had dropped out of the presidential race over press reports about an affair. I have always felt that a person's personal life was their own business and not that of the public at large, but Mary Anne felt that Dick had lied to her publicly when he denied having had an affair. She insisted that it was a matter of his integrity. By August, Dick announced that he would not run.

After that, Dick was freer to be himself. Before his term ended, his liberal side came through when he pardoned a group of female prisoners who had been abused in their marriages and killed their husbands. He also commuted the sentences of prisoners on death row, a decision that was later reversed by the courts.

Even though Dick's political philosophy was much more liberal than mine, I thought he was a good governor, a real innovator, and one of the best campaigners I've ever known—bar none. He was my choice to run for governor in 1998, but try as I might, I couldn't convince him to do it. That's a shame because I believe he had a legitimate shot at being governor or John Glenn's successor as a U.S. senator. I was disappointed, but I respect his decision. He paid his dues.

GEORGE VOINOVICH

George Voinovich may be the most fortunate politician I've ever known. He's been a member of the Ohio House, a Cuyahoga County commissioner, mayor of Cleveland, and a governor, and with the possible exception of one or two elections, he was never in a really tight race.

I don't know if it would have made any difference, perhaps not, but for the first time in my life I thought long and hard about running for governor—something reporters speculated about for years. In 1978 I was not serious. In 1982 I was semi-serious. I was serious in 1990. I wasn't ready for it in those early years, but by 1990 it was my time if I wanted to run.

I had a clear shot in the primary as far as the major Democratic officeholders went. They all indicated to me that they would not run if I chose to do so. Beyond that, the problem I struggled with was that the name "Riffe" had never been on a statewide ballot and "Voinovich" had. I had done polling in 1981 and 1989 and made some real gains statewide, but I still would have had to do an awful lot to get my name recognition to where it should be. Raising the necessary money was the least of my concerns.

By contrast, whether the Republican nominee would have been George Voinovich or Bob Taft, both came from large metropolitan areas. You have to think about things like how do I deal with a Voinovich. Northeast Ohio traditionally has been a Democratic stronghold, but George Voinovich was mayor of Cleveland, and he had won before as a county commissioner, county auditor, and lieutenant governor. The only time he ever lost was when he ran for the U.S. Senate against Howard Metzenbaum in 1988.

There were other factors to consider, including the fact that my father's health was failing, and I wasn't feeling so great myself and probably was feeling some of the effects of my yet undiagnosed vascular disease as well as a lifelong sinus problem. Besides, as Bob Dole found out in the 1996 presidential campaign, you can't campaign for the top spot and be a legislative leader at the same time. When you're a legislative leader, you've got to be there in the legislature running things. When it came down to that, I just couldn't get it in my mind that I really wanted to run for governor.

To be honest, prior to becoming governor, George Voinovich really didn't make much of an impression on me. The whole time he served in the House, from 1966 to 1972, I was in the minority and didn't really have any dealings with him. I recall that he was close to Speaker Chuck Kurfess, but that's about the extent of my recollections.

He served as lieutenant governor only a short time in 1979 before running for mayor of Cleveland, so he didn't register with me there either. Even if he had served out his term, Jim Rhodes didn't use his lieutenant governors anyway.

His 1988 race against Howard Metzenbaum for the U.S. Senate was memorable only because he got the daylights kicked out of him. Howard was one tough son of a gun. A lot of people who didn't agree with his liberal politics liked him because he fought relentlessly for what he believed in. Voinovich got only 43 percent of the vote.

When he beat Tony Celebrezze to become governor in 1990 and the Republicans captured control of the state Apportionment Board, Voinovich came to Columbus with an attitude. He thought the legislature and legislative leaders would do whatever he said or wanted. We told him that wasn't the way it would be, and it wasn't.

The governor and I weren't seeing eye to eye on a lot of things, not just on the issue of raising new revenue for the budget. I wasn't about to go along with his proposal to privatize all state liquor stores. I wasn't convinced it would save the money his party predicted, because closing those stores would put a lot of people out of work.

As always, the budget ended up in a conference committee, and it was slow going. We had to adopt a thirty-day interim budget before all sides could come to terms on something the governor would sign. When we finally did, he got in his licks by vetoing about thirty line items, then put his name to it, and said the budget was "reasonable," balanced, and "got the job done."

Within months of enacting the budget in July 1991, things started to go sour. Spending was higher than expected and revenues were lower than expected. By December the governor was calling for budget cuts in the 3 to 6 percent range and "sin" tax increases on alcoholic beverages, cigarettes, and tobacco to cover a projected deficit of nearly $1 billion.

That didn't fly with me at all. First, I didn't feel it was to the point where we needed to raise taxes. Stan Aronoff didn't either. We wanted to give it more time to see if things improved since we were almost into another election year. Second, if you can avoid it, you don't take up controversial issues in an election year unless it's after the election.

I wasn't about to take up a tax increase, so the governor had to settle for the legislation authorizing a $100 million expenditure of "rainy day" funds, an acceleration of certain tax collections, the reappropriation of some money, and the use of other reserves.

As January 1992 drew to a close and Governor Voinovich signed the bill, we had taken care of any problem with the first fiscal year of the budget. That wouldn't be the end of it though. The Office of Budget and Management was projecting that fiscal year 1992 would be just as bad.

The governor continued to harp on taxes. He just didn't get it. Regardless of what type of tax you're talking about, when you're in an election year it's never a good time to raise taxes. This is what Stan and I were arguing with the governor about privately, trying to get him to understand that it would be difficult for members to vote for any type of tax increase at the time. We tried to make him understand that we had to be sure a tax increase was needed, and if it was, we were ready to assume our responsibility to pass one.

In April 1992 the governor was threatening to go into the districts of Democratic members and campaign against them if they didn't support his tax increases. In June he accused me of sticking my head in the sand "like an ostrich" because I asked him to delay making any budget cuts until we had a clearer picture of what was happening with state revenues. The way it looked to me, if anybody had his head in the sand it was George Voinovich because he sure as heck wasn't passing any tax bill in the House without my support.

It probably bothered some Republicans more than it did me, but little more than a year before, Voinovich was campaigning on "doing more with less" and "no new taxes." Now that he was in office, some members of his own party thought he was breaking his word.

In the past I never worried too much about Republican governors campaigning against my candidates. It didn't make a whole lot of difference as far as I could see. But this time was different because we didn't draw the lines, and there was little margin for error if we were to keep the majority. I've never gone spoiling for a fight with a governor, but if George Voinovich went on the attack against our candidates, I wasn't going to take it lying down.

I signed off on two secret weapons to use against the governor if necessary. First, we produced a TV commercial holding George Voinovich's feet to the fire on his campaign pledges, and it was a real zinger. The ad was called, "Promises Made, Promises Broken," and I would have to put it up on the air big-time if necessary. Second, my campaign staff worked up a plan to dispatch "truth squads" that could go in before or after appearances by the governor. The idea was to set the record straight for the public and the news media if he went after our candidates.

All this was supposed to be a secret, but one day I got a call from Paul Mifsud, the governor's chief of staff, saying he had a copy of a confidential memo about the truth squads. He said he found it in a men's room at the Hyatt Regency of all places. It didn't bother me so much that Paul knew about the truth squads, what concerned me was that something confidential was stolen or leaked out of our campaign. Not only that, the *Cleveland Plain Dealer* got a copy and reported, "In case Voinovich does detour from the high road, the campaign-planning document obtained by the *Plain Dealer* indicates that House Democrats are prepared to:

- Muster "truth squads" to counteract statements Voinovich makes while campaigning for GOP House candidates. "As much as possible, we want people who are local to the applicable media market," the document says.

- Determine what kind of donations Voinovich is seeking for House Republican nominees. "If we could muddy the waters by attacking Voinovich on squeezing special interests, this could be of use either by the truth squad or individual (Democratic) candidates," according to the document.
- Preempt Voinovich by scheduling a "positive media hit" for Democratic candidates in the Voinovich's cross-hairs by publicizing "a negative against the Republican opponent," or by recruiting local Republicans to publicly support Democratic nominees.

I never could pin down exactly how that memo got out, but I suspect some wise guy on our side thought they'd send a signal to the governor's office not to mess around with us. It's a good thing nobody owned up to it because I wouldn't stand for leaks.

As it turned out, neither the commercial nor the truth squads were necessary. The governor never went after our candidates the way he said he would. While he was on a September trade mission to the Far East, the Republicans may have done some polling that showed we were going to keep the House majority. And I know some friends of mine, Jim Rhodes and John Wolfe among them, warned the governor that if he didn't start working with me, he would never get anything done. I didn't ask them to do that; they knew that more would come of cooperation than confrontation.

Right after he returned from his trade mission, George Voinovich called me. "I know you're going to keep the majority. Look, I've been listening to the wrong people. All along you've told me that you'd assume your responsibility to make sure that budget was balanced. I should have believed you then," he said. "I'd like to get together with you after the election. We've still got budget problems, and I know if it's going to get resolved, you've got to be with me." That was a real turning point in our relationship.

Outside of two or three commitments he had made to appear with Republican House candidates, the governor said he would stay out of the House races. He honored those commitments by just going through the motions. He never did say one bad word about our candidates, and he never put a dime of his own money into the Republican's House campaign fund. After the election, in which we held the House majority by a 53-46 margin, George Voinovich was a new governor. (Sometimes it takes a while to get the hang of working with the opposite party in a legislature.)

In December 1992 the administration continued to project a deficit of $250 million for the fiscal year. There were only six months left to balance the budget, it was after the election, and there was no longer any reason to put off consideration of a tax increase. The governor, Stan Aronoff, and I were in agreement that something had to be done.

The governor wanted two separate bills: one to raise the taxes necessary to eliminate the deficit and another authorizing roughly $1 billion in capital improvements. I said there was no way I would agree to that because I had been down that road before, and I knew exactly what would happen—a lot of House members, mostly Republicans, would vote against the tax increases and for the capital improvements. No sir. The only way I'd go along with it was if both the taxes and the capital improvements were in one bill. It was like a light went off in the governor's head. He had taken his share of criticism from Republicans over pushing for tax increases, and he knew what I said was absolutely right. Later on the governor said that was one of the smartest moves he made in his first term.

The tax bill was a grab bag of taxes, including a number of "sin taxes," but I also made sure one thing I wanted was in there: an increase in the personal income tax to 7.5 percent for persons earning more than $200,000 a year. It may not have amounted to a lot in terms of total revenue, but I didn't want people saying that only the little guy buying a pack of cigarettes or a bottle of beer was footing the bill.

The bill was introduced on a Tuesday and by Thursday it cleared the House and the Senate on bipartisan votes and was headed to the governor.

It's not as though the first two years of the Voinovich administration were without successes. It was his idea to create a special fund within the budget in 1991 to help address inequities in school funding.

We also passed a package of economic development bills in 1992 focusing on tax incentives to prevent businesses from fleeing Ohio for more favorable taxes, particularly across the Ohio River from Cincinnati to Kentucky. That was right in Stan Aronoff's backyard, and as Senate president, he asked and I agreed to come back in session during the 1992 campaign to take up the bills. I had no problem cooperating on it and added a bill of our own to Stan's, speeding up the expenditure of bond proceeds for local infrastructure projects. Probably the most significant of the three bills was one to provide a corporate tax credit for businesses that expand and provide permanent, productive jobs.

Two years later we went even further by passing a package of five bills—two House and three Senate—creating various tax credits and incentives to stimulate business locations and expansions. These were all attempts to keep our tax structure from discouraging business growth in the state.

Looking back, I can't imagine a more interesting time in the economy of this state than the period during which I served. Ohio's population and industrial strength reached an all-time high in my early years; we struggled with recessions, plant shutdowns, high unemployment, and population losses during my middle years; and by the time we reached the Voinovich administration, unemployment was low again. For the first time Ohio had more service-sector jobs than industrial jobs. We clawed our way back from the dark days of the 1970s and 1980s to where people didn't think of Ohio as a "rust belt" state anymore.

The difference between the first two and last two years of George Voinovich's first term was that he came to realize that whatever success he enjoyed legislatively was due in part to Stan and me and our respective caucuses. That made for a considerably better working relationship.

Since the budget was no longer a problem, the governor set his sights on other goals. One that became a major issue during 1993 was reforming Ohio's workers' compensation system, which the governor labeled "the silent killer of jobs" in his 1993 State of the State Address. There were undeniably problems in workers' compensation that affected both injured workers and employers. To me, the choices were to strike the best compromise we could or postpone the inevitable, and I could see no good in doing that. I determined that the best thing to do was reach some sort of compromise and move on. Even John Hodges, president of the Ohio AFL-CIO, agreed with me that something had to be done.

Just as I had done in the past, I got the major parties with a stake in workers' compensation together to try to work out a compromise. I threatened to make my own compromise if business and labor didn't work together on it. Finally, after a lot of bickering and posturing, an agreement was reached, but at the last minute labor backed out. We could either let the whole bill fall apart or pass it, so I said to heck with labor and pushed the bill through.

What some of the labor people didn't understand was that my primary goal was to take workers' compensation reform off the table as an issue, because George Voinovich was making political hay with it. By signing the reform bill we had passed, the governor had compromised his ability to use that issue as a political weapon. The bill made a number of changes in the administrative operation of the bureau to speed up the process and crack down on fraud. As it was, the legislation did not decrease benefits, but it did bring workers' compensation under managed care, which labor did not like.

After I retired, however, the governor went ahead and did what he probably wanted to do all along—take over control of the bureau. While labor may not like it, what that means is the success or failure of the bureau to serve business and injured workers will fall squarely on the shoulders of the governor. The extent to which labor's concerns are addressed by the bureau also will fall to the governor.

As we approached the latter part of 1993, I could see that things were not shaping up well insofar as the Democrats' statewide ticket and that George Voinovich could be handed another easy election in running against state Sen. Rob Burch of New Philadelphia. When George Voinovich captured 72 percent of the vote on election day, the only suspense was over how much his margin of victory would be.

As my career drew to a close, I didn't feel I ever really knew or understood George Voinovich. He was a different kind of person from, say, Jim Rhodes who loved working with and mixing it up with people. George Voinovich is more of a manager who takes care of the store. He told me he didn't like campaigning, didn't like going out to make political speeches, and didn't like debates. Jim Rhodes liked everything about politics, and he was always thinking. His mind was going ninety miles a minute. He had ideas coming out of the woodwork.

During my time in office, Voinovich received the best press that I can remember of any governor, including Jim Rhodes. I don't think he's been scrutinized the way other governors have been. I don't know why. He worked at his press relations, there's no doubt about that, but others have too and didn't get those kinds of results.

I would have to say my dealings with George Voinovich were more in the nature of a business relationship. I was never able to develop any kind of a personal relationship with George Voinovich. It just wasn't there.

Epilogue

I feel a bit like George Bailey in the movie *It's a Wonderful Life*. As I write this I am battling cancer. It will be a tough fight that takes all the strength I have. The choices I face are to fall into a state of despair or to embrace life as I always have. Well, I've never been a quitter, and I'm not about to quit now.

Not everything turned out the way I would have wished personally, politically, or governmentally. That's life. I have no regrets. Right or wrong, I've lived with my decisions, because, if you accept the call to lead, you can't second-guess yourself. I will go to my grave knowing that whatever mistakes I made in life are far outweighed by the good that the House and the Ohio General Assembly as a whole were able to do. No one has had a more satisfying political career than me.

While this book focuses mostly on the past, I believe there are lessons in it for the future. Everywhere I go in Ohio I can see where the state can take credit for progress that no individual can claim. It takes teamwork to make government and politics work. It does make me proud, however, to know that I played some small part in the progress.

Although I am not in public life anymore, public affairs will always be a part of my life as they have since my childhood. I am concerned about the future of Ohio. I've witnessed changes in public life that trouble me. I also see cause for optimism. I believe citizens and public servants can make a difference.

In government, there is a tendency today to see only what is bad or not working. Almost unnoticed are the many good things that government at all levels does for people, day in and day out. Much of this is taken for granted. That has always been the case to some extent, but never in my lifetime has government been less appreciated than it is today.

I find this ironic, and it bothers me greatly. The quality of education, health care, job training, transportation, environmental protection, and any number of other areas of government services are so much better today than they were when I first entered the legislature; the difference simply boggles my mind. Sometimes I look back on it and think: How did we get it all done?

Somehow the connection between government and the people it serves has to be reestablished. I honestly don't know what the answers are. Perhaps a part of the solution is for government to do a better job of communicating with the public. I base this on my own experience. We tend to underestimate how smart citizens are, if only given the information they need to make decisions. As I have related in these pages, I took plenty of tough votes in my day—often at odds with constituents in my district—but I always went to great pains to speak directly with the public. Politicians simply must hold a dialogue with the public they serve.

I'm not so sure the phrase "actions speak louder than words" applies to government the way it did in my time. Today, even when the actions of government are good and responsible, they are more likely than ever to be distorted by various sides of a given issue for political gain without regard to how it reflects on the institutions of government. The image of government and its ability to function have suffered in the process. It's imperative that government reestablish and maintain close and constant lines of communication with the public. This is not only a responsibility but a matter of survival if good government is to prevail.

It is a given that government should be held accountable for its actions. As long as term limits for state legislators are in place, however, I see accountability getting worse rather than better. This is another irony that I am convinced will come back to haunt our state—an irony because the idea behind term limits was to improve the quality of state government. It is my firm belief that, in reality, term limits will produce lawmakers who are less committed to the long haul and more dependent on special interests due to lack of a base and resources upon which to run. It also stands to reason that the governor will become proportionally more powerful because of the vast resources at his or her disposal relative to less experienced and established state legislators. And, of course, the governor's obligation is to the state as a whole, while our senators' and state representatives' politics are much more local in nature.

Perhaps most troublesome about term limits is that unelected bureaucrats and special interests will see their power increase so that the public will, in fact, have even less influence over the direction of government.

In 1992, the year term limits were passed on the statewide ballot, I was in the fight of my life to retain majority control of the Ohio House. Had it been just about any other year, I would have done everything in my power to defeat it. As it was, it was all I could do to win the majority again under Republican-drawn district lines.

In 2000, when the first legislators were forced out of the Ohio House and Senate, the public would see the good cast out with the bad—assuming a significant number of legislators stayed that long. We saw many talented representatives and senators leaving early rather than let the clock run out on them. Institutional knowledge, wisdom that comes with experience, and the ability to forge effective legislative coalitions suffer.

Unless we do away with term limits, state government will be harmed. It is my sincere hope that leaders with political courage will take up the fight to repeal term limits after the public has had an opportunity to witness its effects.

Another issue that I find deeply troubling is that leaders don't stand up for what they believe in like they used to. Why? Because those who do stand up for the greater good often fall victim to single-issue politics, the power of negative advertising, and shallow or biased news coverage. I was fortunate enough to build an organization that insulated me and my caucus from such influences so that we could more freely exercise our authority.

Yet contrary to what some of my critics have said, neither I nor the Democratic Caucus was all-powerful during the time we held the majority. There is no stronger force in politics than the popular vote. The beauty of our democracy is that no matter how many campaign dollars are spent or how many lobbyists try to influence legislators, ultimately the power rests with the people. That is something politicians should never forget.

Often it takes tremendous political courage to do what is right. As a teenager, I saw it in people like my father and Franklin Roosevelt. As a young man, I saw it in Harry Truman and Jim Rhodes. As a mature legislator, I saw it in all the governors and many of the legislative leaders with whom I served. It is taking a position when you know you are going to catch hell for it. When we passed the infamous "90 percent tax increase" in 1983, it took courage knowing full well that the Republican Party would exploit it for political advantage. And yes, while there were casualties, the voters of Ohio overwhelmingly rejected a repeal because they knew the tax increase was needed. Our political courage was rewarded, principally in terms of the vital benefits and services that were delivered to the people of Ohio.

It is my hope that future generations of leaders will understand that the public may not always agree with their decisions, but that it will recognize and appreciate the political courage demonstrated in voicing them.

I also worry about how the changing nature of politics has caused a decline in friendship and civility among members of the legislature. This growing divide is evident not just between members of opposite parties, but even among members of the same party. Thank goodness I served during the time I did. For most of my career, neither the public nor the people with whom I served were cynical about their government. It has always been true in politics that you fight to win. But for most of my career, we could be friends or at least civil to each

other when the election or floor fight was over. I don't recall the contempt that many legislators today hold for their colleagues.

Ohio is not unique in this phenomenon. Legislative scholar Alan
Rosenthal, who has interviewed me on numerous occasions over
the years, has written about the breakdown of civility in legislatures
around the nation. Congress recently held a retreat so that members
could learn how to better get along with each other. This trend is not
healthy because it leads to less understanding and tolerance of others' viewpoints. It creates gridlock. It skews legislative priorities.

Much of my success in politics was due to the fact that I had friends
all over the map, Republicans and Democrats; business and labor;
blacks and whites; Protestants, Catholics, and Jews; rich and poor;
and on and on. There is no way I could have achieved what I did were
it not for the diverse network of friends I built up over nearly forty
years. My advice to those who follow me in state government is that
friendship and respect among colleagues is more than good politics,
it's good for the soul and the right thing to do.

Two other disturbing trends in politics that somehow need to be
reversed are negative campaigning and the enormous amount of
campaign spending. Both accelerated tremendously during the 1980s
and 1990s, and there's no denying that I was a part of the latter.

I attribute the rise in negative campaigning to the late Lee Atwater,
who helped engineer Republican victories, including President Ronald
Reagan's. It worked, particularly on television. By 1990 we were starting to spend significant amounts of money on television advertising
in state legislative races, and negative advertising became more pro-
nounced. Today negative campaigning is everywhere, and I hate it.

I define negative advertising, first, as advertising that focuses on
the opponent rather than your candidate. Second, it tends to take information out of context in order to put things in the worst possible
light. I never did like it, and the few times I went along with negative
advertising it was generally in response to a negative attack from the
other side.

As the public grows increasingly weary of politicians attacking
each other, I believe more and more candidates will refocus on the

issues. In the meantime, it is the responsibility of leaders to resist the win-at-all-costs approach to campaigns. It produces a short-term gain that results in long-term damage to the political process.

More than anybody, I created the model for big money, caucus fund-raising in Ohio. As a leader, I saw ample financial resources as a necessity in order to keep the House majority. What I didn't anticipate was the enormous cost of TV advertising, polling, and direct mail. My first caucus fund-raiser in 1973 raised $88,000, and it was one of the biggest political fund-raising events this state had seen outside the political party organizations. Today that amount of money is peanuts. In the 1970s and 1980s TV advertising was used comparatively little in legislative races. Polling and direct mail were used sparingly.

You can argue about whether fund-raising is driving up costs or costs are driving up fund-raising. In reality, it is both. But I will tell you this: Those who are making all the money out of this are political consultants, television stations, printers, pollsters, and radio stations. I know of no politician, including myself when I was still in office, who wouldn't want to spend less time raising money.

Unless the U.S. Supreme Court reverses itself, it will remain unconstitutional to limit campaign spending in cases where public financing of campaigns is not involved. My hope is that the court does reverse itself, or that there is a movement to amend the U.S. Constitution so that it is not an infringement of freedom of speech to cap spending in campaigns. Otherwise, I wonder where it will stop.

I don't know that people today are all that different from people of my generation. During my upbringing, cities were smaller, there were no suburbs, labor-intensive manufacturing jobs were plentiful, a high school education could take you places, and we were competing against other cities and other states, not nations on the opposite side of the globe. Everybody's looking for someone to blame for changing circumstances, but my experience has taught me that the answers are rarely that simple.

It wasn't so long ago, for example, that schoolteachers were among the most respected people in the community. Today schoolteachers have been targeted by politicians who want to blame our education problems on them. Yet schoolteachers are no more responsible for our educational problems than politicians are for all the unsolved difficulties that afflict our society.

The world of politics has long been rough and tumble, but we always had heroes. There are few political heroes today. Public cynicism has grown so great that elected officials today must spend an inordinate amount of time deflecting public criticism, not to mention political sniping and news reporters more interested in conflict and controversy than public policy.

I can say without reservation that the vast majority of legislators and governors I ever worked with were good, honest, hardworking men and women dedicated to serving the public. That remains true today. Unfortunately, the public at large cannot see what I see. What they know about their elected officials comes to them through many filters, if at all.

Elected officials must bear a part of the responsibility for this. Again, part of their obligation as public servants is to know, listen to, and communicate with the public they serve. But the public also has an obligation to participate in their government. Voting is the least of it. Citizens have the capacity to make their feelings known to their elected representatives between elections if only they chose to exercise it. They can organize. They can stay informed about current events that have a direct impact on them, and they can act accordingly.

The news media also shares the burden for both the perceptions and misperceptions that the public holds about government and politics. During the first half of my career, politicians could fraternize with reporters and not feel like targets or adversaries. We didn't have a complicated set of rules regarding what was on or off the record. There was a greater degree of trust and fair play in the way politicians and reporters dealt with each other. While the reporters of old might not have been as well educated, they tended to be more mature and straightforward in the way they covered the news.

That changed with the likes of Jack Anderson, and it picked up steam in the 1980s and 1990s. Soon, reporters were fixated on writing exposes rather than covering the news. Too many news people wanted to hang a trophy on the wall instead of enlightening the public about the formation of public policies that would have a huge impact on their lives.

I never had a problem with a reporter if he or she was fair to me. I am simply concerned that fair play has become less common among news organizations than it used to be. All I knew how to do was be fair and honest with responsible reporters and ignore those who weren't— all the while making sure my constituents or caucus got the straight information from me.

Because of this often-hostile environment, many citizens think twice about going into public service; they know there is a good chance they will become the target of vicious attacks or distortion. I understand their hesitation. When I was charged in 1995 with failing to report honorariums I had received prior to retirement, there was a media frenzy. The implication was that I had accepted money from special interests and tried to hide it. When later that year the charge was dismissed, it was hard to tell from the news coverage. Why? Because I plead guilty to failing to report interest income on some investments, including certificates of deposit. The distinction was lost to the reading and viewing public and, no doubt, public cynicism was enhanced.

Nevertheless, it would be wrong to assume that I am pessimistic about the future. I am not. I believe that much of what happens comes in cycles. Someday it will become apparent that our system of government and politics is not broken; we simply need to go back to some of the values that worked so well for so many years—values such as fairness, honesty, the honoring of commitments, service, duty, consistency, and respect.

Public service is noble. Teamwork and cooperation are virtuous. Compromise is not a dirty word. Republicans and Democrats can agree to disagree and shake hands at the end of the day.

Most of all, I hope we can return to a time when politicians, the public, and the press can believe—if not the best in people—at least not the worst in people. Certainly I made my share of enemies over the years, but I had many, many more friends. My friends and supporters were what sustained me. With very few exceptions, whether I agreed with them or not, I saw value in every legislator and citizen I came to know. I believed in them, and that faith was returned to me manyfold.

Afterwords

"A good father will leave his imprint on his daughter for the rest of her life."

—James C. Dobson

I have always been a daddy's girl. I don't remember when it began. I just always remember being one.

I remember sitting in the bathroom watching him shave and wrestling with him on the living room floor. I remember wanting him to tuck me into bed at night and getting angry when he called me Pumpkin Head. I was so proud when he was the fireman to slide down the pole during my school field trip to the fire station and when he spoke to my elementary school on what being a state representative was all about. We had a special relationship.

We also shared a unique professional relationship. I have interacted with Vern Riffe as his daughter and as a lobbyist. I had to learn to call him Mr. Speaker and to think of him as Mr. Speaker. It is from that dual perspective that I would like to share some personal thoughts about our Mr. Speaker.

Deciding to accept a lobbying job was difficult for me. I had a lot of questions. Would my father let me into his political world? Could I make it in his world? Would others let me succeed in my father's domain?

But perhaps the most perplexing question was whether being a lobbyist would interfere with my relationship with my father.

I struggled with these questions for days. The answers simply eluded me. I finally decided that I had to have a frank conversation with Dad. I invited him to lunch. It was then that I received my first official, non-family lesson in the school of Mr. Speaker politics.

I asked him what he thought about his daughter becoming a lobbyist. He very quickly responded that it wasn't important what he thought. What did I think? I asked him if he thought it would ever come between us. I will never forget his response. He looked directly at me and said, "I can look you in the eyes and tell you no just as easily as I can anyone else." And on many occasions he did just that. I won a few, and I lost a few. For the next ten years we shared this father-daughter and Mr. Speaker-lobbyist relationship.

When Mr. Speaker decided to retire, I had a very different set of questions. Could I make it in my father's world when my father wasn't in it? Would others let me succeed when Dad wasn't there? But this time I didn't need to talk to Dad to find the answers or the courage to go it alone. All I had to do was remember what I had learned from Mr. Speaker. "Order and organization are paramount to action." "Compromise is not a dirty word." "You can't get anywhere alone." "When you do a good job for the people, you do a good job for your party." "Loyalty, loyalty, loyalty." "Be honest and fair with all people regardless of their political affiliation." "Always keep your commitments." The list goes on and on.

Vern Riffe was an extraordinary father and public official. There is no one who compares—not in this state, not in this country. He will always be my friend, my mentor, my hero, and my father. The one and only "Mr. Speaker."

VERNA RIFFE BIEMEL

People always ask me, "How does it feel to be the grandson of 'The Speaker'?" My reply is that I never knew "The Speaker." The only person I knew was papaw. I know the man who would come home on Friday evenings, relax in his chair, and eat a banana. I was very close to my grandfather, and when he passed away it took a big part of me with him that will never be replaced.

My life is very hard without him around to give the advice I have needed growing up. There is not a day that goes by that I don't think about him, and I am truly papaw's boy.

I would like to thank the people who made Vern Riffe what he was and what he still is—a legend. Finally, thank you, Papaw. There will never be a grandfather as great as you. You are what keeps me going. If it wasn't for you, I would never have wanted to be a politician like you. I know I can never fill your shoes, but I will carry on what you started. I am forever grateful that you are my grandfather. I love you.

VERNAL G. RIFFE IV

Index